Application of Information Technology in Libraries

Application of Information Technology in Libraries

P. VENKATA RAMANA
Associate Professor & Head
Library and Information Centre
Jawaharlal Nehru Architecture and Fine Arts University
Masabtank, Hyderabad -500 028.
Andhra Pradesh, India.

Ess Ess Publications
New Delhi

Application of Information Technology in Libraries

ISBN: 978-81-7000-698-5

₹ 1200/-

First Published 2013

Published by:
Ess Ess Publications
4831/24, Ansari Road,
Darya Ganj,
New Delhi-110 002.
INDIA
Phones: 23260807, 41563444
Fax: 41563334
E-mail: info@essessreference.com
www.essessreference.com

Cover Design by *Patch Creative Unit*

Printed and bound in India at Salasar Imaging Systems.

Respectfully dedicated
To
My beloved Grand Mother
Late Smt. P.Venkatamma
&
My beloved Parents
Smt. P. Manchalamma
&
Late Sri. P. Ganganna

Contents

Dr. B.R. AMBEDKAR OPEN UNIVERSITY
డా. బి.ఆర్. అంబేద్కర్ సార్వత్రిక విశ్వవిద్యాలయం

Road No.46, Prof.G.Ram Reddy Marg, Jubilee Hills, Hyderabad-500 033

Prof. V. CHANDRASEKHAR RAO Ph (O):040-23680469
Dept of Lib & Inf. Science Email: drvcsrao@gmail.com

Foreword

Information Technology (IT) has tremendous impact on all the sectors of the society. Libraries and information centres are not an exception. IT has brought enormous changes and radical transformation in the functioning and management of modern libraries. IT has profoundly changed library operations, information resources. Information services, staff competencies and users' expectations.

Today, Libraries are facing variety of challenges of information explosion, IT revolution and network evolution on one side, decreasing library budgets, increasing cost of print based information resources, growing electronic information resources, emergence of digital/virtual libraries and ever rising users' expectations for complex information requirements on the other side. IT has virtually unlimited potential in enhancing the capabilities of modern libraries not only to meet these challenges but also to satisfy the ever growing demands of users efficiently and effectively. Today every library is striving hard to use modern technologies not only to just automate, but also to increase the efficiency and effectiveness of information services.

The effective utilization of emerging technologies has become inevitable for the survival and successful management of modern libraries in a dynamic digital information environment and global knowledge society.

Dr. P. Venkata Ramana's book *Information Technology Application in Libraries* is very timely and quite relevant to the present trend of modernization of library and information centres, especially in Automation and Networking.

I hope the book will be quite useful to the decision makers, practicing library managers, library science teachers, research scholars and all other library and information science professionals who are planning to introduce, use and manage the modern technologies in their libraries.

V. Chandrasekhar Rao

Preface

The digital technology is rapidly transforming the whole world. Information Technology (IT) plays a vital role in today's global knowledge economy. The world is witnessing an information technology revolution radically transforming all the aspects of human life. With the expanded use of information technology in all the spheres of human activities. IT has proved to be a boon for the modern society.

The impact of information technology is enormous and global in its magnitude, pervasiveness and usefulness. IT is a driving force for change and transformation in libraries. IT has transformed the role of libraries creating new challenges and opportunities. The accelerated pace of technological developments have profoundly affected all the aspects of libraries. Information Technology has an immense potential in enhancing the capabilities of libraries to increase the efficiency, productivity and effectiveness of library operations and services.

The application of information technology to library operations and services has become a key to the success in satisfying ever-changing complex information demands and expectations of increasing number of users. Because of the rapid revolutionary technological advancements accompanied with numerous advantages, use of IT applications in libraries has grown tremendously in recent years. The proper exploitation of new technologies in library is no longer a matter of choice but a matter of survival in an era of rapidly changing technology and global knowledge society. Libraries now use IT not only to automate their activities but also to provide many innovative information services to the users. Today, the success of a library is increasingly dependent on the most effective utilization and strategic management of modern technologies in libraries.

The book has been organised into seven chapters followed by Select Bibliography and Select Library and Information Science Technology Journals.

Chapter 1 provides a brief introduction to information technology. It introduces definition and discusses major components of information technology including evolution of computers, generations of computers, computer hardware, software, types of computers, multimedia, databases, communication technology, networks internet and publishing technology. A brief review of latest technological advancements and innovations is also provided.

Chapter 2 presents the reasons for information technology applications in libraries and briefly reviews global and national scenarios of the current trends in IT applications in libraries. It also discusses the impact of IT applications on library operations including acquisition, classification, cataloguing, circulation, serials management and information services, staff and users.

Chapter 3 presents the historical background, growth and development of universities and university libraries in the country. It also covers the establishment of central universities their objectives, profiles and libraries. A brief information about INFLIBNET is also provided.

Chapter 4 provides objectives, scope, methodology and significance of the study. It presents the results of an analysis of data regarding the status of use of IT in Central University Libraries. It discusses library collection, users, staff, budget, infrastructural facilities, computer facilities, software packages used, planning approaches adopted for IT implementation, development of databases, computerised library operations, and information services, bibliographic standards, networking and resource sharing etc., of Central University Libraries in India.

Chapter 5 presents the results of the analysis of data about the perceptions on the impact of using IT applications in house-keeping operations, information services as perceived by staff and users of CU Libraries in India.

Chapter 6 discusses the rationale for IT applications in libraries, key factors in strategic technology planning and strategies for managing technological change in libraries and IT skills required for changing role of library professionals in managing modern libraries in digital environment.

Chapter 7 presents the summary of findings, conclusions and suggestions made to Library Management, INFLIBNET and Government. It provides areas for future research in IT applications in Libraries and also discusses the future challenges of emerging rapid technological advancements.

This book is designed to educate and develop librarians who can effectively manage the planning, design, selection, implementation, usage and administration of emerging and converging information and communication technologies in libraries.

This book is valuable reading for policy decision makers, practicing library managers, working library professionals at all levels, university teachers, research scholars and students of library and information science, library software development firms and all other library professionals involved in planning, implementation and management of modern information technologies in libraries.

Acknowledgements

I wish to record my sincere thanks and deep sense of gratitude to Dr.V.Chandrasekhar Rao, Professor & Head, DLIS, Dr.B.R.Ambedkar Open University, for his invaluable guidance, constant encouragement and constructive suggestions in completing this book.

I am highly thankful to Dr. D. Vijay Kishore and Dr. P. Padmavathi, JNAFAUSPA for their good support and cooperation.

I am extremely thankful to Prof. A.A.N. Raju, Prof. N. Laxman Rao, Dr. J. Yadagiri Reddy, Dr. V. Viswamohan and Dr. S. Sudarsan Rao of the DLIS Osmania University, for their constructive suggestions and kind cooperation.

My special thanks are due to Dr. E. Rama Reddy, University Librarian and all the Library staff members of University of Hyderabad for generously sparing their valuable time for discussion and providing needed information.

I express my sincere thanks to all the University Librarians and the library staff of all Central Universities for kindly responding to my letters and providing needed information. These include Prof. Noorul Hasan (AMU), Dr. P.K. Jayaswal, (Assam Univ.), Sri. A.K. Katna, (BBRAU), Sri. Ramjee Singh, (Banaras Hindu Univ.), Sri M.L.Saini, (Univ. of Delhi), Dr. Neela Jagannathan (IGNOU), Dr. Khalid K Farooqui (JMI), Sri.B.N. Rao & Sri Mahesh chand (JNU), Mrs. Lucy

Bendang (Nagaland Univ.), Dr. Lalit P. Pathak, (NEHU), Dr. P. Ramanathan (Pondicherry Univ), Dr. M.N. Borah (Tejpur Univ.), Dr. S.G.Nandi, (Visva-Bharathi).

I am highly thankful to the Osmania University, Hyderabad for the facilities provided for research for awarding the degree of Doctor of Philosophy in Library & Information Science, and for the generous permission accorded for publication.

My thanks are due to Prof. LS. Ramaiah, Dr. P. Vyasamoorthy, Sri. Srinivas (ICRISAT), Ms. Prasanna (Motorola, Hyd), Sri Satyanarayana (BHEL, Hyd), Dr. C. Raghavendra Rao (UOH, Hyd) and all other library professionals for their valuable help, assistance and cooperation.

I record my gratitude and sincere thanks to all the authors and editors whose works I had consulted and formed source material in the preparation of this work.

My special thanks goes to my wife Mrs. P. Subhashini and my children Master P.Venkat Sudhir and Kumari P.L.Deepti for their support and cooperation in completing this work.

I am highly thankful to Sri. Sumit Sethi of M/s Ess Ess Publications for publication of this work.

P. VENKATA RAMANA

Abbreviations And Acronyms

ACU	Association of Commonwealth Universities
ADISc	Associateship in Documentation and Information Science
A&I	Abstracting and Indexing
AIU	Association of Indian Universities
AI	Artificial Intelligence
ALA	American Library Association
ALU	Arithmetic and Logic Unit
AMU	Aligarh Muslim University
AP	Andhra Pradesh
ARPANET	Advanced Research Projects Agency Network
AU	Assam University
BBAU	Babasaheb Bhimrao Ambedkar University
BHEL	Bharath Heavy Electricals Limited
BHU	Banaras Hindu University

BLISc	Bachelor of Library and Information Science
CAS	Current Awareness Service
CALIBER	Convention for Automation of Libraries in Education and Research
CCF	Common Communication Format
CDROM	Compact Disk Read Only Memory
CDS/ISIS	Computerised Documentation System/Integrated Sets of Information System
COPSAT	Content Pages of Science and Technology
CPU	Central Processing Unit
CSIR	Council of Scientific and Industrial Research
CUC	Calcutta Universities Commission
DAE	Department of Atomic Energy
DBase	Data Base
DBMS	Database Management Software
Dept.	Department
DELNET	Developing Library Network
DESIDOC	Defence Scientific Information and Documentation Center
DOE	Department of Electronics
DOS	Disk Operating System
DOT	Department of Telecommunications
DRDO	Defense Research and Development Organisation
DSIR	Department of Scientific and Industrial Research
DTP	Desktop Publishing Software
DVD	Digital Video Disc

E-Mail	Electronic Mail
ENIAC	Electronic Numerical Integrator and Calculator
ERNET	Education and Research Network
ETD	Electronic Submission of Theses and Dissertations
FTP	File Transfer Protocol
ICAR	Indian Council of Agricultural Research
ICHR	Indian Council of Historical Research
ICMR	Indian Council of Medical Research
ICRISAT	International Crops Research Institute for the Semi Arid Tropics
ICSSR	Indian Council of Social Sciences Research
IGNOU	Indira Gandhi National Open University
IIT	Indian Institute of Technology
ILL	Inter Library Loan
ILMS	Integrated Library Management Software
I-NET	Network Sponsored by Department of Telecommunications
INFLIBNET	Information and Library Network
INSDOC	Indian National Scientific and Documentation Centre
IP	Internet Protocol
IRC	Internet Relay Chat
ISDN	Integrated Services Digital Network
ISO	International Standards Organisation
ISP	Internet Service Provider
IT	Information Technology
IUC	Indian Universities Commission

JANET	Joint Academic Network
JMI	Jamia Millia Islamia
JNU	Jawaharlal Nehru University
KB	Kilo Byte
LAN	Local Area Network
LIBRIS	Library Software available in India
MAN	Metropolitan Area Network
MANUU	Maulana Azad National Urdu University
MARC	Machine Readable Catalogue
MB	Mega Byte
MGAHV	Mahatma Gandhi Antharrastreeya Hindi Vishwavidyalaya
MLISc	Master of Library and Information Science
M.Phil.	Master of Philosophy
MS DOS	Micro Soft Disk Operating System
NCSI	National Center for Science Information
NEHU	North-Eastern Hill University
NEP	National Education Policy
NIC	National Informatics Center
NICNET	National Informatics Center Network
NISSAT	National Information System for Science and Technology
N-LIST	National Library and Information Services Infrastructure for Scholarly Content
NPE	National Policy on Education
NPUL	National Policy on University Libraries
NU	Nagaland University

OCLC	Online Computer Library Centre
OHP	Over Head Projector
OPAC	Online Public Access Catalogue
PC	Personal Computer
PG	Post-Graduation
Ph.D.	Doctor of Philosophy
PLANNER	Promotion of Library Automation and Networking in North Eastern Region
PU	Pondicherry University
RAM	Random Access Memory
SAIL	Steel Authority of India Ltd.
SDI	Selective Dissemination of Information
SIRNET	CSIR Network
SPSS	Statistical Package for Social Sciences
SOUL	Software for University Libraries
TB	Tera Byte
TCP	Transmission Control Protocol
TIFR	Tata Institute of Fundamental Research
TISS	Tata Institute of Social Sciences
TU	Tezpur University
TV	Television
UG	Under-Graduation
UGC	University Grants Commission
UK	United Kingdom
UNESCO	United Nations Educational, Scientific and Cultural Organisation

UNIMARC	Universal Machine Readable Catalogue
UOD	University of Delhi
UOH	University of Hyderabad
UP	Uttar Pradesh
URL	Uniform Resource Locator
USA	United States of America
VB	Visva Bharati
VC	Video Conferencing
VCR	Video Cassette Recorder
VDU	Video Display Unit
V-SAT	Very Small Aperture Terminal
WAN	Wide Area Network
WB	West Bengal
WP	Word Perfect
WS	Word Star
WWW	World Wide Web

List of Tables

Map

1

Introduction to Information Technology

1.1 INTRODUCTION

Information Technology plays a vital role in today's global knowledge economy. We cannot imagine a modern society without information technology (IT). IT has tremendously transformed our lives directing our destinies by enhancing our abilities to perform multiple tasks. IT has become an integral part of all the spheres of human activities. IT has become an inclusive technology as it does not exclude any area/ field from reaping the benefits of technology. IT is used for information, communication, education, entertainment and a variety of other activities in our daily life. The rapid revolution of digital technologies has created not only wide range of opportunities for the society but also offered variety of new challenges. The digital technology is rapidly transforming the whole world radically. IT has proved to be a boon for the modern society.

The impact of information technology (IT) is enormous and global in its magnitude, pervasiveness and usefulness because of its most distinguishing features of dramatic decrease in cost, size and tremendous increase in processing speed, storage and communication capabilities. IT is the most pervasive force influencing virtually all the spheres of human activities all over the world. IT has profound effect on the progress and development of human civilization.

The dream of librarianship is to serve the information needs of users timely, efficiently and economically. IT has transformed the way people generate acquire, access, use communicate and share information across the globe. With the use of IT, expectations of users for precise, relevant and easy to use information have risen dramatically. Libraries all over the world realised that demands and expectations of their information consumers are rapidly increasing at a rate with which any library with limited resources can hardly cope with through conventional means. Libraries now use IT not only to automate their activities but also to provide innovative information services to the users. Therefore, it has become imperative on the part of libraries to revise their approach, reorient their mode of operation and utilize innovative technologies in order to provide personalized, speedy and cost-effective services to the users.

Panda (1995:23) stated that the important traits of IT that makes the computerization in the libraries exigent can be summed up as: increased computer power leading to speedier and cheaper computer processing, cheaper data storage facilities, digitization of multimedia information, faster data transfer between different systems and media, improved telecommunications such as ISDN, decreased size and cost of equipment, increased reliability of hardware and software, wide availability of electronic information resources and online book vendors.

The major factors and challenges forced the libraries to adopt IT can be summed up as:

- Information explosion
- Rapid and constant technological developments
- Shrinking library budgets

- Escalating price of documents
- Ever growing e-resources
- Greater level of users' expectations for instant results
- Rise of competitors (commercial information service providers)
- Insufficient library collection.
- Changing trend from collection possession to information access provision.
- Inadequate physical facilities in terms of space, furniture and equipment.
- Inability to provide efficient and effective services with manual methods

IT offers tremendous opportunities to provide solutions to some of these major challenges now libraries are facing. IT has great potential for variety of applications in libraries as it contributes to improved quality, increased productivity, more efficient operations, better resource sharing and more effective services to users. Early library automation efforts proved that libraries using IT have improved the efficiency and effectiveness in their operations and services. Libraries have now a wide range of IT based solutions from which they can select the best mix of services to meet the needs of their users. They are, therefore, forced to change, adopt and exploit new technologies to remain successful in satisfying the changing complex information needs of their users.

This chapter provides an introduction to information technology, which can serve as foundation for understanding the technologies used in this book. It covers the definition of IT, major components of IT such as computers, communication, Internet and other technologies.

1.2 INFORMATION TECHNOLOGY: DEFINITION

Information is the collection of facts gathered through various sources. Information plays a vital role in drawing useful conclusions and taking effective decisions. For decisions to be useful, information must be accurate, timely, complete, precise and relevant. Technology is the application of science for practical purposes of solving problems. Technology makes information gathering fast and easy. Technology helps to save time and energy by providing convenience at work. Information technology refers to the management and use of the information using computer-based tools such as computer hardware, software and other technologies. Information Technology is the use of computer and communication technology for the processing, storage, retrieval and communication of information. The phrase Information Technology refers to the set of technological devices used for the creation, gathering, processing, storage, retrieval and delivery of information. The technological devices include computers, communication devices, micro electronics, software and other products.

According to the Information Technology Association of America (ITAA), Information Technology is "the study, design, development, implementation, support or management of computer-based information systems, particularly software applications and computer hardware." IT deals with the use of electronic computers and computer software to convert, store, process, transmit and securely retrieve information.

UNESCO defines Information Technology as "The scientific, technological and engineering disciplines and the managerial techniques used in information handling and processing; their applications; computers and their interaction with men and machines and associated social, economic and cultural matters" (Peltu, 1982).

A L A Glossary of Library and Information Science defined IT as "the application of computers and other technologies to the acquisition, organisation, storage, retrieval and dissemination of information" (American Library Association, 1983).

Moll (1983) opines in its widest sense that IT can be said to involve:

> "...... various means of obtaining, storing and transferring information using computer, telecommunications and microelectronics for fostering development process."

The British Department of Industry defines Information Technology as "the acquisition, processing, storage and dissemination of vocal, pictorial, textual and numerical information by a microelectronics based combination of computing and telecommunications" (Longley, 1985).

According to Olsen (1989), the convergence of three key technologies, viz., computers, telecommunications and microelectronics, and the development of a whole range of media (magnetic, optical and now magneto-optical), software, products, and services constitutes the package being called information technology.

According to Viswanathan (1995), broadly Information Technology may be said to be that technology which is used for information management, which involves acquisition, processing, storage, retrieval and dissemination of information. As reprography, printing and publishing are all activities involved in information management, the corresponding technologies become part of IT.

According to Murthy (1999), the information technologies that are relevant to libraries mainly include: (i) Computer technology, (ii) Telecommunication technologies, (iii) Reprographic technologies, (iv) Library technologies, and (v) Technical communication.

For the purpose of this study, the term 'Information Technology' is used to cover all of those technologies which include personal computers as well as a variety of technologies controlled by those computers including application software, databases, CD-ROMs, networks, communication devices, electronic information products and several other compatible devices used in libraries.

1.3 COMPONENTS OF INFORMATION TECHNOLOGY

Information Technology is a broad term that encompasses wide range of sub-technologies. It is the convergence of computers, communication and micro-electronic based technologies. IT is undergoing rapid revolutionary innovative developments. Successive developments in IT are tremendously enhancing their capabilities resulting into better technological devices, innovations, products, services and quality solutions. In recent years, IT has expanded so rapidly to include a wide array of devices, information products and services that transformed the role of a library into a gateway of accessing global information resources.

This section provides an overview of major components of computer, communication and other relevant technologies used in libraries.

1.4 COMPUTER TECHNOLOGY

The computer is the key component of modern information technology. Computer Technology has transformed every sphere of human life all over the world. Computers have affected all the activities of modern life. Computers have become indispensable in every field of work due to ease of use and utility. As computers have become easier to use, people found them very useful in daily life. Computers are enriching our lives in many ways by enhancing our abilities and increasing our skills, efficiency and productivity. Modern computer's increasing capabilities have contributed for the growing use of computers in all sectors in the society. Today, we cannot imagine life without computers. Computers are now being widely used in diverse areas for various purposes such as office, education, business and industry, science and technology, media, banking, publishing, medicine, transportation, government etc.

1.4.1 Computer

Oxford Advanced Learners Dictionary defines computer as "an electronic machine that can store, organize and find information, do calculations and control other machines".

A computer is an electronic device that can receive, store and process data based on a set of instructions called a program. A computer accepts input (data), process it, stores it and produces output (information).

Computer is an electronic device that performs diverse operations with the help of instructions to process the information in order to achieve desired results. Computer performs many functions such as arithmetic calculations, logical operations and information processing, storage, retrieval and communication.

Data, Information and knowledge : Computers are information processing machines. Computer is a machine that can receive data, process data and converts it into useful information. Data refers to facts, figures, statistics, text and instructions. Data as such does not convey any meaning or conclusion. Information is the result of processed data i.e. meaningful facts. Data can be defined as a set of isolated and unrelated raw facts, figures, text and instructions which have little or no meaning simply because they lack context for evaluation. When the data is processed and converted into a meaningful and useful form, it is known as information. Information can be defined as a set of organized and validated collection of data. Knowledge is the act of understanding the context in which the information is used.

1.4.2 Characteristics of Computer

Today, computers have become more powerful and widely used tools due to less cost, high processing speed, large memory capacity, increasing capabilities and usefulness. Computers enable us to be free from drudgery of tedious, repetitive ad laborious activities and thus make our lives easier, faster, better and more comfortable. Because of these powerful characteristics, computers have been extensively used in offices, homes and a large number of diverse fields. Computers have gained greater importance due to the following characteristics.

Speed : Computers process data speedily and perform

calculations extremely fast. The speed of calculations has increased exponentially in recent years. Computers can do thousands of calculations at a very high speed. Computers are capable of doing the most complex tasks in minutes. Today, powerful computers can perform 100 million calculations per second. Computers can complete in minutes the huge tasks that a person would take years to complete.

Accuracy : Computers process data and perform all kinds of complex calculations very accurately as per the instructions given to them. Most of the errors attributed to the computers are really human errors such as program error, procedure error and erroneous data.

Reliability : Modern computers ensure high degree of reliability. Computers are widely used because of their performance reliability. Computers consistently perform all the assigned and repetitive tasks accurately and perfectly.

Storage Capacity or Memory : A computer has huge memory capacity to store vast amount of data and information. A powerful computer can store billions of characters, thousands of images and make them available for ready use.

Tirelessness : Computers can perform repetitive tasks continuously for days and months with the same speed and accuracy without any fatigue and tiredness.

Versatility : Computers can do wide variety of multiple tasks simultaneously. Computers are increasingly used in diverse applications. Computers are used in office, education, research, industries, banks, railways, entertainment, engineering etc. The number of areas for which computers can be used continues to grow very fast.

1.5 EVOLUTION OF COMPUTERS

Modern **computer** has transformed all the spheres of human **life.** The **evolution of computer** is a long gradual development from Abacus to modern computer. The term computer originally meant a person capable of performing numeric calculations with the help of a mechanical computing device. Computer technology has a long and interesting history. The process of inventing calculation tools useful to human activities explains the evolution of computers. The significant events in the **evolution of computers** are listed below:

- The Abacus is the earliest calculating tool invented by Chinese mathematician named Abacus in 1450 BC to aid man's basic arithmetic operations like addition, subtraction, multiplication and division. The abacus consists of a rectangular wooden frame with rods carrying round beads.

- John Napier, a Scottish mathematician invented Logarithms in 1617 to compute approximate values of calculations including multiplication, division and exponents.

- William Oughtred invented Slide rules in 1621 which was used as a ready reckoner for carrying out complicated calculations. Today, pocket calculators have replaced the logarithmic tables and slide rules.

- Blaise Pascal a French Mathematician invented the first functional mechanical calculator *called pascaline* in 1642 to carryout arithmetical operations.

- Charles Babbage designed a Difference engine for computing logarithms (1822) and Analytical engine (1833) for following instructions from punched cards. Analytical engine was more sophisticated complex machine which could perform any mathematical operations automatically. Charles Babbage being the pioneer in the development of computer was called as the father of modern computer.

- The origin of the electronic calculator could be traced to the Turing Machine of Alan Turing in 1930 leading to the era of computers.

- In 1942, Lady Augusta Ada Love Lace became the world's first programmer to work upon Babbage's designs thus contributing to the history of computers.

- Howard Aiken designed a large-scale electromechanical computer called mark I in 1944 which was a major step forward in the evolution of computers.
- John Eckert and John Mauchly developed the first general purpose electronic computer -Electronic Numerical Integrator and Calculator (ENIAC) in 1946 at the University of Pennsylvania in the USA.

The inventions of transistors and integrated circuits in 1960's were great advancements over vacuum tube technology leading to the next generations of digital electronic computer. By 1990's personal computers using microprocessors become part of everyday life. Advances in technologies continued to produce cheaper, smaller and more powerful computers contributing to the explosion of computers in all facets of modern life. Subsequently, the computers have been undergoing tremendous transformation in the size, speed, storage capabilities and applications leading to the emergence of different generations of computers.

1.6 GENERATIONS OF COMPUTERS

The history of development of a computer can be classified into different stages. Each stage of major technological innovation resulting into smaller, cheaper and more powerful, more efficient computers with a period of about 10 years is known as a generation. Based on the technological advancements, modern computer systems have gone through a series of six generations during the evolution process. Each successive generation of computers used latest technology characterized by higher processing speed, large memory capacity, smaller size, improved reliability, increased performance and reduced cost than the previous generation.

1.6.1 First Generation Computers

The First generation computers available during late 1940's and early 1950's used thousands of vacuum tubes for the central processor, magnetic drums for memory, punched cards for input and output and machine language for human-machine interface. These computers were huge, bulky, expensive and complicated machines that consumed a lot of electricity, generated more heat, occupied large space and needed specialist operators. The first electronic digital computer, ENIAC developed in 1946 can be treated as origin for the first generation computers. It weighed 30 tons, occupied the space of a two car garages and contained 18000 vacuum tubes. It costs half a million dollars at 1946 prices. It could perform 5000 additions or 350 multiplications in one second. It could complete in one day the calculations that would have taken a whole year to do manually.

1.6.2 Second Generation Computers

Second-generation computers started in the early 1960's used transistors. Transistors were faster, far cheaper, much smaller, and required less energy and produced less heat than vaccum tubes. These computers used punched cards for input. IBM 700 Series computers belong to this generation. High-level languages like FORTRAN were developed and used as human machine interface language. Compared to the first generation, these were faster, compact, lower in cost and easier to maintain them.

1.6.3 Third Generation Computers

The third generation computers started in 1964 replaced transistors with integrated circuits. Chips were cheaper, cooler and faster than transistors. This increased the speed and efficiency of computers. Operating systems were the human interface to computing operations. Keyboards and monitors became the input-output devices. Third generation computers had higher speed, larger storage capacities and lower prices. IBM/360 family and DEC – PDP/8 belongs to this generation.

1.6.4 Fourth Generation Computers

The Fourth generation computers saw the reduction of computer components to microscopic dimensions. These computers are made using Very Large Scale Integrated Circuits (VLSI). Thousands of integrated circuits placed onto a silicon chip made up a microprocessor. Computers built using microprocessors known as microcomputers, which constitute the fourth generation computers. Many computer companies such as Intel, Sun, Apple, Compaq etc. began developing their own microprocessors and microcomputers. Computers began to rapidly increase in speed, reliability and power while becoming more compact, cheaper and more user-friendly from the 1980's onwards resulting into the personal computer revolution. The first home personal computer is made by IBM in 1981. The other significant development was that these computers could be linked together to form networks leading to the emergence of Internet. PCs in the home have become highly popular for the use of work, games, music, video and accessing the web. Computers have increased their role from professional and business machines to entertainment and educational tools.

1.6.5 Fifth generation computers

The first four generations of computers were basically built to handle numeric and data processing applications. The fifth generation computers are the development of intelligent thinking machines to create a human like computer. These computers developed during 1990s used ultra large scale integration and logic based languages to handle sophisticated non-numeric applications. The three characteristics that can be identified with the fifth generations computers are mega chips, parallel processing of several instructions and artificial intelligence which comprises expert systems, natural language processing, speech recognition, vision recognition, knowledge processing, and robotics. Super computer is emerged with new technological developments.

1.6.6 Sixth generation computers

The sixth generation computers are very large sized super computers. These computers facilitate various national and international networks in transmitting huge quantities of data across the world. The Centre for Development of Advanced Computing (C-DAC) developed Asia's second largest super computer "PARAM-

10000" in 1998 is an example of sixth generation computers. It could perform 100,000,000,000 mathematical operations per second.

1.7 CLASSIFICATION OF COMPUTERS

Today, computers are available in different sizes and types designed for different purposes. The use of different types of computers has made life more comfortable, highly convenient, smooth and fast paced. The size and speed of a computer varies considerably from very small to very big. A wide range of computers are available today in the market ranging from a personal computer to a super computer. Based on physical size, performance and application areas, computers can be classified into four categories namely micro computers, mini computers, main frame computers and super computers.

1.7.1 Micro Computers

Micro computer is a small, low-cost digital computer which uses microprocessor. Micro computers are also known as personal computers (PCs) as they are intended to be used by one person at a time. Many individuals purchase micro computers for personal use either at home or at office. Personal computers are the most widely used computers which have found application in daily activities of the modern world. Personal computers are suitable for general purpose tasks like word processing, programming, e-mailing, internet surfing, digital documentation and multimedia games. The physical characteristics and fast processing capabilities of high speed, accuracy and low cost of personal computers account for their wide usage and high popularity.

The micro computers include PCs, Desktops, Laptops, Handheld computers, Tablet PCs, PDAs and notebook computers, workstations, palmtops etc.

Personal Computers: Computers used by the individual persons.

Desktop Computers: A desktop computer is designed to be permanently kept on a desktop.

Desktop Computer

Source: *http://www.herat4soo.com/308518*

Laptop / Note Book computers: Laptops computers are portable computers with lightweight and can be easily carried in a bag. Today, laptops are becoming faster, slimmer and cheaper with enhanced features and functionalities.

Laptop / Note Book Computer

Source: *http://www.dell.com/us/p/laptops*

Laptop Computer: The main difference between desktop computer and laptop is their size, portability, mother board and human computer interface.

Hand held computers or palm tops: Handheld / Palmtop computer is a computer that can be hold in hand, pocket or purse and used in mobility. Ideally, a palmtop is used for storage of personal information like phone numbers, appointments, addresses, pictures and such other small data.

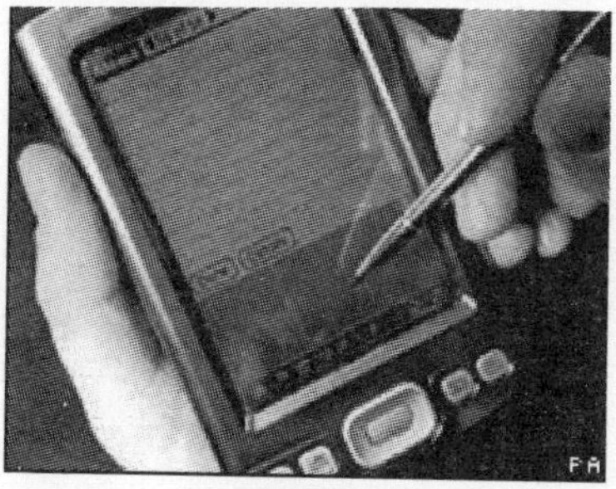

Palm Top

Source: *http://news.bbc.co.uk/2/hi/uk_news/scotland/6202003.stm*

Tablet Personal Computers: Tablet PCs are mostly used in graphics work. It is an electronic device that utilizes digital ink to write or draw directly on the monitor.

Tablet Personal Computer

Source: *http://libraryportal.wordpress.com/2011/01/24/tablet-pc-will-be-replacement-of-books/*

Personal Digital Assistant (PDA): PDAs are lightweight, hand-held computer designed for use as a personal organizer with communication capabilities. PDAs are intended to fulfill the needs of the mobile people by providing real-time message communications and a variety of personal services such as notes, calendars and diaries.

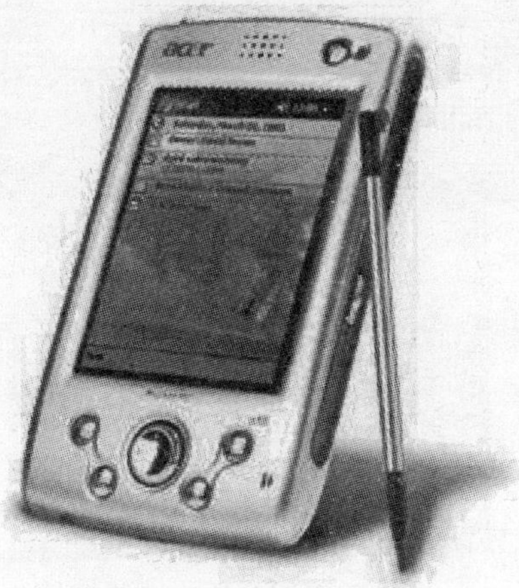

Personal Digital Assistant

Source: *http://www.bullcitymobile.com/FridayFlashbackThePDA*

1.7.2 Mini computers

A mini computer is a small digital computer which can process and store less data than a mainframe but more than a micro computer. A mini computer is multi-user digital computer capable of supporting from 10 to hundreds of users simultaneously. Mini computers are used in industries, research organizations, colleges and universities. Mini computers are smaller, slower and less expensive and less powerful than mainframe computers. Examples: PDP 11, IBM (6000 series).

1.7.3 Mainframe Computers

Mainframes are large, high capacity powerful multi-user computers capable of supporting many hundreds or thousands of users to work simultaneously. It allows simultaneous access to multiple users and supports a large number of input and output devices. Mainframe allows its user to maintain large information storage at a centralized location and be able to access and process this data from different computers located at different places. They are used for centralized processing functions by large organizations for the purpose of research, engineering works, meteorological calculations, graphics etc. Example: IBM's ES 000, VAX 8000.

Mini Computer
Source: *http://www.governmentauctions.org/labels/business.asp*

1.7.4 Super Computers

Super computers are the special purpose machines with highest processing speed. Supercomputers are extremely fast, expensive and the most advanced powerful computers that can perform hundreds of millions of instructions per second. It allows multiple users to interact with the CPU simultaneously through multiple types of input devices. It also provides outputs in a variety of forms and supports a large number of output devices. They are used for very large complex scientific, research and technical applications including engineering designs, weather forecasting and nuclear physics. Examples: CRAY-3 and PARAM Padma.

Super Computer
Source: ***http://en.wikipedia.org/wiki/File:Columbia_Supercomputer_-_NASA_Advanced_ Supercomputing_Facility.jpg***

1.7.5 Servers

Servers are computers that provide service to other computers called clients over a network. Web servers, file servers and e-mail servers supply web pages, files and e-mails to computers respectively that need access to them.

1.7.6 Thin clients

Thin clients are computers that do not have complete hardware found on other computers. Thin clients essentially rely on other computers over a network to perform most of their processing functions.

1.7.7 Future Computers

With rapid innovative technological advancements, computers, in future, would become further faster, more smaller, more reliable, more mobile and more powerful with enhanced user-friendly multimedia capabilities.

1.8 COMPUTER HARDWARE COMPONENTS

The main purpose of a computer is to process data into useful information for taking effective decisions. The physical parts or components that make up computer are called hardware. Computer receives data from input devices, stores it in memory and processes it in central processing unit and displays and prints the results or useful information through output devices. The computer consists of central processing unit, memory unit, input devices and output devices. Figure 1 shows different components of the computer.

1.8.1 Central Processing Unit (CPU)

CPU is a micro processor and a brain of a computer. CPU interprets, coordinates the operations and supervises the instructions.

The CPU consists of three units.

Arithmetic and Logic Unit (ALU): ALU is the intelligence of the computer. ALU performs arithmetic calculations, logical operations

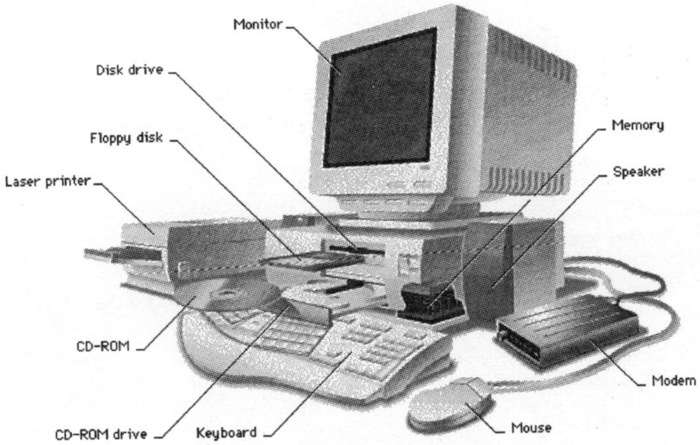

Components of Computer Hardware
Source : *http://www.warepin.com/classifications-of-computer-hardware-systems/*

and comparisons on the stored numbers and the results are transferred to memory unit.

Control Unit: The control unit executes the program instructions. It coordinates, directs and controls the activities of all other units of a computer. The control unit gives command to transfer data from input device to the memory, from the memory to the ALU. It also transfers the results from ALU to memory and to the output device for printing. It works like the central nervous system of the human body.

Memory Unit: Computer has storage capacity known as memory. Memory unit stores programs, data and final results. Memory consists of two types of memory - Read Only Memory (ROM) and Random Access Memory (RAM). ROM is a memory used to permanently record programs and instructions by the computer manufacturer which cannot be altered. RAM is a memory used to temporarily store information as is being entered. RAM and ROM called as main or primary memory. When you enter data into computer, the data will be stored in RAM. The other types of memory include virtual memory, cache memory and buffers.

1.8.2 Input devices

An input device accepts instruction and data from the user and communicates them to the computer for further processing. There are many input devices. The most common input devices are key boards, pointing devices (mouse, touch pad), trackball, joystick, light pen, digital camera, barcode readers, scanners, speech recognition and hand writing recognition devices.

Mouse Pointing Pen Trackball Trackstick Keyboard

1.8.3 Output Devices:

Output is the data that has been processed into useful information. Once data has been entered and processed, the output will be provided through output device. Output devices are used to communicate information from the computer to the user. The most common types of output devices are monitors, printers and plotters. The three basic types of printers are dot matrix, inkjet, and laser.

1.8.4 Storage Devices and Media

Secondary/ external storage is used to store data and programs. It enables to store large amounts of data. Secondary storage involves both storage devices and storage media. The storage device is the device used to read and write data on the media. The storage media is the actual materials used to store the data. For example drives are storage devices and disks are the storage media.

Secondary storage media fall into three main categories – magnetic, optical and solid state.

- **Magnetic Storage** is commonly used with floppy disks, hard disks and magnetic tapes. Magnetic tapes are used as archival storage for large volume of data.

- **Optical Storage** is used with CDs, CD-ROMs and DVDs. Optical disks have much higher storage capacity than magnetic disks.
- **Solid State Memory** is used in small devices such as organizers, cameras, phones, hand held computers and smart cards.

In addition to the above, many other components are required for the computer to work efficiently. For example, every computer requires a bus that transmits data from one part of the computer to another.

1.9 COMPUTER SOFTWARE

A computer system consists of hardware and software. Computers cannot work without software. Software controls the work of a computer. Computers need instructions to perform any task. A set of instructions which indicate the tasks to be performed and controls the sequence of operations is known as program and set of programs is called software. Software refers to a set of programs written by programmers using a programming language to perform certain tasks. Software is responsible for controlling, integrating and managing the hardware components of a computer and to accomplish specific tasks.

Programming Languages: Programming languages are computer communication languages used to write computer programs to communicate with computer. A programming language consists of all the symbols, characters and usage rules that enable people to communicate with computers. There are many programming languages used for different purposes. The popular languages are Basic, Cobol, Fortran, C++, Perl, Visual basic etc.

Computer software can be categorized as System software and Application software.

1.9.1 System Software

System software helps the user to run the computer system. System software is a software that controls, integrates and manager all the resources and components of a computer system. Some examples of system software are operating system, device drivers, language translators and system utilities and some fundamental utility programs such as disk formatters, file managers, text editors etc,. Some of the system programs include assembler, computer and interpreter.

Operating system: Operating system (OS) is the most important system software required to operate a computer. OS provides user friendly interface between the computer and the user. It allows the user to create files, folders and manage directories. It also manages memory hardware and software. The basic functions of an operating system are the management of processes, memory, files, devices, security and user interface. The popular operating systems are MSDOS, Windows, UNIX, Linux etc.

1.9.2 Application Software

Computers perform different tasks or applications. Software used to perform specific task or application is called application software. Application software is set of programs that make the computer to perform specific application like payroll accounting, inventory control etc. To facilitate the use of computers in different applications, large number of application software packages is developed for various fields.

There are two categories of application software:

- General purpose software include word processing, spreadsheet, database management, graphic software, desktop publishing software etc.,
- Special purpose software developed for use in specific fields such as libraries, banking, business, industry, science, technology etc.,

The application software packages such as word processing, database management, spreadsheet, desktop publishing are briefly described.

Word Processing Software: Word processing is the most commonly used software for preparation of electronic documents in homes and offices. Word processing has completely changed the nature of work in offices. This software is used to prepare, edit, store, retrieve, display and print letters, memos and reports easily in more elegant style. Word processing software has may features such as deletion, insertion, replacement copying, formatting, spelling checker, mail merge, search and replace, thesaurus, multiple fonts and many more.

Spreadsheet Software: Spreadsheet software is used to create tables to manipulate numbers and to perform various analysis. Spreadsheet is like a large table in electronic form in which row and column titles and input data may be entered and some values may be derived on the basis of other values necessitating arithmetic computations. MS Excel is used to calculate and analyze numbers.

Desktop Publishing Software (DTP): Desktop refers to creation of printed documents using a desktop computer. DTP software is a page make-up utility mainly concerned with appearance of text which includes display of page layout, display of text in different styles and sizes and display of graphic images. DTP software is used to compose, create and provide high-quality printed documents such as newspapers, brochures and other publications using text, graphics, pictures, lines, shapes, patterns, borders etc.

Graphics Software: Graphics Software is software used to convert numerical data into graphic form. It helps to create charts, drawings, manipulate photographs and make presentations. It also provides for three dimensional display and maps.

Data Communication Software: Data Communication Software is software used to transmit and receive digital data between two or more computers. They may be a computer, terminal and a host computer. It allows the dissemination of information to remote users. This data can be further analysed using DBMS or Spread Sheet Software.

Database Management Software (DBMS): Data consists of facts, figures, observations and concepts. Processed data becomes information. Data prepared and organized logically in a structure in machine readable form is called a database. A database is a collection of logically related files. File is a collection of related records and the record is a collection of related fields. Database management software allows storage, modification and extraction of information from a database in an efficient manner.

DBMS can be defined as a collection of interrelated data and software to access that data. The main objective of DBMS is to provide good storage and efficient retrieval of information. DBMS is used to organize and manage databases in the computer. DBMS allows us to store and manipulate large quantities of data easily using the computer. For example, we can sort the names, addresses, grades and produce variety of printed reports using the database. DBMS packages include dbase IV, FoxBASE, Oracle etc.

Library Automation Software is software used to computerize all the house-keeping operations of a library such as acquisition, cataloguing, circulation, serials control and provide computer based information services. Examples: Soul, CDS/ISIS, Libsys etc.

1.10 ARTIFICIAL INTELLIGENCE (AI)

Artificial Intelligence (AI) is the branch of computer science concerned with making computers behave like humans. John McCarthy coined Artificial Intelligence in 1956 at the Massachusetts Institute of Technology. According to him, Artificial Intelligence is the science and engineering of intelligent machines, especially intelligent computer programs. Intelligence is the ability to acquire, retrieve and use knowledge in a meaningful way.

Artificial Intelligence (AI) refers to computer programs, which emulate human intelligence. Examples are making decisions, solving problems and drawing conclusions. AI techniques are being increasingly utilized to enhance database systems especially their user-friendliness. AI is used in game **playing, neural networks** and **robotics**

AI has two branches: natural language processing and expert systems.

Natural Language Processing: Natural language processing (NLP) is the ability of a computer programs to understand human written and spoken languages. Natural Language refers to a language for expressing thoughts and feelings. Natural Language Processing (NLP) involves the interpretation, manipulation or generation of human language by computer so that one can communicate with a computer as one communicates with another person. In natural language processing, a user can interact with a computing using natural human language rather than a structured command language with the help of an interface called natural language interface, which translates the natural language into the application language. One of the important uses of natural language processing is to use human language to search databases.

Expert System: Computers are programmed to make decisions in real-life situations. Expert system is an artificial intelligence application that uses a knowledge base of human expertise to aid in solving problems. An expert system can be defined as Artificial Intelligence programs designed to represent human expertise in a specific domain. The heart of an expert system is knowledge base, which contains facts, rules and other information pertaining to a particular domain. Facts represent accepted knowledge in a certain field (normally possessed by experts) and rules- a collection of IF - THEN statements also called "rules of thumb" for drawing inferences. IF such-and-such is true THEN assume that so and so is true. Typical expert system application areas include medical diagnosis, planning, decision-making, monitoring and design. Potential areas of using expert system in library system are in the application of cataloguing rules and classification schemes and in the design of information retrieval system. Expert system is made up of three basic components: the knowledge base, an inference engine and a user interface. The use of expert systems is growing rapidly because of powerful technological advancements. (Bhardwaj,1995:57).

1.11 USER INTERFACE

User interface facilities easy communication between user and computer. User Interface is a set of commands or menus through which a user communicates with the system. Interface is a means of providing interaction and communication between the user and the computer. The success of any system will depend on its ability to communicate with the user in a language, which is spoken and understood, by both the user and the system (Jones, 1988).

A user interface may be defined as an interactive system through which the lay user can communicate with the software irrespective of its complexity, with little or no knowledge of it, and easily exploit/utilize its capabilities. A good user interface anticipates the user's requirements and assists them to gather information and use necessary tools. User interfaces available in today's market can be categorized as: 1) Menu - driven systems; 2) Command-based systems; 3) Direct manipulation systems; 4) Systems based on artificial intelligence using expert systems methodologies (Gauch, 1992).

The other user interfaces are character-based interfaces, graphical user interfaces, and pen-based interfaces; touch screen interfaces and conversational interfaces.

User- friendly interfaces have been developed in order to make it easier for user both to input data to the system and to use the system output (Rowley, 1993). Better user interfaces facilitate and make it quite easier for the user to use online public access catalogues (OPACs), databases and electronic information resources in networks.

A well-designed interface will enable the searcher to access systems and navigate them transparently (Hulser, 1993). Good design results in increased user satisfaction, usage and productivity, and decreased development and training costs. It has been shown that well-designed user interfaces can increase productivity by 25 per cent and reduce errors by 25 percent (Johnson et al., 1989).

Lot of research efforts are going on to develop more sophisticated, innovative and intelligent user-friendly interfaces and make it easier for users to utilize new technological products, resources, facilities and services effectively.

1.12 MULTIMEDIA TECHNOLOGY

Multimedia is one of the fastest growing and the most exciting areas in the field of information technology. Multimedia offers much richer and more efficient means for effective presentation and communication of information. Multimedia has become highly effective as it combines text, audio, animation, video and graphics for presentation of information.

The word Multimedia contains two separate words multi means many and media means communication mediums/ materials through which information may be transmitted. Multimedia refers to the combined use of several mediums such as text, audio, animation, video and graphics to present information to the user via the computer in an attractive and interactive manner

Multimedia can be defined as seamless digital integration of text, audio, video, animation and graphics within a single presentation in a way that provides users with high levels of control and interaction.

Multimedia applications that allow users to actively interact with the presentation are called *Interactive Multimedia*. When you provide a structure of linked elements through which the learner can navigate, interactive multimedia becomes hypermedia. Hypermedia is an extension of the hypertext to include pictures, sound, movies along with text and links to other documents. Hypertext is the text presented with hyperlinks to have connection to the other related documents.

A multimedia system is a system capable of processing multimedia data and applications. It is characterized by the processing, generation, manipulations and retrieval of multimedia information. The hardware components of a multimedia computer include sound card, graphics card, CD/DVD drive and speakers. The components of multimedia include Text, Graphics, Animation, Video and Sound.

Multimedia has great potential for its application in various areas such as advertising, training, education, entertainment, corporate presentations, electronic reference sources and digital publications.

Virtual reality refers to artificial reality in which the user becomes fully immersed in an artificial three dimensional world completely generated by a computer. Virtual reality can be described as an artificial environment that is created by using special computer hardware and software, which is presented to the user in such a manner that it appears and feels like a real three dimensional world. To enter in a virtual reality world, a user wears special gloves, earphones and goggles all of which receive their input from the computer system (ITL Education solutions, 2009).

1.13 DATABASES

Databases are used to manage huge amount of information. A database is an organized collection of logically related data accessible through computer. The organised collection of information (Database) serves as a base from which the desired information can be retrieved, conclusions can be drawn and decisions can be made by further reorganizing or processing this data.

Data is the raw material from which information is derived as the end product. The term database refers to an organised collection of logically related records accessible through computer. In the field of library and information science, a database is defined as an organized and generally unlinked set of machine readable bibliographic or information source records. A record contains information relating to one document or item. Records are composed of a number of fields. Database may be stored on magnetic or optical media such as disks and accessed either locally or remotely. Catalogues, files and lists of borrowers are all types of databases. Rowley (1993: 67-73) categorized Databases either reference or source databases.

1.13.1. Reference databases

Reference database contain bibliographic, directory, or other citations that refer the user to primary information sources such as a document, an organization or an individual for additional information or for the full text of a document. Reference databases are divided into bibliographic, catalogue and referral databases.

- **Bibliographic databases** : Contain a series of linked bibliographic records, with each record containing some combination of components such as accession number, title, author, source reference, abstract etc. These components do not give the information or the text of the source document, but only point to where the information might be found. These include citations or bibliographic references and sometimes abstracts.
- **Catalogue Databases** : Show the stock of a given library or library network. These databases list the monographs, journal titles and other items of the library but do not give much information on the contents of these documents.
- **Referral databases** : contain descriptive, directory references to information such as the names and addresses of individuals and organizations.

1.13.2. Source Databases

Source Databases contain the original source data. After successful consultation of a source database, the user should have the required information. Source Databases can be grouped according to their content.

- *Full-text databases* contain the complete texts of newspapers, journals, encyclopedias, and other published information sources.
- *Numeric databases* contain numerical data of various kinds including statistical, economic or other survey data.
- *Text-numeric databases* contain a mixture of textual and numeric data (annual report) and handbook data.

1.14 COMMUNICATION TECHNOLOGY

Rapid advances in communication technology combined with accelerating developments in computer technology have offered tremendous opportunities in the field of information management. Developments in communication technology have made possible to access a wide variety of electronic information resources across the globe easily, instantaneously and economically. Computers are used for generation, processing and retrieval of information. Telecommunications are involved in communication of that information. Communication means sending or receiving information. To make the information more useful and easily accessible remotely, it must be transferred from one location to another. The technology used in transferring information is called communication technology. Communication Technology consists of telecommunications and data communications. Telecommunications is the use of telephone, fax, telegraph, radio or television facilities to transfer the information, either directly or via computer. A communication system can be defined as the collection of hardware and software that facilitates inter-system exchange of information between different devices.

Data communication is the transfer of data or information between two devices through transmission medium. It is the transmission or reception of digital information between two or more computers. Data Communication system consists of five basic components such as a message, sender, receiver, medium, and protocol. According to Rowley (1993), the essential components of a communication are a transmitter to send information, and receiver to accept it; a transmission medium (channel) through which the message travels; signals and codes which represent message; and network controls to ensure that the message gets to its destination. Different kinds of communication systems and networks are used under different circumstances for different purposes.

Viswanathan (1995) stated that the communication systems are classified according to the channel used into radio, microwave, satellite, and co-axial cable and fiber optic communications.

The physical components of communication technology include cabling media switching and signaling technologies, communication controls, protocols, codes and standards, digital or analog communications and data or voice communication technologies.

The important applications of communication technologies in information services include access to databases and digital information resources by remote users, electronic file transfer, electronic messaging, electronic data interchange and sending online databases as well as network databases etc.

Based on signal characteristics, telecommunication networks are classified as telephone, telegraph, telex and data networks.

1.15 COMPUTER NETWORKS

Computer Network is a system of connecting two or more computers to share information and resources. Technical dictionary definition of network implies "Computer and communication links that permit computers to communicate with each other and to share programs, facilities, data and knowledge bases".

A computer network is a system of interconnecting multiple computers. A computer network consists of a set of communication channels inter connecting a set of computing devices or nods that can communicate with each other. The nods may be computers, terminals, workstations, or communication units of various kinds distributed over different locations (Malwad, 1995).

The main objective of a computer network is to share all resources, which include computing devices, software, human resources, databases, digital information products and services etc.

1.15.1. Types of Networks

According to the geographical area covered, networks can be classified into three:

Local Area Network (LAN) : LAN is a network that interconnects computers in a small geographical area such as office, home or building.

Metropolitan Area Network (MAN) : MAN is a network that interconnects a number of computers spread over a metropolitan area such as a city or town. e.g. CALIBNET, MALIBNET etc.

Wide Area Network (WAN) : WAN is a system that interconnects a number of widely dispersed computers over a large geographical area such as cities, states, countries or even the whole world. e.g. Internet, INFLIBNET, JANET.

LANs, MANs, and WANs are generally interconnected in hierarchical manner to form a global network called network of networks i.e. Internet.

Based on the purpose, networks can be classified into two categories (Haravu, 1993).

Infrastructure networks are those that provide the hardware, software protocols and freeways for the free flow of information. Networks like ERNET, I-NET, NICNET, INDONET etc., come under this category.

Application networks are those that are setup by or for a specific community to serve well-defined end-users. Library Networks like DELNET, CALIBNET, and MALIBNET etc belongs to this category.

Library Network: The US National Council for Libraries and Information Services offered a comprehensive definition of Library Network as "two or more Libraries and / or other organizations engaged in a common pattern of information exchange, through communication, for some functional purpose. A network usually consists of a formal arrangement whereby materials, information and services provided by a variety of types of libraries and/or organizations are made available to all potential users. Libraries may be in different jurisdictions but agree to serve one another on the same basis each serves its own constituents. Computers and telecommunications may be among the tools used for facilitating communications among them. The basic purpose of Library networks is for resource sharing among institutions, organizations, libraries etc.

1.15.2. Network Topologies

Network Topology/structure refers to the way in which the computers are linked together in a network either physically or logically. Network Topology indicates the mode of connection of the computers and other equipment including the communication links in a network. It is the geometric representation of the relationship of all the links. There are five basic topologies: Bus, Ring, Star, Tree and Mesh. More complex networks can be built as hybrids using two or more of the above basic topologies.

Bus Topology : Bus Topology network uses a common bus/ backbone/cable to connect all the computers with terminators at both the ends.

Ring Topology : In ring topology, computers are placed on a circle of cable without any terminal ends. Every node has exactly two neighbours connected to form a ring for communication purposes.

Star Topology : In star topology, devices are not directly linked to each other but are connected through a hub forming the shape of star.

Tree Topology : A tree topology combines characteristics of linear bus and star topologies. It consists of groups of star-configured workstations connected to a bus backbone cable.

Mesh Topology : In mesh topology, every node has a dedicated point-to-point link to every other node.

1.16. INTERNET AND WORLD WIDE WEB HTTP:// EN.WIKIPEDIA.ORG/WIKI/INTERNET

Internet brought a great revolution in global communication system. Internet is the largest world-wide network of networks enabling all kinds of computers to communicate and share information across the globe. It is a global source of information resources accessible through computer networks at anytime by anyone from anywhere in the world. Internet has dramatically improved personal communication and interaction among scientific research community and enabled them to access a vast range of latest information resources at their desktop computers. Today, Internet is being increasingly used for academic, research, social and commercial purposes. Internet is the fastest growing information system for delivering wide variety of resources, products, tools and services.

The word Internet is derived from two words – Interconnection and Networks. Internet is the largest worldwide system of computer networks - a global network of networks which allows the users to access and share information. Each of these networks comprises tens of thousands of computers. The high level of Internet connectivity has contributed for the fastest communication, easy information access and effective sharing of wide range of resources and services across the globe. It is the most powerful and landmark technological advancement in the field of Information Technology (IT). Internet is the world's largest and fastest growing network of networks. Internet is growing at an astounding rate connecting millions of users located all over the world. The users figures vary widely and change very rapidly day by day. Internet contains wealth of information resources on almost all the fields of knowledge.

1.16.1. Evolution of Internet

The Internet traces its origin back to 1960s, when the US Government funded Department of Defence's Advanced Research Projects Agency (ARPA) to create a computer network that continues to function in the event of a disaster such as a nuclear war. ARPA developed ARPANET (Advanced Research Projects Agency Network) linking US scientific and academic researchers that became the precursor to the modern internet. By 1970s, ARPA helped in the development of a new protocol known as TCP/IP (Transmission Control Protocol/ Internet Protocol) a common communications standard for ARPANET for transferring data between the networks. In 1980s user net newsgroups and electronic mail were emerged. Internet really became popular in the 1990s after the development of World Wide Web (www). In 1991, Tim Berners-Lee of the European Organisation for Nuclear Research (CERN) in Geneva released World

Wide Web. The CERN team developed the protocol based on hypertext (HTTP) that makes it possible to connect content on the web with hyperlinks. Initially, the Internet was largely a text-based system. Subsequently, the www permitted access to information using a Graphical User Interface (GUI) and the use of hypertext links to access information across the network. Now, the web sites are able to provide users with a range of experiences such as pictures, multimedia and interactivity. With the growth of Internet, the quality, quantity and variety of information has also grown enormously. The Internet today is repository of every consumable type of information.

1.16.2. Basic Internet Terms

The understanding of following basic Internet terms enables to utilize the Internet resources and services. (ITL Education solutions, 2009).

Web Page : The World Wide Web consists of files called web pages, which contain information and links to resources throughout the Internet. A web page is an electronic document written in a computer language called HTML (Hyper Text Markup Language). These web pages are linked together through a system of connections called hyperlinks, which enable the user to jump from one web page to another by clicking on a link. On the web, user navigates through these pages of information according to his/ her interests.

Web site : A website is a set of related web pages linked through hypertext links published by an organization or individual. Normally a website contains a home page along with other additional web pages. Each website is owned and updated by an individual, company or organization. It is an area on the web which is accessed by its own address known an URL (Uniform Resource Locater).

Home Page : A home page is the starting point or a door way to the website like the table of contents of a book, the home page usually provides an overview of what could be found at the website.

Web Browser : To use web, you need software called browser. A browser is a computer program that access web pages and display them on the computer screen. It is the basic software that is needed to find, retrieve, view and send information over Internet. To access the web, the user requires web browser. The most popular browsers are Microsoft Internet Explorer, Netscape Navigator, and Mozilla Firefox etc.

Uniform Resource Locator (URL) : Each web page has a unique address called Uniform Resource Locator (URL) that identifies its location on the Internet. Web browsers utilize the URL to retrieve a file from the computer on which it stores. The format of URL consists of five parts Network protocol, Server domain name, domain type, file path or directory and file name. Example: *http://www.university.edu/history/syllabus.html*

Domain Types : A domain type represents the type of organization or country to which the host belongs. Some of the important domains on the internet are given below:

- .com - for commercial business
- .edn - for educational institutions
- .gov - for government agencies
- .mil - for US military sites
- .net - for a network
- .org - for non-profit organizations
- .int - for international entities

After the domain name, the domain type such as .com is displayed. A domain type represents the type of organization and country to which the host belongs. Domain types have been assigned to identify and locate files stored on host computers in countries around the world. These are called country codes such as au for Australia, in for India, uk for United Kingdom and so an.

Hypertext and Hyperlink : The web is a network of billions of interlinked documents called hyper links or highlighted words. Hypertext refers to the text that connects to other documents.

Hypertext is a method of instant cross referencing. Hyperlink refers to a hypertext document that takes you to some other part of the same document or to different web page/site. Hyperlink is used for organising information and link related documents together using words and graphics. Hyperlinks are the foundation of web and serve as means of effective information retrieval from the web.

Internet Service Provider (ISP) : An Internet Service Provider is a company or an organization that provides access to the Internet. An ISP has multiple Internet access methods including dial-up, Digital Subscriber Lines (DSL), Cable Modern leased line, Broad band, and Integrated Services Digital Network (ISDN). While choosing ISP, Many factors should be kept in mind such as speed, consistence, reliability and price of the internet access and also other additional services.

Web Server : Server is a computer equipped with server software, which provides a specific kind of service to the client software running on other computers. It is a computer that answers requests from user's computers. The primary function of a web server is to deliver web pages on the request to clients. This means delivery of HTML documents and any additional content that may be included by a document, such as images, style sheets and scripts.

Transmission Control Protocol/ Internet Protocol (TCP/IP) : TCP/IP is the basic communication protocol of the Internet. It defines the language that your computer users to communicate with other computers. It allows programs on user's computer to communicate properly over the internet. The function of TCP/IP is to route blocks of information from a source to a destination over a complex network – Internet.

1.16.3. Internet Applications and Services

Internet has become the vast repository of information. The uses of Internet are constantly growing and expanding very rapidly. Today, Internet has vast range of applications and provides access to wide variety of services such as electronic mail, file transfer, World

Wide Web, Internet telephony, text messaging, and multimedia file sharing, interest group membership, interactive collaboration, video conferencing, electronic commerce, vast information resources and many more. Some of the important applications/services provided by the Internet are briefly discussed in the following sections. (ITL Education solution, 2009).

1.16.3.1. World Wide Web (WWW or Web)

The World Wide Web is a system of interlinked hypertext documents accessed via the Internet. The documents are formatted in a markup language called HTML (Hyper Text Markup Language) that supports links to other documents, as well as graphics, audio, and video files usually accessed by web browsers from web servers. Web browsers make easy access to the World Wide Web. With a web browser, one can view web pages that may contain text, images, videos, and other multimedia, and navigate between them via hyperlinks. Two of the most popular browsers are Firefox and Microsoft's Internet Explorer (http://en.wikipedia.org/wiki/World_Wide_Web).

The World Wide Web is the most popular and widely used service on the Internet because it is so easy to use and rich in information resources. It presents text, images, animation, video, sound and other multimedia in a single interface. The Web is not synonymous with the internet. It is a subset or part of the internet. The Internet is the decentralized global network of computers that transfer information where as Web is one of the applications / services that runs on the Internet. It is a collection of text documents and other resources, linked by hyperlinks and URLs, usually accessed by web browsers from web servers. Most web pages contain hyperlinks to other related pages and files, source documents, definitions and other web resources. The operation of the web relies primarily on hypertext as it is a means of information retrieval. Hypertext is a document containing words called links that connect to other documents. A single hypertext document can contain links to documents and resources throughout the Internet.

Web is a client server-based distributed hypertext multimedia information system. The use of web has changed the way people access, organize, use and publish information on the Internet. The major features responsible for the rapid growth and widespread usage of web are:

- It combines multimedia information such as text, audio, video, images etc.
- It allows many users to simultaneously access the same information
- It is highly interactive embedded with hypertext links
- Web is global in nature permitting unrestricted dissemination
- Web has achieved a high degree of user-friendliness in its interface
- Anyone can develop their own information website and inexpensively make it available to millions of people

1.16.3.2. Electronic Mail (e-mail)

E-mail is a store and forward system that does not require the simultaneous online presence of senders and receivers. E-mail is the most popular service on the Internet used for communication of information and interaction with each other across the globe. It is the quickest, cheapest and most efficient means of two-way communication. E-mail has made it possible to transfer messages instantaneously to any corner of the world without the expense associated with long distance STD telephones calls. It has been widely used now by many for communication, correspondence and information delivery purposes. It saves time, money, effort and other resources.

1.16.3.3. File Transfer Protocol (FTP)

One of the most popular internet applications is file sharing between users of different computers. File Transfer Protocol is software used to copy files from one computer to another scattered across the Internet. File transfer protocol is system of rules and a software that enable a user to log on to another computer and transfer information between it and user computer. TCP enables file sharing over the internet. It was the first internet service developed for easy exchange of files. FTP allows the user to get access to the files stored in a remote computer and can upload and download files from the remote computers. It can be used to transfer files, data, articles, software and other useful information from the Internet.

Transferring files using e-mail is not a good choice, if the file size is large or when there are many files. FTP sites can consist of hundreds of files with information on books, music, software games, images, sounds, multimedia, course work etc., FTP can be done using the command prompt browser and various GUI based FTP software such as cute FTP and WS-FTP.

1.16.3.4. Telnet

The word "Telnet" is derived from telecommunications and network. Telnet is a protocol that allows a user to log on to a remote computer and use it as if it is being used locally. It means that someone in Hyderabad could connect to a computer in the US library of congress and search the OPAC the same way as someone located at a terminal in the library. When the user types in commands they are executed on the remote computer. The user's monitor displays what is taking place on the remote computer during the telnet session. Telnet is a utility which allows user to log on another system and use various services available on that host. It can be used to access many library OPACs, bibliographic databases and other CDROM and online databases.

1.16.3.5. Internet Relay Chat (IRC)

Internet Relay chat is a service on the Internet that allows people to communicate in real time and carry on conversations via the computer with one or more people. It provides the user with the facility to engage in simultaneous online conversations with others from anywhere in the world. Chat is an instant communication service.

1.16.3.6. Chatting and Instant Messaging

Chat programs allow users on the Internet to communicate with each other by typing in real time. They are sometimes included as a feature of a web site where users can log into chat rooms to exchange comments and information about the topics addressed on the site. Chatting has become quite popular with all kinds of Internet users.

1.16.3.7. Internet Telephony

Internet telephone is the use of the Internet rather than the traditional telephone service to exchange spoken information. To make telephone calls over the Internet. Voice over IP (VoIP) is used as on cost-effective alternative to traditional telephone service. The main advantage of Internet telephony is that telephone calls are virtually free to users who already paid for Internet connection.

1.16.3.8. Video Conferencing (VC)

Video Conferencing uses the same technology as IRC but also provides sound and video pictures. It enables direct face-to-face communication across networks. A video conferencing system has two or more parties in different locations which have the ability to communicate using a combinations of video, audio and data. Video conferencing provides real-time visual communication. VC has many benefits as a tool for both teaching and learning activities.

1.16.3.9. Newsgroups (Usenet)

Newsgroups are international discussion groups that form on a particular topic and helps in gathering information about that topic. They provide a forum for users to discuss topics of mutual interest. The information or articles are posted to the newsgroup so that others can read, reply and comment on them. Most newsgroups exist on a network known as "Usenet" which contains thousands of newsgroups.

1.16.3.10. Mailing lists (List Server)

The Internet has large community of individuals who carryout active discussions, organized around topic-oriented forums that are distributed via e-mail. This method of internet communication is known as mailing list. It enables people with similar interests from all over the world to communicate and share information with each other. The mailing list groups are administered by a software program known as list server.

1.16.4. Internet Search Engines

Internet provides access to a wealth of global information resources. The explosive growth of heterogeneously organized information resources on the Internet is making it very difficult for anyone to search, locate and timely access the required relevant information. There are some programs that help the searcher to browse/surf the net websites and locate required information on the Internet known as search engines. Search engines help to locate specification information and find specific sites on the Internet. A search engine is a searchable database of Internet files collected by software called a spider. It allows the user to enter keywords of a particular topic and retrieve information about websites containing those keywords. When users search the web using a search engine, they are provided with the links of all the searched web pages. Search engines are brokers of information-sites created to help people to navigate the Net. Search engines are the retrieval tools for HTML documents on the web. They have robots and spiders which go into every web document and search for specific information. The search engines locate required websites on a particular subject, save the surfing time and provide a list to enable the user to find the sites of his interest. They enable the users to get maximum benefit from the Internet. The search engines facilitate searching net documents using keywords, phrases. Boolean operators, exact matches, concepts, free natural languages query etc.

Internet provides various search engines to facilitate easy searching and location of specific required information. The popular search engines *www.google.com, www.altavista.com, www.excite.com, www.gopher.com, www.hotbot.com , www.infoseek.com, www.lycos.com, www.yahoo.com , www.webcrawler.com, www.magellan.com*

1.16.5. Internet Resources

Internet is a vast repository of universal information resources. It has become an effective means of enriching and updating the information resources of libraries. It helps in building information sources in libraries in more easily accessible form and in most economical way. Internet has become viable complement to the library. Information sources on the Internet supplement the in house collections in libraries.

There is an enormous growth in the number of websites on the net providing access to various information sources. The important information sources available on the Internet are: databases, electronic journals, full text documents, technical reports, bulletins, theses, dissertations, scientific publications, library catalogues, reference sources, patents, standards, education materials, information about societies, fellowships, grants, universities etc. Libraries must strive to make use of these vast, growing Internet-based information sources and services to meet changing complex information needs of users.

Internet could be used to support library acquisitions, technical processing, serials control, reference and information services, and development of digital information resources. Internet has become an effective channel for marketing of library and information products and services at global level.

1.17. REPROGRAPHIC AND MICROGRAPHIC TECHNOLOGY

If a library wishes to extend reading facilities outside the library premises, then it has to offer generous reprography services to its users. Reprography means reproduction of printed or written matter. Reprography includes microcopy, micrographics, and photocopy, duplicating and in-house printing technology.

The impact of modern technology on library management started with the developments in micrography. The earliest example of miniaturization was most probably found in micrographics field in

1939, where filming of documents resulted in tremendous reduction in filing and storage area needs. In addition to excellent space utilization, micrographics provide efficient storage, fast retrieval, archival quality, durability and security as well as other benefits. Micrographics include microfilms, microforms and computer output microfilm etc. During the late 1930s, libraries began making microfilm copies of rare documents, newspaper files as a means of conserving storage space and preservation as the paper copies generally have a rapid decomposition rate.

1.18. PUBLISHING TECHNOLOGY

New Technological innovations such as digital computer, word processing programs, desktop publishing, electronic publishing and web publishing technology have profoundly transformed the publishing industry.

Word processing program can be used to type, add, edit, delete, move, copy and insert the text very easily and instantaneously. Desktop publishing is the process of using a desktop computer to layout pages and adds graphics for printing most complex and sophisticated documents such as brochures, letterheads, logos, charts, newsletters, manuals catalogs, reports and books.

With the emergence of huge capacity storage technology, wide spread usage of internet, networks, intranets and multimedia technologies, electronic publishing has become increasingly popular as it saves lot of money, time, papers, printing, binding and distribution costs. Electronic publishing is the process of publishing and distribution of documents in electronic formats by using computer, communication and electronic technologies. The number of DVD titles, reference sources, secondary periodicals, newsletters, journals, journal articles, books, monographs, reports and conference proceedings published in electronic form has been growing very rapidly in recent years.

The latest development in electronic publishing is web publishing. Today, Internet has become the most widely used popular channel for publishing a wide range of digital information resources across the globe. The trend of web publishing is growing rapidly day by day owing to the wide spread usage of internet and the emergence of more powerful technological advancements.

1.19. TECHNOLOGY TRENDS

Information Technology (IT) has been undergoing rapid revolutionary developments for the last three decades due to its most distinguishing features of decreasing cost, size and increasing capabilities and pervasiveness. The storage and management of huge information in paper documents has become extremely costly, time consuming and labour intensive. Information storage medium has drastically changed over the years from clay tablets to optical media. Optical media is now widely used for compact storage of huge quantity of information in text, audio, video form and speedy dissemination to the needy around the world. One megabyte of information on paper might cost on an average $4, on diskette perhaps $1.7 and on CD-ROM might average $0.0024 or even less (Martin, 1994).

Roffe *et al* (1995), stated that a core component of IT is the semi-conductor chip which, since the early 1980s has not only decreased in size and cost but has also increased steadily in capacity and complexity. These developments have enabled computers to evolve from room-size machines to palm-size devices.

Soubra (1995) stated that IT is a revolutionary technology evolved with great rapidity leading to (i) decreased cost of information and data processing, (ii) speedier information processing, (iii) decreased size and increased reliability of equipment, (iv) digitalization of information, and (v) growing importance of software. Microprocessor capacity and performance improvements were about a thousand fold and, in storage about a hundred fold.

Chen (1997) stated that during the last decade, there have been endless and dramatic technological changes in all three major areas of IT - computing, communications and content. We have witnessed the advent of personal computers, world-wide packet networks, optical disk and other mass storage media, interactive video technology, image technology, digitizing and scanning technology, computer graphic technology, and the growth in size, variety and number of databases.

Moore (1997) stated that the impact of information technology arises from three of its characteristics. First, it is an enabling technology applied in a wide range of different circumstances. Second, the capacity of the technology has been increasing at an exponential rate. Finally, and perhaps most important, the cost of the technology has fallen rapidly over the same period and, again, seems likely to continue to do so.

Tedd (1997) reported that very large-scale integration of the electronic components that comprise any computer has resulted in a huge increase in the power available and a decrease in the cost of processing. The speed of processing and the amount of information stored in main memory have increased dramatically over the years with a parallel decrease in their costs.

The rate of advancement in storage technology has been truly amazing. Research in storage technology has created storage solutions such as holographic storage, blue laser and Millipede-each offering digital storage densities that are orders of magnitude greater than anything we know and use today. Holographic storage incorporates the use of lasers, optics, image sensors and special crystals that respond to laser light (D'Souza 2002).

The parallel rapid developments in computer processing speed, storage facilities, multimedia, software, communications and networks enabled libraries to automate their operations efficiently and provide high quality information services effectively.

1.20. CONCLUSION

Information Technology has changed dramatically during the last three decades. IT has become all pervasive due to its distinguishing features of decreasing, cost, size and increasing speed, storage and communication capabilities. Today, IT has become an integral part of all the human activities. Information Technology is a broad term that encompasses wide range of sub-technologies. IT refers to the devices and tools used in the generation, gathering, processing, storage, retrieval, communication and delivery of information. IT includes computers, software, databases, communication, networks, internet and publishing technology. Successive developments in IT are tremendously enhancing their capabilities resulting into better technological devices, innovations, products, services and quality solutions. In recent years, IT has expanded so rapidly to include a wide array of devices, information products and services that are transforming the role of a library into a gateway of accessing global information resources. It briefly discussed about different components of IT such as computer, communication and other related technologies.

1.21 REFERENCES

Aksoy, Pelia and DeNardis, Lawra. (2006). Introduction to Information Technology, New Delhi: Cengage Learning, 410p.

American Library Association. (1983). The ALA Glossary of library and information science. Chicago: ALA.

Association of Indian Universities. (1998). *University Institutions in India.* New Delhi: AIU. 32p.

Balaguruswamy, E. (2009). Fundamentals of Computers. Noida: Delhi: Tata Mcgraw Hill.

Bhardwaj, J.M. (1995). Database Management Systems. Application of Information Technology. Block 3. Unit II,56-57. New Delhi: IGNOU.

Burger, Jeff. (1995). Multimedia Studio for Windows. New york: Random House Electronic Publishing, 390p.

Collin, Simon. (1996). Multimedia made simple. New Delhi, Asian Books Pvt. Ltd, 145p.

Curtin, Denis, P (1998). Information technology: the breaking wave. Boston: Mcgraw –Hill, 300 p.

Chen, Ching-Chih. (1997). Multimedia technologies, (pp.206). *World Information Report* (1997/98). Paris: UNESCO.

Dakshinamurti, G. (1985). Automation's effect on library personnel. *Canadian Library Journal,* 42 (December), 343-351.

D'souza, Marco. (2002).Technology next: Store more!. Digit, August: 31-36.

Gauch, S. (1992). Intelligent information retrieval: an introduction. *Journal of the American Society for Information Science*, .43(2), 175-182.

Haravu,L.J.(1993). Library automation and Networking in India: An overview of recent developments 40(1), 32-40.

Haravu, L. J. (1995). Strategies for the adoption of New Information technologies. In CALIBER-95: *Information Access Through Networks.* (working papers for CALIBER-95, Hyderabad, 10-12February, 1995. Ahmedabad: INFLIBNET Centre.

Hulser, R.P. (1993). Overview of graphical user interfaces', Computer in Libraries 13(2), 18-23.

Hauptman, R. & Anderson, C. L. (1994). The people speak: the dispersion and impact of technology in American libraries. *Information Technology and Libraries,* 13(4), 249-56.

Information Technology Association of America, Informarmation Technology Definition. www.lcanitblog.com/featured/information_technology/ (Accessdn10.1.13).

Introduction to Information Technology, (2006). Information Technology Education Solution. Delhi. Dorling Kindersley, 648p.

Isaacson, Walter. (1997). "Driven by the Passion of Intel's," Time, Dec.29 1997-Jan.5, 1998.

Johnson, G.I.,Clegg, C.W. and Ravden,S.J. (1989). Towards a practical method of user interface evaluation. Applied Ergonomics, 20(4), 255-60.

Jones, W.P. (1988). As we might think?: Psychological considerations in the design of a personal filing system', in Guindon,R.(ed.), Cognitive Science and its applications for Human-Computer Interaction. Hillsdale, NJ: Erlbaum. 235-88pp.

Jones, Dorothy E. (1989). Library support staff and technology perceptions and opinions. *Library Trends*, 37(4), 432-56.

Jones, Dorothy. (1999). Ten years later: Support staff perceptions and opinions on technology in the work place. *Library Trends*, 47(4), 711-745.

Kuppuswamy Rao, K and Umapathi Rao, Y.V. (eds). (2002). Information Technology: A foundation course. Hyderabad: Dr. B.R.A.O.U. 169p.

Longley, D. & Shain, M. Macmillon. (1985). *Dictionary of Information Technology* (2nd ed.). London: Macmillan.

Malwad, N.M. (1995). Networks and their classification. In Applications of Information Technology Block 4. Unit 13, p.28. New Delhi, IGNDU.

Martin, Katherine. (1994). Understanding the forces for and against electronic information. *CD-ROM Professional*, 74(July/August), 129-134.

Moll, P (1983). Should the Third World have Information Technology. *International Federation of Library Associations Journal.*9(4),296-308.

Moore, Nick. (1997). The Information Society, *World Information Report* (1997/98)(pp.271-283). Paris: UNESCO.

Murthy, S.S. (1999). Role of libraries in the New Millennium of Information Technology. *DESIDOC Bulletin of Information Technology,* 19 (4-5), 3-10.

Neelameghan, A. (1998). Information technology applications in enterprises: Opportunities and challenges. *Information Studies,* 4 (1), 13-32.

Olsen, J. K. (1989). Strategic issues in information with special reference to developing countries. *IAALD Quarterly Bulletin,* 34(3), 119-125.

Olsgaard, J.N. (1989). The physiological and managerial impact of automation on libraries. *Library Trends,* 37(4), 484-494.

Panda, K.C. (1995). Computer-based acquisition control. *Application of information technology.* Block 2, Unit 6.(pp.17-35). New Delhi: IGNOU.

Panda, K.C. and Gautam, J.N. (1999). In'fo Technology (IT) on the Cross' road: from abacus to Internet. Agra: Y.K. Publisher, 272p.

Peltu, M. (1982). Information technology: An overview. In Taylor, H. (Ed.). *Information management and organisational change* (pp. 81-86). London: Aslib.

Rajagopalan, R. (1985). You and the Computer. New Delhi: Children's Book Trust, 133p.

Roffe, Pedro. Aning, Kwaku & Tesfachew, Taffere. (1995). Overview, *UNCTAD Advanced Technology Assessment System.* Issue 10 Autumn, P.V.

Rowley, J.E. (1993). *Computers for libraries,* 3 (Rev. ed.). London. Library Association Publishing, 311p.

Soubra, Yehia. (1995). Trends and current situation in the diffusion and utilization of information technology. *UNCTAD Advanced Technology Assessment System.* Issue 10 Autumn, 49.

Suresh K. Basandra. (1999). Computers Today, New Delhi: Galgotia Publications.

Su, Shaiao-Feng. (1993). Attitudes of academic library professionals towards computer-Based systems in Taiwan. *Journal of Librarianship and Information Science.* 25(3), 143-152.

Tedd, Lucy A. (1997). *An introduction to computer-based library systems,* (2nd ed.). chichester: John Wiley.

Viswanathan, T. (1995). *Overview of computer technology unit 1. Application of Information technology* (MLIS-06), (pp.5-30). New Delhi: IGNOU.

World Wide Web: From Wikipedia, the free encyclopedia. http://en.wikipedia.org/wiki/World_Wide_Web

2

Information Technology Applications in Libraries

2.1 INTRODUCTION

Rapid advances in the digital technology have brought revolutionary changes in the concept, organization, functioning and management of library and information systems throughout the world. The impact of these changes affected all the aspects of library operations, information resources and information services, staff skills requirements and users expectations. The accelerating pace of technological developments has tremendously increased the ability to access, store, process, communicate and deliver effective information services in libraries. Worldwide libraries have been exploring new technologies as a means of providing better and faster access to vast array of information resources and efficient information services to their users. IT has a huge potential for providing wide range of new opportunities and offering better solutions to achieve greater levels of efficiency, productivity and higher standards of quality services in libraries.

Mayor (1997), Director-General of UNESCO stated that the developments in information processing and communication technology are at the heart of many of the transformations that have marked the latter half of the twentieth century. The phenomenon of the Internet highlights the accelerating pace of these developments and their potential impact on economic, social and cultural life. We are embarked upon an information revolution that promises to open a new era in human history, with consequences as far-reaching as those of the agricultural and industrial revolutions.

2.2 REASONS FOR IT APPLICATIONS IN LIBRARIES

Several people have given varied reasons that contributed to the IT applications in libraries. Library automation is one of the major applications of IT in libraries. It implies the change from manual system to the application of computers and other modern techniques to library operations and services.

According to P.S.G Kumar (1987:296), some of the major factors that contributed to the introduction of computerisation in Indian libraries include (i) Greater speed, (ii) Increase in efficiency, (iii) Capability to handle large volume of data, (iv) Flexibility to numerous manipulations, (v) Improved quality in service, (vi) Economy in power, (vii) Availability of hardware and software facility, (viii) Responsibility thrusted on the organisation, and (ix) To enhance the prestige.

Griffiths and King (1989) stated that the main effect of technological change is the availability of more sophisticated, more reliable, more efficient and less expensive information systems, services and products. The use of automated systems in libraries help to improve the efficiency of library operations and the effectiveness of services provided to the library users.

Laxman Rao (1993:97) consolidated the factors contributed for library automation under the following: (i) economy, (ii) improvement of services, (iii) management information, (iv) co-operation and centralisation, (v) prestige, and (vi) research.

Rowley (1993:4-5) stated that the four broad objectives of library computerisation are: to accommodate an increased workload, to achieve greater efficiency, to introduce new services, to benefit from cooperation and centralisation.

According to Haravu (1995), the main reasons why academic and special libraries seek the application of IT solutions are to (i) obtain increased operational efficiencies, (ii) relieve professional staff from clerical chores so that they are available for user oriented services, (iii) improve the quality of services, (iv) provide new services hither to not possible, (v) improve the management of their physical and financial resources, (vi) facilitate wider access to information for their clients, (vii) facilitate wider dissemination of their information products and services, (viii) enable their participation in resource sharing library networks, and (ix) enable rapid communication with other libraries and professional peers.

According to Wright (1995:26), the most frequently cited reasons for library automation are: (i) lower costs of maintaining automated systems, (ii) improvement of library services, (iii) improved collection management, and (iv) increased ability to share resources among libraries.

According to Satyanarayana (1996:142), the broad objectives of library automation are: to improve the efficiency of library functions, to provide the type of services which were hither to not possible, to relieve the professional manpower of tasks which are routine, repetitive or clerical, to improve the cost efficiency of library operations.

Lancaster and Sandore (1997) listed better reasons as: to cope with increasing demands, to reduce staff or prevent staff increases, to allow more jobs to be performed by clerical or para-professional staff, to improve existing services, to provide new services, and to collect better data to aid overall management of the library.

Venkataramana and Chandrasekhar Rao (1998) stated that, effective use of IT in libraries offers the following benefits:

- Increases efficiency in operations

- Eliminates repetitive nature of works
- Improves the quality and range of services
- Facilitates easy and wider access to all kinds of information sources
- Facilitates faster information communication
- Increases morale and motivation of library staff
- Facilitates cooperation and resource sharing
- Saves time, space and resources
- Improves productivity and image of the library.

2.3 TRENDS IN IT APPLICATIONS IN LIBRARIES

Since 1960s, worldwide libraries have been using technology in general and computers in particular to automate a wide range of administrative tasks library operations and information services. During the last decade, IT has played an increasingly influential role in library management system as they have immense capabilities in handling and processing huge volume of information held in libraries. A large number of studies investigated the utilization of technological applications in library and information centers all over the world.

2.3.1. Global Scenario

The status of information technology applications in libraries in different countries of the world is briefly discussed in this section.

Australia : Luce (1991) discussed the impact of information technologies on the growth and development of cooperative resource sharing networks in Australia. The manipulation of data by computers using CD-ROM or personal computer LANs has created a number of opportunities for libraries, which could affect resource sharing. The development and use of sophisticated telecommunications capabilities is critical to the technological growth and development of resource sharing networks among lioraries in Australia.

Cleary (1994) explored accelerating impact of information technology and telecommunication networks on higher education and academic libraries in Australia. IT acted as a catalyst for change in the university sector though the use of Australian telecommunication networks, such as AARNet, access to online databases, and electronic publishing.

Belgium : Van Borm and van Borm (1991) presented a short history of library computerisation in Belgium describing library networks, software packages and union catalogues.

China : Lin (1988) reviewed the development of computerised library services in the Chinese People's Republic. He discussed the important role of the National Library of China and recent developments in computerised acquisitions, cataloguing, circulation control, union catalogues of periodicals, and on-line cataloguing in China.

National Library of China (NLC), Beijing, played an important role in the national standardization of bibliographic control and in library automation and networking in 1991. It developed an integrated library automation system with Japan's NEC, Inc. This system is capable of handling acquisitions, cataloging, circulation, and OPACs. More than forty libraries were using the system (Tang, 1994).

Academic libraries in China were actively employing new information technologies and establishing networked information systems, both at home and abroad. China's academic libraries have made efforts to utilize the advanced technologies from other countries. In order to move successfully into the new millennium and meet the challenges offered by the globalization of information (Zhu, 1998).

Denmark : Hein (1989) traced the beginnings of library automation in Denmark. The common database for local authority library systems now called BASIS, is used by 110 library systems. The interest in library automation has been increasing rapidly and there were a number of experiments in the field.

Barnholdt (1992) stated that in 1988 it was decided to establish a microcomputer based cataloguing and information storage and retrieval system to provide the university's institute and departmental libraries with a local cataloguing and search tool. This move will increase cooperation, avoid unnecessary duplication of titles and enhance the ALIS database contents.

Hong Kong : The technological advancement can be seen everywhere in Hong Kong. There are seven higher educational institutions in Hong Kong funded by the government. These seven university libraries have made their online catalogs also on the Internet accessible through their university homepages. (Fong, 1997).

Hungary : Mader (1995) briefly reviewd the development of library automation in large research and university libraries in Hungary. Sets out the plan for library automation including details at the organizational level; hardware supply; network developments; and the outline of a library automation strategy for Hungary.

Iran : Hossein Farajpahlou (1994) surveyed 42 Iranian academic libraries and observed that computerisation of library services started in the late 1970's revealed a growing trend. Out of 21 responded libraries, nine (31%) libraries were already using computers, seven (24%) were installing computers, five reported that they would have computers in next year and the remaining eight (27%) were planning to buy and install computers in the future. Though, there are locally developed and commercial software, CDS/ISIS software is playing a major role in computerization of library services in Iran.

Jordan : Younis (1990) traced the historical development and the factors affecting the library movement in Jordan. He studied the use of computer applications in 333 libraries in Jordan. The problems that obstruct the use of computers are the lack of trained staff, funds, physical facilities, software, users' indifference, and administrative factors. Recommends solutions to improve libraries' chances to adapt new computer technologies to improve their functions and services to users.

Kenya : Agalo (1998) discussed the emerging trends in the Kenyan academic and national libraries in the wake of current technological advancements and found slides, audio-tapes, radio, microforms, computers, photocopiers, videos, filing telephones, televisions, internet access, fax, CD-ROMs, CD-I, OPACs in most of the libraries.

Lithuania : Maceviciene and Tolusis (1995) provided an up-to-date account of library automation in the 15 Lithuanian academic libraries. The major development in academic library automation is specifically related to the integrated systems embracing essential functions of a library. Half of the Lithuanian academic libraries have CD-ROMs of library collection building. The insufficient knowledge of the library staff on the usage of modern information technologies and the poor financial situation of parent institutions are some of the problems faced by the libraries.

Malaysia : Ming (1996) presented a broad review of the likely future impact of computers and information technology (IT) on university libraries, highlighting the potential role of information professionals as intermediaries between information producers and end users. Focuses on their changing roles amidst new challenges and opportunities that IT offers.

Yaacob and Harun (1996) investigated the impact of new technologies on the management of libraries in Malaysia. User training is an area undertaken seriously by libraries and information centres. Most established libraries and information centres in Malaysia have embarked on library automation, or are in the process of implementing it. They state that in 1994, 50 libraries automated fully using different software packages. The number has increased dramatically to 169 in 1995 with the additional application of advanced IT. There has been a close correlation between the librarian's attitude towards IT and the speed of the library automation.

As a part of Vision 2020, the Malaysian National Library plans to become a world-class library with high-tech facilities. Out of total of nine universities and four technical colleges in Malaysia, five universities provide Internet access to their library catalogs. With the improvement in telecommunication technology, libraries in Malaysia will be able to provide better services and take advantage of resource sharing (Fong, 1997).

New Zealand : Lin (1997) studied the impact of IT on library organizations including library structures and staff and found significant impacts within university libraries in New Zealand. In these libraries, IT is on its way to change their organizational structures and to produce significant impacts on library staff.

Nigeria : Eniya (1991) reviewed the state-of-the art of computerisation in Nigerian libraries. Computerization of library services is intended to ensure accuracy, efficiency, effective information management, reliable user services, enhanced inter library co-operation and library prestige. Till 1985, libraries are mostly at the trial stage. University and research libraries and the National Library of Nigeria are leading the race to computerize their services.

Pakistan : Khan (1995) studied the impact of new information technologies on society, organizations and libraries in particular. Examined to what extent IT has been implemented in the university libraries in Pakistan, taking into account some of the efforts regarding for the improvement of libraries and their services. Discussed the factors inhibiting IT transfer in developing countries and made a number of recommendations for the overall improvement of information services in Pakistan.

Malik (1996) reviewed the status of library software and library automation training in Pakistan. Library automation was started in Pakistan in 1980s and many libraries were computerised after 1987. He has discussed about various library software packages and the role played by the library schools and professional associations in imparting training on library automation in Pakistan. He revealed that the libraries face the problems of inadequate funds, lack of standard software package, proper training etc.

Singapore : Pong (1990) traced the development of

computerisation of library operations in Singapore from 1970-1989. Although the initial interest of Singapore libraries in the application of computers can be traced back to the 1960s, serious considerations to computerise library operations were only taken in the 1970s. He concluded that with Government emphasis on computerisation, computers and related technologies are becoming increasingly important and are likely to dominate the library scene of Singapore in future.

Spain : Keefer and Jimenez (1992) reviewed automation efforts from 1960s, which have increased in the past 5 years, coinciding with the introduction of new software packages. The pace of automation and the software solution chosen vary according to the type of libraries. Some networking and cooperative ventures have begun recently, especially among university and research libraries.

Taiwan : Lee and Chuang (1994) stated that the rapid progress of library automation in Taiwan in the 1990s has been attributed to three main factors: good planning for automation; joint efforts among librarians to move towards automation; and, most importantly, the government's financial support in implementing automation.

Sung (1994) reviewed the development of library automation and networking in Taiwan which began in the 1970s. Computerized catalogues and union periodicals lists were produced and online reference databases and online shared cataloguing were made possible by the advent of digital communications networks, including Taiwan Academic Network (TANet).

Li (1997) stated that library automation in Taiwan began in the 1970s and has been marked by an impressive array of achievements since the 1980s. In 1988, thirteen universities and colleges in Taiwan had automated library systems. By 1992, the number had increased to twenty-three. In 1994, there were forty-six institutions with library automated systems, a 254 percent jump in six years. As a developing country, Taiwan's achievement in library automation has been remarkable.

United Kingdom (UK) and other European Countries : Woods (1986) summarised the history; current position; and future plans of automation in the UK university libraries. He covered: acquisitions, cataloguing, circulation control, serials as well as staffing and networking.

Sippings (1987) surveyed the use of technologies and found that 80% of those surveyed were using some sort of computer and that 95% of these were using business packages such as word processing or spreadsheets on them.

Brindley (1989) stated that Universities in UK have been major users of computers. Joint Academic Network (JANET) encouraged a diversity of networking activities in universities. IT has increased impact on all the main strands of higher education – teaching, research and administration – during 1990s.

Hayter and Heery (1989) stated that IT has made forceful impact upon academic libraries. Many services provided for library users have benefited from the use of computers. In many university and polytechnic libraries the work of cataloguers, issue desk staff, acquisitions librarians and interlibrary loans staff has been profoundly changed by the introduction of computerised services. The survey shows that the majority i.e. 86% of senior staff in UK academic libraries now make at least some use of IT in their day to day work. Most computer-users i.e. 72% of library staff use some kind of network. The most popular use of IT amongst 68% senior library staff is for word processing followed by e-mail with 60%.

Furness and Graham (1996) surveyed the use of IT in 170 special libraries in 1994 in UK. He found that 95% of the libraries surveyed use computerisation for some of their operations and services. The library catalogue proved to be the most popular area for automation with 80 per cent of the respondents having an online public access catalogue (OPAC) followed by acquisitions (50 per cent), serials control (46 per cent) with automation of circulation and interlibrary loans systems being 43 per cent and 30 per cent respectively. 71 per cent of the organisations surveyed subscribe to commercial online services. 62% purchase CDROM databases and 46% use internal databases.

McKenna and Forrester (1998) reported that the consensus in UK higher education was that automation of local library holdings is giving way to the use of the World Wide Web (WWW) for the delivery of global cataloguing information.

The literature covering more than one European country is being reviewed below.

Wood (1990) described library automation and information technology initiatives in Europe. The development of LIB-1 and LIB-2 studies covering computerised library catalogues; library housekeeping-systems; computer based user-related services; inter loans are dealt together with the resulting Action Plan and pilot projects.

Central and Eastern European libraries employed automation on only a small scale in the 1970s and 1980s, and with a few notable exceptions did not implement large-scale integrated systems until the 1990s (Gyeszly 1991).

Larsen (1992) found that more than 1,300 large integrated library systems are installed in the EC member countries. This figure represents a growth rate of more than 525 per cent over the last 5 years. The number of suppliers of large integrated systems has increased from 12 in 1986 to more than 30. More than 3,600 small integrated systems have been installed by some 40 different suppliers shown in a study carried out in 1991.

Walckiers (1992) presented an overview of library automation in Europe. He discussed computerised library functions, integrated library systems, Local Area Networks, Wide Area Networks, union catalogues, national bibliographies, standards of bibliographic records, subject headings and classifications, CD-ROMs and online bibliographic databases, pilot projects, book preservation and the impact of technological change on libraries.

Borgman (1996) reported the results of a mail survey of seventy research libraries in six Central and Eastern European countries. Results showed that these libraries are acquiring automated processing systems, CD-ROM databases, and connections to computer networks at a rapid rate and that automation activity has increased substantially since 1989. 'Access' is their top reason to automate, which appears to mean placing the catalogue online with better search capabilities and putting items on the shelves faster. Co-operation and standards are highly ranked automation goals.

Cockrill (1997) discussed the issues of 23 qualitative interviews conducted at a random sample of UK and German university libraries. Issues discussed include: impact of economic recession on university funding; rapid growth of IT in all areas of academic life and its impact on libraries; online access to external databases (including the Internet). In the UK, the fundamental changes in the higher education system have led to a substantial increase in demand on university libraries but without increases in finance. Similarly, in Germany, the most prominent issues have been the massive increase in student numbers and the changes in IT, networking and automation.

United States of America (USA) : Brimsek (1990) reported the survey results of 4116 individuals with a response rate of 38.4%. Of the 33 technological uses, word processing was cited most often (88.7%), followed by online searching (87.3%), fax (72.8%), and telecommunications software (70.3%). The application of technologies was perceived by 88.9% to increase the level of service provided, 75.9% a greater level of user satisfaction, and 86.4% indicated an increased level of job satisfaction due to new technologies.

Metz (1990) discussed trends in the way the US university is approaching the issue of electronic formats: university libraries are providing commercial or private data bases for their communities; the ownership versus access approach to the evaluation of libraries; libraries are using new technology to automate old processes before using it creatively; libraries are concerned about the higher cost of electronic information; some universities have merged their library and computing units on campus; higher user expectations; and use of alternate information sources.

Hauptman and Anderson (1994) surveyed 800 different types of American libraries and reported that out of 238 respondents, majority of libraries have the most technology. Large academic and research libraries are now almost entirely dependent on technology, but even small special and public libraries can hardly function without computers, modems, CD-ROM readers, fax machines and other equipment. Results indicated that only one third of respondents have online public access catalogues (OPACs) or use electronic mail, and less than 50 per cent have access to CD-ROMs. Concluded that, as money tightens throughout the 90s, libraries will have to seek out new technologies as a means of delivering quality information services at a reasonable cost.

2.3.2. National Scenario

Libraries in India are at a critical juncture due to the pressure created by technological changes, shrinking library budgets, high cost of documents and increasing information needs of users. Recognising the fact that use of IT opens new avenues for better services, an increasing number of libraries and information centers have computerised their activities in India. During the recent years — the library and information centers have become more active to computerise their operations and services.

India : Computerisation started in India when punched cards were used during late 1950s and early 1960s for some applications in the insurance sector and census operations. It started with the installation of the first computer at the Indian Statistical Institute (ISI), Calcutta in 1955. INSDOC was the first in experimenting with computers in information processing work in 1964 using IBM 1620 Model II available at Delhi School of Economics for processing data pertaining to Roster of Indian Translators and for production of author and subject indexes for Indian Science Abstracts. During 1970s DRTC (Bangalore), BARC, TIFR (Bombay), IIT (Madras) and BHEL (R&D) (Hyderabad) are some of the other organisations where computers have been used for production of information products & services (Rajan and Satyanarana, 1987).

P.S.G.Kumar (1987:275) surveyed 37 institutions covering about 82 computerised programs in operation. 21 out of the 37 institutions have computerised only one operation. Six of them have computerised a couple of operations. Nine out of the 37 have computerised three to eight library operations. RRC, TIFR and BARC have not only taken the lead in introducing computerisation at the earliest, but have also tried to evolve a comprehensive computerised system.

Vyasamoorthy (1989) reported the developments and advantages of computers and areas for application of computers in libraries. He stated that there is sharp contrast between library automation in India and abroad. Almost all automation adventures abroad started with academic (university) libraries. In India, all such work has started with special libraries. In India there are about 50 organisations involved in the use of computers for library work.

According to Haravu (1993:32), the main players in the area of library automation in recent years have been special libraries of R&D institutions. The emphasis in most of the special libraries has been on database development and information retrieval services. With the exception of a few university libraries such as those of IIT Kanpur and Hyderabad University, the university sector has not been very active.

Laxman Rao (1993) studied planning and implementation of automated circulation system for Osmania University library system and indicated various benefits of automated circulation system.

Konnur and Rajendra (1994) discussed the applications and advantages of computers in library work and information services provided to users and the problems faced in Poona University Library.

K.P.V. Kumar (1994) considered malignant effects of IT and examined in detail the likely impact of IT on Indian society and the preparations India has to make to reap the maximum benefits from it.

R.P. Kumar (1994) surveyed the usage of modern technologies in different types of 300 libraries in India. He found that some of the libraries have automated their routines while majority of them are still in the planning stages. He examined the impact of modern technologies on these libraries and problems faced by them. 'He' suggested measures for implementation of modern technologies.

Biradar (1995) reported from a survey of 339 libraries responded out of 1213 government-funded academic libraries. Of these, 64 per cent have PCs, 16 per cent have LAN, 9 per cent have UNIX systems, 46 per cent have library automation packages, 23 per cent have CD-ROM drive, 2 per cent have CD-NET, 11 per cent have online facility, 45 per cent have microfiche reader/printers and 23 per cent of them are members of a library network. Further, it was found that out of the 156 universities, 72 universities have responded and 60 per cent of them have PCs, 7 per cent have LAN, 6 per cent have UNIX, 43 per cent have library automation packages, 17 per cent have CD-ROM drives, 3 per cent have CD-Net, 1 per cent have online facility, 42 per cent have microfiche reader-printers and 64 per cent of them are members of library networks. They subscribe to 34 CD-ROM databases.

Gopinath (1995) observed that the developments in IT have been revolutionizing the library and information services. He stated that the technology is evolving rapidly and is providing additional facilities such as network access, electronic document delivery, information interfacing and modeling facilities etc., IT has to be built on a flexible frame to provide instant, conducive approaches towards identification, location, access, retrieval and usage of the information to satisfy the end users.

Vijaykumar (1995) conducted a research to study professional attitude towards library computerisation in university and special libraries in Andhra Pradesh (A.P.).

Rashid (1996) presented a literature review of significant developments in library automation. He discussed the development of library management systems, the advantages of an integrated system and the role of office automation systems in libraries. Outlines recent and future developments in information retrieval systems; online public access catalogues (OPACs); CD-ROMs; and networking.

Sujatha (1996) carried out a study on resource sharing and networking of university libraries in Andhra Pradesh (A.P.). She suggested the networking of university libraries in the state to promote the sharing of resources as there is a large scale duplication of serials and books in these libraries.

Kaula (1997) observed that over the last two decades, libraries have become increasingly aware of the revolutionary impact of developments in information and communication technologies on their key functions. The new developments challenge the library's traditional role, as electronic information products and services, open up a previously unimaginable array of options. With the reduced importance of physical libraries as predicted, librarians and information specialists will need to be proactive and promote their special services to their user community. Much of the future will undoubtedly be decided by our own response to the new technology. If we pretend it does not exist, or run away in fear, it will unquestionably destroy the value and growth of the profession. If we embrace the technology and exploit its capability to the full, it can only broaden and fulfill our professional aspirations. But, technology has to be used as a tool to render assistance to achieve our goal of the profession to serve the end-user as providers of information, pin-pointedly, expeditiously and exhaustively. It is time to embrace these challenges, to grasp the future and push ourselves forward.

Mukesh Saikia (1997) briefly discussed the application of information technology in Tezpur University Library. Described the hardware/software procured for library automation and the creation of database of library holdings using CDS/ISIS. The problems of North-East in having E-Mail, due to insufficient nodes of national networks like SIRNET, I-Net, ERNET, etc are also discussed.

Rama Reddy (1997) discussed the management of data

correction of books database for the data entered during retrospective conversion operation and regular cataloguing function using a different format other than LIBSYS. He briefly described the books database of the case study of the University of Hyderabad.

Ravichandra Rao (1997) discussed the status, problems and the future of automation in academic libraries in India. He stated that automation activities in academic libraries slowly picked up with the support from INFLIBNET, UGC, NISSAT and other similar agencies combined with increased awareness of IT and its applications among librarians. They are beginning to use E-mail, CD-ROMs, LAN, machine-readable catalogue, etc for sharing their resources.

Ansari (1998) reviewed the computerisation activities in 14 universities of Bihar and found that 4 have received financial assistance from INFLIBNET for computersation of their libraries. He discussed certain problems and offered a few suggestions for improvement of computersation process in university libraries of Bihar.

Chaya Devi (1998) conducted a survey by interviewing the three university librarians viz. Andhra University Library, Osmania University Library and Sri Venkateswara University Library of Andhra Pradesh to assess the computerised services offered by them. She found that the impact of IT is not yet felt much in these libraries. Though, these libraries have certain hardware and software facilities, the proper services are not reaching the academic community to the expected extent. She provided a few suggestions for improving the computerised information services to users.

Neelameghan (1998) stated that application of the emerging information and communication technologies (ICTs) in enterprises offer opportunities as well as pose challenges to managers. Keeping these in view, appropriate polices and strategies have to be adopted to derive optimal benefits. He briefly discussed various opportunities and added value that ICTs can provide to enterprise activities and to the management.

Ramaiah (1998) observed that the essential things required

for automation of a university library are: good collection, adequate finance, suitable computer hardware, user-friendly computer software, staff training and user training.

Vivekanand Jain (1998) stated that Banaras Hindu University (BHU) has a computer center with campus LAN and ERNET facilities. He provided the hardware and software facilities of BHU and describes the developments due to the INFLIBNET programme in the university. He felt that due to the large size of databases, BHU requires a huge amount of money, trained manpower and proper planning for automation.

Chandran and Ramesh Babu (1999) conducted an opinion survey to study the attitude of 50 staff members towards use of IT in 16 academic libraries. They found that the library staff have good interest in automating library services and expressed greater appreciation for new technology as it can help in providing better services to their patrons. They also found that insufficient funds is the major reason for poor state of IT applications in libraries followed by lack of support by administrative authorities and lack of trained staff.

Lakshmana Moorthy (2000) carried out a survey to assess the impact of electronic media on 344 library and information centres of scientific, research and developed institutions and universities in India, and received 153 (44.5%) responses. He covered infrastructure, computers, operating systems, library automation software's, database development, networks, databases, digital libraries and impact of electronic media on library system.

Rama Reddy (2000) stated that IT has created greater opportunities in the libraries in the 21st century. The users demands are forcing the application of new technologies, new modes of access to knowledge resources and new techniques of knowledge search etc in the libraries. The professional librarians need to enrich their knowledge with updated collection and services and utilization of modern technologies. The libraries have to devote part of their funds to access electronic resources and databases. As the digital storage costs are reduced and the electronic services become more useful, affordable, available and usable, users will eventually work in a virtual library system.

Kannappanavar and Vjayakumar (2001) surveyed the use of IT facilities, in-house databases, access to networks, library services and barriers to IT applications in two agricultural university libraries in Karnataka. He found that none of the university libraries is having databases and full implementation of IT applications.

2.4 IMPACT OF IT ON LIBRARIES

The rapid advances in IT have increased their capabilities to store, process and retrieve huge volume of information easily, speedily and more accurately at less cost in Libraries. The information is growing exponentially with the use of modern information technologies. The management of massive volume of information has created the problems of access, storage, processing, retrieval and dissemination in libraries manually. IT has enabled libraries to manage this explosive growth of information effectively. IT has great potential to increase the efficiency of library housekeeping operations and to improve the effectiveness of information services. Libraries need to effectively utilize the full potential of IT for the efficient management of modern libraries. T has tremendous impact on library operations, staff competencies, information resources and services, resource sharing networks and users expectations.

The use of Information Technology (IT) has offered many benefits for libraries and users. Both libraries and users have gained for innovation and investments in technology. IT helped libraries to manage information management operations efficiently in order to provide easy access to information resources and services. Libraries utilised technology have achieved varying degrees of success in increasing operations efficiency and improving user services. IT has enhanced not only speed, convince and comfortability but also boosted customer satisfaction. Libraries can be more responsive to the used demands and services with the use of new technology.

Ekpenyong (1991) listed the following benefits of library automation in Nigeria.

(i) It improves service by doing the manual work better, faster and more effectively

(ii) It provides services and products that are not feasible with the manual system

(iii) The system eliminates skilled clerical and cataloguing labour

(iv) Book catalogues and accession lists can be produced automatically

(v) Shelf list data stored by the computer can be automatically analysed to determine Subject strengths and weakness in the library collection.

(vi) Extensive subject bibliographies can be compiled .

Abifarin (1993) surveyed the availability and use of information technologies in 30 Nigerian University libraries. He stated that 10 (58.82%) out of 17 of the respondents recognised the benefits of information technology. He found that 58.82% of respondents indicate easier and quicker access to information, 52.94% improved communication and 47.06% improved productivity. Among all the listed constraints in the use of IT, lack of funds was the common cry of the 10 (58.82%) respondents.

Badu (1993) surveyed staff and students to study the impact of the use of microcomputers on the University of Ghana library. He found that 50% of the library staff were very excited and felt it would improve services, gained library a better corporate image and some satisfaction to staff. Respondents stated that borrowing transaction through computer is completed rapidly compared with manual transactions, which took minutes instead of seconds.

Sharma's (1993) study conducted on the use of computer in libraries of higher education showed that the time taken in processing 500 books in a library manually as well as through computer was 1000 hours and 60 hours respectively. The point to be noted here is that the time required for typing/data entry was the same number of 40 hours for both the systems. This showed that a computerised system is about 50 times cost-effective compared to non-computerised one for the university libraries.

Ganpule and Waydande (1994) stated that library automation brought an efficiency in house-keeping jobs in IIT (Bombay) Library. It helped to bring the list of additions weekly instead of fortnightly with improved quality.

Hauptman and Anderson (1994) surveyed 800 different types of American libraries and found that technology results in an improved perception of our role, status and upgraded our image among patrons. Reported that libraries lack enough money and staff training. Staff felt technological innovations put more pressure and are stressful.

Himmelfarb (1999) stated that we are experiencing a revolution, not only in library services but in the very conception of the library. Now, with the electronic revolutions, it is not only the library catalogue that is computerised but the computer can call up a variety of other catalogues, indexes, databases, CD-ROMs, Internet, as well as books, journals, newspapers, archives, even manuscript collections from other libraries. Potentially, at least, the electronic revolution makes even smaller libraries the equivalent of libraries in major research universities and scholarly institutions.

From the above review of the articles by various library and information experts, the benefits of using IT in LICs may be consolidated as:

- Improved efficiency of library operations
- Improved quality of existing services
- Introduced new services
- Improved Collection Management
- Improved accuracy and control
- Increased ability to share resources

- Improved image
- Improved management information
- Eliminate duplication of efforts
- Rapid communication
- Perform tasks not possible by the manual system
- Improved uniformity and standardisation
- Improved users satisfaction
- Facilitate effective utilisation of funds and
- Facilitate to market library services.

2.5 IMPACT OF IT ON HOUSE -KEEPING OPERATIONS

Libraries use IT for two purposes - housekeeping operations and information services. Library housekeeping operations are a group of activities that enable the performance of day to day functions in a library. The efficiency of a library depends largely on the performance of its housekeeping operations. Libraries have to perform various activities related to acquisition of documents, technical processing of acquired documents, and maintenance of collection, serials, management and circulation of documents known as housekeeping operations. Most of these activities are highly labour intensive and routine clerical works performed slowly and expensively by people. Most of the activities within library are inter-related, inter-linked, inter-dependent and mutually supportive for the overall mission of the library. IT can be used in performing most of the repetitive works of library in a desired number of times speedily, accurately, efficiently and economically without fatigue and wastage of time. IT enabled to interface and integrate each function with the other, saves lot of staff time as the same data need not to be entered at every stage. Moreover files are interlinked so that deletion, addition and other changes in one file can automatically activate appropriate changes in related files. Bibliographic data once entered in machine readable form can be used repeatedly in different operations for various purposes. The use of IT with its immense capabilities of acquiring, storing, processing, retrieving and disseminating information with high speed and accuracy has made a tremendous impact on library housekeeping operations. These operations are amenable to computerization for efficient performance. Libraries use IT for the efficient management of various housekeeping operations.

Library is a complex system consisting of various sub-systems and components. These sub systems are responsible for separate groups of related activities such as acquisition, technical Processing, circulation, serials control and maintenance etc. Each subsystem has some common procedures and activities irrespective of the type or size of a library. Since the functions and activities of different sub systems are closely related, integrated combined efforts lead to better library services. IT is used for the following house-keeping operations.

- Acquisition System
- Classification
- Cataloguing
- Circulation
- Serials Management
- Inter Library Loan
- Management Information Reports
- Networking and Resource Sharing

2.5.1. Acquisition System

Acquisition System is concerned with procurement of required books for the library. It includes finding book selection sources, searching and selection of books required, placing of orders with a wide range of suppliers, keeping track of orders, receiving and recording of their receipt, settlement of invoices and maintaining detailed accounts of funds. Computerised acquisition system performs above activities more easily, speedily and efficiently.

Computerized acquisition helps in selection, ordering, procuring books and other library materials. It helps in preparing subject-wise budget allocations. While selecting, ordering, accessioning books, libraries will be using most of the same bibliographical details of documents such as, author, title, imprint, collation etc. In this process, computers enable libraries in making use of the same data available in different files without entering it again each time.

Functions : Computerised acquisition system performs the following functions

- Book selection
- Pre-order checking of duplicate books
- Print purchase orders
- Send reminder/cancellation letters
- Invoice processing
- Accessioning received items
- Update vendor file
- Print accession list/register
- Send notification to the users
- Print fund utilization account
- Print vendor performance report.

Harbour (1994) made a comparative study on the flow charts of a highly simplified example of a manual and automated acquisition and cataloging system. He found that the number of steps in the computerised process can be reduced by roughly half. Automated system eliminates five tasks such as typing order records; filing order records; typing catalogue cards; filing catalogue cards and updating budget figures. Even, if each of these five take only one minute per item, this represents a considerable annual time savings. For example, if 10,000 items are ordered per year, the time saving will be: $5*10^4/60=833.3$ hours or almost 22 man weeks.

2.5.2. Classification

According to Kumar (1987:262), computerisation provides the following benefits in classification (i) Helps the classificationist in the selection of isolate terms, grouping and arranging them in hierarchical sequence, (ii) Helps a classifier in synthesizing the class numbers, (iii) Saves time by avoiding reference to the schedules of scheme for classification on and often, (iv) The constructed class number can easily be used as a query language in a typical retrieval system, and (v) Improves accuracy and speed in classification.

2.5.3. Cataloguing

Cataloguing is one of the important functions, which link users' requirements to the documents in a library. Computerised catalogue is the most efficient tool in retrieving information about the documents in a library easily and quickly.

Catalogue of holdings can be prepared easily on the computer by importing the bibliographical details of the documents from acquisition file with additional data from library staff. Once the catalogue of holdings is available on the computer, the documents can be searched, retrieved and rearranged in any way as desired. The time consuming work involved in the manual preparation of catalogue cards is greatly reduced by using computers.

Computerised catalogue performs the following functions

- Easy preparation of library catalogue
- Provide many access points and in depth subject cataloguing
- Provide remote access to multiple users simultaneously
- Easy preparation of national union catalogues.

Woods (1986) stated that in manual system, all cards had to be drafted, checked, typed, proof-read, corrected, sorted, filed and the filing checked. If any book is moved to a new location, withdrawn or lost, all the cards had to be found and corrected. A catalogue based on computer file needs only one amendment to correct all the entries and has various other advantages: Additional entries can easily be made.

September (1990) stated that (i) The growing complexity of the card catalogue and the increasing cost of catalogue maintenance were identified as important factors for library automation, (ii) The database would provide cataloguing data, information about books not yet catalogued, books on order and items in circulation, (iii) As collections in libraries especially university libraries, expand and grow, it becomes more difficult to maintain the manual card catalogue, and (iv) Human errors occur as a result of misfiling. Misfiling of cards makes it impossible to retrieve materials easily.

According to Rowley (1993:245), computerised cataloguing system offers many benefits such as (i) The catalogue record has become the central bibliographic record for the library management system as these records can also be used in other functions, (ii) Interchange of catalogue records has led to greater standardisation, (iii) The availability of union catalogues has facilitated more effective inter library lending, co-operative acquisition policies, co-operative resource sharing activities, (iv) No filing or other routine catalogue maintenance is required of catalogues, (v) Different catalogue formats can be choosen for different catalogue locations, (vi) Extracts from the main catalogue database may be printed or consulted online, and (vii) The cataloguing procedure has become more structured, with a significant proportion of stock being processed quickly.

Converting a manual catalogue to a machine readable one is very expensive. Eniya (1991) reported that International Institute of Tropical Agriculture has used an integrated library software package for retrospective conversion of the card catalogue. The data conversion exercise reduced 1,70,000 card catalogue entries to only 24,000 automated catalogue records having about 50 fields in each record.

2.5.4. Circulation

Circulation refers to the lending of documents to maximum users for their effective utilization. Circulation procedure in a conventional system is very lengthy and consumes much of staff time in repetitive works. The circulation system must be simple, speedy and effective. The use of technological devices such as computers, barcode scanners and its software in circulation helps in performing these routine operations easily and quickly. Academic libraries are the most suitable candidates for computerisation of circulation-control systems as they frequently have high-volume of circulating transactions per day. It saves lot of time for staff as well as users. It helps in maintaining up-to-date membership records and in finding out latest status of documents under circulation.

An automated Circulation system should perform the following functions

- Rapid charging and discharging of documents
- Renewal of loans
- Reservation of documents
- Send reminders for overdue documents
- Calculation of fines
- Sending fine notices
- Printing fine receipts
- Maintenance of membership records
- Provide circulation statistics

P.S.G Kumar (1987) stated that an automated circulation system should perform the following functions: (i) Provide information on the location of the item on loan at the bindery, on reserve, being recatalogued, etc., (ii) Give details of items on loan to a borrower, (iii) Record of reserves, alerting the library staff on return of a reserved item by a borrower and print a book available notice to the one reserved, (iv) Print recall notices for items on long-term loan, (v) Renewal of loan, (vi) Alerting library staff about over-due items and printing of over due notices, (vii) Calculation of fines, printing of the fine notices, recording receipt of fines and even printing of fine receipts,

(viii) Calculation and printing of statistics of various types, (ix) Analysis of summary statistics, (x) Provision for handling special categories of borrowers and special types of materials, (xi) Printing due date slips: automatically generating orders for lost books, and (xii) Provision for inter-library loan transactions.

Ganpule and Waydande (1994) stated that circulation activity was considered on priority basis for computerisation in IIT (Bombay) Library. Circulation being a major and most difficult activity that takes place on a large scale in library dealing with all the users, has a high visibility factor. Computerisation of this activity would have immediate impact on the users, as the benefits of automation would immediately be transferred to the users.

2.5.5. Serials Management

Serials management refers to the acquisition of journals magazines and other periodicals publications. Serials include periodicals, newspapers, annuals, journals, memoirs, proceedings, transactions etc., of societies and monographic series. Serials are distinguished from monographs by their ongoing nature. The continuing nature of serials subscriptions creates problems and makes it a complex process requiring a separate control system. Computerisation helps in the efficient management of serials in libraries.

Computerisation has been considered as effective instrument for serials management in libraries. Computers help in periodicals subscription and subsequent monitoring of the receipts of individual issues. In computerized serials management, it will be easier to detect and control the non-receipts of the periodical issues by sending timely reminders to suppliers. It helps in maintaining record of budget sanctioned and amount expended for different categories of serials.

Ravichandra Rao (1983) stated that an automatic serial control system should perform the following functions:

Ordering : Ordering new journals; Renewal/discontinuation; Sending reminders; Receiving the journals,

Reader Services : Preparation of a list of periodicals received; Preparation of a list of periodicals cancelled; Preparation of a list of holdings; List of holdings with their status (i.e., on shelf, in binding, in circulation etc.), and

Management Services : keeping track of amount spent on subscriptions, binding etc.; Estimation of the budget for the next year; Announcement of the missing serials for recording the same.

2.5.6. Inter Library Loan

Inter Library Loan system deals with the process of borrowing items from other libraries. Development of ILL system has been relatively slow in India as compared to western countries due to lack of access to catalogues of other libraries collections in manual system. Now it is gaining momentum due to present library conditions with improved technological capabilities and network developments.

Typically computerised Inter Library Loan system offers the following benefits: (Rowley, 1993) (i) improved ILL transaction control and management, (ii) Off line preparation and storage of messages, (iii) Elimination of filing, searching, sorting and preparation of reports, (iv) Reduction of staff time required to process ILL requests, (v) Enter the requests and the computer will create the forms and keep track of all the details of all records, (vi) Easy to download and upload ILL records, (vii) Update ILL records automatically by entering record numbers, (viii) Print downloaded ILL records using flexible formatting options, and (ix) Maintains data, generate forms and produce various reports.

2.5.7. Management Information Reports

Management needs accurate and reliable information for taking right decisions.

In today's library environment of decreasing budgets and increasing accountability and demands, library managers are called upon to monitor the functioning of the library regularly to assess the efficiency of library operations in order to make decisions about changes in the way library functions. A computerised library system provides comprehensive, reliable, relevant, up-to-date and specific information useful to the management quickly on various library activities required by the management for taking effective decisions.

Management needs accurate and reliable information for taking right decisions. Computerized library can provide comprehensive, relevant and up-to-date information quickly on various library activities required by the management for the following purposes.

- Budgetary control
- Preparation of accounts
- Maintenance of records
- Library statistics
- Generation of reports

Cortez (1983:22) defined a management information system as '... an automated library system with design features to help in the performance of management decision-making. It has dual function to support day-to-day library operations as well as to provide management with useful information for decision making'.

Bichteler (1987) stated that automated system allow more objective, quantitative and monitoring of work. Rowley (1993: 259) stated that most of the library management systems offer an extensive set of standard reports relating to transactions in various functions in the system.

Wright (1995:118) stated that in automated integrated online library systems, a wide range of reports can be generated from the systems about every part of library activities. The availability of appropriate statistics and summary report related to a particular library function makes planning, evaluation and justification of the library's service much easier. Computer based system can provide a variety of complex information in all library operations for many library management decisions.

2.5.8. Networking and Resource Sharing

Advancements in technology, coupled with the ever-changing needs of users, are pushing computer networking to new heights, both in terms of capabilities and the importance of sharing resources efficiently.

Pong (1990) stated that the Singapore Integrated Library Automation Service (SILAS) system has 30 institutions with online access to the database via 116 terminals. The main function of SILAS is to provide online shared cataloguing facilities to participating libraries, which can cut down drastically the costly and time-consuming process of creating bibliographic records from scratch. Thus duplication of effort in cataloguing is avoided. For the network as a whole, the estimated average cataloguing hit rate is over 60% for libraries with general science and technology collection, the hit rates go beyond 80%. The availability of participant's holdings information in national union catalogue facilitates inter-library loans and helps libraries in rationalising their acquisitions.

In the Western Europe, library automation was laid on a foundation of cooperation and exchange among libraries (Higginbotham, 1993).

2.6 IMPACT OF IT ON INFORMATION SERVICES

Libraries, renders various information services to meet the different needs of their users in order to save their time due to information explosion, increasing specialization and increasing need for quick access to relevant information. Information services are to be provided to users not only on demand but also in anticipation of their needs.

Libraries use IT to increase the efficiency and effectiveness of their information services. Computers enable libraries to develop database of their collections and make them easily accessible to users. In an automated library, once databases are developed many services such as bibliographic service, Indexing service, CAS, SDI etc. will be automatically generated from them and the users can have direct access to them. Computerisation offers a variety of computer-based information products and services including access to external databases, CD-ROMs etc. Net working has enabled libraries to share their resources more effectively especially in the present days of increasing document prices and decreasing library budgets. Computerisation of different housekeeping operations enabled libraries to provide various kinds of information services to the users effectively.

Libraries are experiencing a significant impact of IT on information processing, sources and services. Rapid technological developments enabled libraries not only to improve the quality of existing services but also to offer a wide range of new services to users.

An automated library provides the following information services.

- Development of databases
- Online public access catalogue (OPAC)
- Reference Service
- Current awareness service (CAS)
- Selective dissemination of information (SDI) service
- Bibliographic Service
- Literature Search Service
- Online search service
- CDROM search service
- Internet service

2.6.1. Development of Databases

Libraries use IT to create in-house databases of their holdings and make them easily accessible to users. Bibliographic databases refer to machine-readable records of bibliographic information. Computerised databases provide easy and user-friendly access to the information resources and form sound foundation for efficient information services. One of the fundamental characteristics of computer based information retrieval is that the database at the heart of the system may be used as the basis for a plethora of different products ranging from CD-ROM, through online access on an external host to printed indexes and current awareness bulletins (Rowley, 1993:115).

2.6.2. On-line Public Access Catalogue (OPAC)

Library Catalogue is the most important tool to locate reading materials in the library. One of the major advantages of computerization is the computerised on-line catalogue popularly known as On-line Public Access Catalogue (OPAC). OPAC provides easy access to the library catalogue through computer. OPAC is a computerised database of the library holdings, which can be searched in many powerful ways than manual card catalogue. OPAC can be conveniently and quickly searched locally, online, through networks, Internet and can also be made available on CD-ROM format.

OPAC is a gateway to find information in libraries and provides facilities to browse, search and locate information. OPAC also shows the current status of a book, whether it is available on the shelf or issued. If issued, the book can also be reserved. OPAC also provides remote access from outside the library through Local Area Network (LAN) or from anywhere in the world through web. OPAC accessible through web is called web OPAC. The web OPAC is more simple, popular and easy to access and use. OPAC has the facility to display, download or print the catalogue records. The OPAC provides simple and advanced search facility to search an item by author, title, corporate body, conference name, subject headings, keywords, class number, series name, accession number or combination of any of two or more.

Rowley (1993: 247) stated that OPAC supports more sophisticated searching and allow consultation of issued records as well as on-order items. It also offers powerful sorting capabilities and printing options. Other features include number of ways of displaying search results, access from remote locations, searches statistics, generation of hard-copy catalogues and creation of catalogue on CD-ROM.

2.6.3. Reference Service

Reference service is the provision of assistance to individuals seeking information. Reference service is one which provides the answer to users' question or information needs. Answers take as many forms as questions. Reference service is usually provided in response to a question ranging from simple inquiries to complex search requests. These questions can be classified into two categories (i) ready reference questions requiring straight forward factual responses and (ii) long range literature searching involves preparation of bibliographies on specified topics.

Libraries are able to provide better, faster and effective reference services to the users with the development of computerized bibliographic databases and the availability of various electronic reference sources.

Asynchronous tools such as e-mail, FAQs, and interactive tools like chat rooms, virtual reference desk, and ask-a-Librarian are replacing the conventional means of post, phone or in-person reference enquiries. Ask-a-Librarian allows the user to click on ask-a-librarian link to send a formatted enquiry to the librarian. The librarian either provides an answer, links to resources or links to a subject expert.

2.6.4. Current Awareness Service

Current Awareness Service (CAS) refers to the review of received publications, select the items of interest to the organization and bring them to the notice of all the interested persons. The main objective of CAS is to keep the users up-to-date with current trends and developments in their field of interest. CAS appears in various forms such as title announcement, contents list, indexing and abstracting services, digests, etc. The Information Bulletin' is one of the popular forms of CAS adopted by many libraries and information centres. Libraries using computers can provide current awareness bulletins easily and speedily. Libraries now compile current awareness bulletins using predefined search strategy from the database either on CD-ROM or online periodically. Internet has enabled a lot of innovations in contents, methods of production and distribution of current awareness products. Web tools such as Listserv, Weblog, Webzines and e-newsletters provide latest information on hot topics, new ideas and opinions, and also an opportunity to discuss wide range of issues. Web resources enable libraries to provide variety of web-based current awareness services to their users.

2.6.5. Selective Dissemination of Information Service

Selective Dissemination Information (SDI) is the personalised information services rendered more effectively by the computers in automated library. This service helps to send the selected relevant updated items to the individual users. SDI provides access to current literature acquired by the library according to users' requirements. The concept of SDI is that an individual is notified of items of interest to him. SDI is truly formalized by the computer. SDI can be provided using external and internal databases. SDI is a tailor made CAS designed to serve the individual users directly. It is a selective notification of current items of information to the individual user. In SDI, user profiles of personal interests will be stored. The items which match the user profile are brought to the attention of the user. This process is laborious which takes lot of time manually. Use of computers has made SDI Service simple, faster and more effective. Many scientific and technology research and development libraries provide effective computer based SDI services to their users form the items they have received. Computerised SDI would provide better coverage than the manual service. Today, electronic mail can be used as an effective method of providing SDI service. For example, library can run an in-house SDI daily against newly received items and the useful references can be sent through electronic mail direct to the individual user.

2.6.6. Bibliographic Information Service

Bibliographic information services form the basic and important services rendered by the library and information centers. The services which provide information about books and other reading materials are called as bibliographic information services. These services are very valuable in libraries not only to make users informed of the current literature available in their field of interest but also to save considerable amount of time of the users.

Research survey revealed that a significant amount of time of the users is wasted in searching bibliographic information. Compilation of bibliographies and reading lists is one of the most important activities in libraries. It is a very tedious and time consuming work manually. With the availability of OPAC and bibliographic databases, bibliographic information services have become more easier convenient, efficient and cost effective for the users. Electronic databases also provide unique search options such as keyword, subject, author, source, year of publication etc. and variety of display formats. Web-based services facilitate full-text searches and link to full-text of the documents. Dialog, STN and Silver Platter are some of the popular database companies that offer bibliographic and reference databases on CD-ROM and online platforms.

2.6.7. Literature Search Service

When a user wants a comprehensive literature on a particular subject, he needs to do literature search. Literature search involves conduct of retrospective searches of literature on the subject interest of the individual user. Retrospective search service is of great value to the user as it provides a comprehensive survey of literature on the subject of interest to the user. The retrospective literature search can use both internal & external databases. The manual literature search process consumes considerable time, energy and money. Libraries prefer automated searches as it is cost effective compared to manual searching.

Bibliographic databases provide effective and speedy search facilities. With the development of machine readable catalogues and bibliographic databases, literature searching has become relatively easier, more effective and less time consuming process. The advantages of automated searching over manual include speed, currency, convenience, accessibility to combine search elements to do both more complex and specific searches and the ability to modify search strategy immediately.

2.6.8. On-line Search Service

On-line Search Service refers to the mounting databases on a computer and making necessary arrangements for such databases to be searchable from a large number of remote user terminals. Some of the major database hosts are: DIALOG, DATA-STAR, ESA/IRS, QUESTEL, STN international, ORBIT search service etc. The advantages of online searching over manual include speed, currency, convenience, access, ability to combine concepts and search elements to do both more complex searches and more specific searches, ability to modify the search strategy immediately.

2.6.9. CD-ROM Search Service

Optical discs have become increasingly important as a medium for the storage and dissemination of information during the early 1990s. Optical discs represent alternative means of accessing information to online commercial databases.

O'Leary (1990) stated that using CD-ROM databases at the point of use or in the library was found to have considerable effect on budget in a number of academic institutions and in one case CD-ROM virtually replacing online searching. This is particularly applicable to academic institutions, because of the high customer base, fairly predictable fixed type of demand and the frequent requirement for historical rather than current information.

Akeroyd (1991) observed that, since the installation of CD-ROM network at South Bank polytechnic library, demand has been so great that within three months, file server access had to be doubled. It has been found that its use has significantly reduced online expenditure, and led to a substantial increase in the number of inter-library loans from students.

Biddiscombe (1991) stated that the networking of CD-ROMs is now being run successfully in a number of academic institutions.

CD-ROM based information service has created positive benefits for the image of the library as a provider of information. The bibliographic database on CD-ROM will alert users to documents whose existence they would not otherwise have expected. This may lead to fuller exploitation of existing library resources and more demand for documents that can be acquired via library networks and inter library loan (Rowley, 1993:176).

Smith (1993) reported that 82% of academic institutions used CD-ROMs and found them invaluable for end-user searching. All respondents generally agreed that CD-ROM searching was far more relaxing and far more fun than online searching.

CD-ROM has a number of advantages over online. There are no telecommunication charges, costs are known in advance. It is intended for the end user and consequently can save staff time. Users do not have to worry about generating high bills through lengthy or complex searches or simply practicing searching techniques and downloading is generally easier (Bevan, 1994).

Yaacob and Harun (1996) stated that the application of CD-Net should be promoted so that CD-ROM databases can be networked to allow affordable access to more users.

2.6.10. Document Delivery Service

Document delivery service is the most important and critical services rendered by LICs. Document delivery service refers to the supply of a copy of the documents to users on demand either in print or electronic form.

Many libraries have made their OPACs accessible in their websites. Many library networks such as INFLIBNET and DELNET developed union catalogue of periodicals holdings of large number of universities. Users can search for required documents from these databases and request them from concerned library. IT has made the electronic document delivery service easy, simple, cheap and instantaneous. BLDSC, ADONIS are some of the examples for document Delivery Services.

2.6.11. Internet Service

Internet is the world's largest repository of information. Libraries use internet technologies and applications to provide wide range of innovative services to the users. Libraries provide access to wide variety of web based information resources and services.

Internet is a network of thousands of computer networks spanning around the world. Internet being vast information source enable libraries to provide a variety of information services to users. Innovative use of Internet technologies enable us to reach both local and distant users much more easily and effectively than hitherto possible. In addition to bibliographic and catalogue information, we can extend information content to cover full text, images, animations and full multi-media (Ressler and Trefzger: 1997).

According to Rajasekhar (1998), the applications and services a librarian can provide on the Intranet and the Internet may include catalogue databases, current awareness bulletins, externally purchased databases, CD-ROM databases, remote information services, internal newsletters, reports and journals, and Internet information sources.

2.7 IMPACT OF IT ON LIBRARY STAFF

Human resources are the key to the successful use of any technology in a library. The greatest challenge faced in the deployment of IT is the requirement and development of skilled human resources. Staff who can support and comply with the computer and network environment is essential for effective IT implementation. IT has tremendous impact on various aspects of library staff.

2.7.1. Staff Attitude towards IT implementation

Positive attitudes and actions of staff involved in IT use are regarded as crucial for the successful implementation of a new system. The attitudes of library staff members toward a proposed automation project fall into fairly distinct categories. Fortunately, for the sake of progress toward automating libraries, the great majority of staff members are open-minded, reasonable and enthusiastic people who showed a genuine interest in learning more and being included in training and orientations. A second group exhibits attitudes ranging from indifference to hostility. Some of these employees, driven by fear or a strong preference for the status quo, are truly resistant to automation. They may have an irrational fear of technology (Walton, 1982).

According to Luquire (1983), 'to deal with the new technology and maintain balance between human considerations and the technology of library automation, better understanding of the complexities of the perceptions and attitudes of people is mandatory. Most of the process of human and organisational management is at the mental and psychological plane rather than the physical.

Shaw (1986) found more positive than negative reactions (176 compared to 30). Staff feels happier if they are consulted in the automation process and kept informed of developments. A year after automation, he found that staff felt that services were better and faster than before. Much research has suggested that the style of implementation and consultation with the workforce is more significant in gaining employee acceptance of new systems than actual changes in the jobs themselves.

Kiesler et al (1987) found that there was even a segregation between those who worked on the automation project and those who did not. The 'library technologists', who were usually young, gaining special influence within the library. Hence a new social order is being established in some libraries with different people gaining rewards, recognition and influential power for their technological skills. There was evidence of some ill feeling about this from the other staff.

Klerk and Euster (1989) found that the technical services staff, accustomed to the detail and specificity required by a computer are adapting easily.

Prince and Burton (1998) found that senior academic-related staff were largely disinterested in technology, the more recently qualified staff being more positive adopters of innovation.

According to Dobb (1999), without a very committed and energetic staff willing to share their skills and enthusiasm for library work with our patrons and with each other every day, our organisation could not really progress in using technology.

Jones (1999) conducted a survey on 218 support-staff perceptions and opinions about technological change in three university libraries and received from 118 respondents i.e. 54%. Most have now experienced a high-tech work environment for a long time. Regarding personal reactions to working with new technologies, out of 118 respondents, thirty-nine people checked only positive terms (excitement, enjoyment, pleasure, competency). Twenty-two respondents checked only negative terms (frustration, inadequacy, dislike, irritation, tolerance). Fifty-seven respondents checked a mixture of positives and negatives.

2.7.2. IT Training for Library Staff

Although all library automation studies and consultants stress the importance of training, their advice does not seem to be getting through to many library managers. In a recent study of special libraries, the greatest source of technostress was found to be inadequate or non-existent training on in-house systems [Bichteler, 1986].

Bichteler(1987) interviewed several academic and public librarians and complained that the training sessions which were too brief, proceeded too rapidly and incorrectly assumed certain previous knowledge. They felt that the whole staff should be trained together rather than training supervisors first and then having the supervisors train others.

Kiesler, Obrosky and Pratto(1987) argue that automation brought about re-skilling of both professional and clerical grades. This is best enabled where a library management style matches task needs and staff abilities without concern over job titles.

Sievert, Albritton, Roper, and Clayton (1988) observed that

resistance may decline with familiarity and experience with automated technology. They found that frequent computer users were significantly less anxious than others. The staff in technical services, who had more experience with the computers, were found to be less anxious than those in reader services. Formal computer courses also seemed to lessen anxiety. Training, therefore, is a useful solution, but it is important that people are given a chance to practice what they have learned.

Corbin (1991) pointed out that to have a basic understanding of computers, maintain good working knowledge and made aware of new developments of automation, a high level of sustained training is necessary for all levels of library staff regardless of their responsibilities or relationship with the automated system.

Johnson (1991) stated that computer knowledge appears to be of more importance as a qualification for advancement. In his study all but one respondent (98.1 per cent) felt that some minimal understanding of automated systems is necessary for promotion. Relating to the changing recruitment policy, 74 per cent believed that in the future computer-literate people will advance far more rapidly than those with just library skills.

Yacoob and Harun(1996) stated that it was not unusual for some staff to find difficulty in adapting to new systems. Routine jobs have been reduced, job designs have changed and new skills are required. This involves retraining of staff and additional staff support.

2.7.3. Staff Involvement in IT implementation

Jones (1989:449) reported that "the feeling of satisfaction increases as the percentage of involvement increases" and showed a decrease in satisfaction as staff involvement decreased.

Statham and Bravo (1990) suggested, "that careful planning and continued feedback are required when introducing new technology....". They also state that "an important underlying issue is the need to involve the affected workers in the planning process. . .".

Daniels (1995) stated that as non-professionals will use new computerized system on a day-to-day basis, they have the power to make it success or failure. Therefore it would be wise to involve them as much as possible in the planning stages, and inform them as much as feasible of all major decisions that will affect their jobs and working environment.

2.7.4. Impact of IT on the size of library staff

According to Johnson (1991) a number of automated libraries shows that non-professional staff are the group most likely to have their numbers reduced by the implementation of a new system. Nearly half (48.2 per cent) of the participants reported a decrease in the number of non-professional or 'clerical' positions as a direct result of automation.

Jones (1999) stated that a large majority of the total respondents report reductions of personnel in all categories – support staff, librarians, and student workers. There was a definite decrease in the number of support staff at each library where these surveys were distributed. However, 57 percent of respondents do not believe technology is responsible for most of the personnel changes. In all three libraries, the largest percentage of respondents (i.e., 53 percent, 68 percent, and 55 percent) said that technology was not responsible for most of the personnel changes.

2.7.5. Impact of IT on Job Structure and Design

Horny (1987) stated that automated systems frequently bring with them opportunities for redesigning the way in which people work as well as in the structure of the whole organisation. Certain jobs may no longer be significant. Others may combine, or become interdependent, due to the way in which functions interrelate within the system. He documents technical services staff reallocations at Northwestern University, with work responsibilities shifted from professionals to support staff and from support staff to students. Reassignments and staff reductions resulted in considerable savings in salaries.

Klerk and Euster (1989) also found that there were fewer professionals working in technical services because of the changes to the cataloguing process and, at the same time, automation has brought about an increased demand on the public service area, where professional librarians now spend more of their time. This is changing the orientation of the library from a warehouse to a client-centred learning centre.

Furuta (1990) stated that the introduction of the bibliographic utilities in the 1970s produced far-reaching changes in cataloging departments by allowing the bulk of the material to be processed more quickly and cost effectively by non-professionals. In turn, that change caused professionals' duties to shift to handling the more difficult items.

Dyer, Fossey and Mckee (1993) stated that technology can have a profound effect on job design and the quality of working life. The introduction of an automated library system brings changes in the working environment, in the nature of the work and job content, in job autonomy and methods of control, in skill requirements, responsibility, status and career paths and in patterns of relationships, work groups and communication.

2.7.6. Impact of IT on Workload of library staff

Daniels (1995) stated that most of the extra work will be concerned with record conversion, inputting of data and bar-coding the material. The potential that computerised systems have for providing a much improved service has meant that workload has increased in two ways. Firstly, the very effectiveness of them, and the fact that they enable staff to do so much more, has led to the creation of more work. Extra work may also arise from tasks such as back up and maintenance - these can sometimes take up more staff time than is originally estimated.

Jones (1999) found that more than half of the total respondents replied that technology increased their workload. The percentages of staff in each library who believed technology has added more responsibilities to their job are even higher: 58 perçent, 64 percent, and 62 percent.

2.7.7. Impact of IT on Job Satisfaction of library staff

Sykes (1986) discovered that library assistants in one academic library gained satisfaction either from contact with the users or from doing the job efficiently led him to conclude that for those who get their satisfaction from the latter, automation increases job satisfaction.

According to Craghill, Wilson and Neale (1989), automation can lead to increased variety, challenge and opportunities for learning and development, especially when the system is being implemented. It can also bring an increased sense of achievement and feeling of usefulness. They assert that job satisfaction is increased in many cases: "mainly by increasing the efficiency and effectiveness with which [staff] are able to do their jobs".

Daniels (1995) stated that non-professional staff in UK college seemed fairly comfortable with the new system to use for the basic functions. Their increased job satisfaction demonstrated better and more efficient services to the users and enhancement of overall image of library. They were impressed by the way, it had led to improve speed, efficiency, accuracy as well as access to materials. One library stated that it had doubled circulation figures and the other two appreciated the drastic cuts in waiting times.

2.7.8. Techno Stress and Other Physical Problems & Solutions

The use of sophisticated information technology continues to become increasingly commonplace in libraries in the new millennium, as it has made possible many exciting new opportunities in managing and using library. Along with impressive achievements in streamlining library operations and improving library services, IT has produced a new set of intellectual, psychological, physical and social barriers to effective library development.

Brod (1984) stated that the main symptoms of stress are many and varied – as many as 194 separate problems have been identified as stress-related. These can be both short and long-term and range from indigestion and irritability to hypertension and heart disease. Techno stress is one particular kind of stress that workers can experience. It is a term defined by Brod as "a modern disease of adaptation caused by an inability to cope with the new computer technologies in a healthy manner".

Dainoff (1986) observed that many problems have been alleviated by improved design of workstations. In order to accommodate a great variety of individual shapes and sizes, the workstation must be flexible and must take into account the integration of chair, terminal and work surface. A second focus of ergonomics in libraries has been the reduction of eye strain and glare resulting from VDT use. These problems can be minimized by a number of techniques such as relocation of the VDT, installing light barriers and filters and using colored screens.

Roose (1986) stated that some of the earliest manifestation of techno stress in our society were health problems related to the use of terminals, evident since the early 1970s. Through the years, ergonomists have investigated visual and musculoskeletal problems, job stress factors, working conditions and psychological states of VDT operators.

Bichteler (1987) reported on technostress in libraries, examining some of the fears, frustrations and misconceptions, which hamper the effective use of computers. Technostress among library staff members may result from poorly designed workstations, inadequate training and inept planning and implementation on the part of management. Library users often have false expectations and a lack of understanding of the system, resulting, at least in part, from inappropriate training. Both staff and users may suffer from fear, insecurity and general apprehension of new technology. Managers can take a variety of approaches to alleviate technostress in staff and patrons.

Statham and Bravo (1990) suggested that loss of control and intensifying job pressures often center around the introduction of new technologies and are associated with stress and physical problems.

They mention better communication, better staff training, staff involvement in planning, and careful timing of installations as some ways to prevent health problems (pp.124-26).

Dyckman (1992) suggested cross-training and diversification of both activity and responsibility as ways to avoid physical problems. Ergonomic workstations with comfortable chairs, wrist rests, and glare controls are also important.

Dyer, Fosey and Mckee(1993) observed that resistance to technology has been found to be greater in libraries with greater centralisation and stratification and not so great in those with a less formal structure. This may be because of the need for a flexible approach to task needs and staff skills. With the enhancement of clerical grades to para-professional, and diminished supervision by professional grades, reported by some libraries, the whole structure could become flatter than before.

According to Daniels (1995), the common physical complaints of VDU workers include hand cramps, pain in the neck and shoulders, back pains, asthenopia, headaches, and general fatigue. These symptoms in some part can be avoided by taking simple precautions - workers should ensure they maintain the correct seated posture at a workstation and take frequent breaks from their work. Employers must help by providing the correct furniture and equipment such as anti-glare screens.

2.8 IMPACT OF IT ON USERS

The major reason for using new technology should be that it will ultimately benefit the end user by improving the range and quality of user and support services. One of the major significant challenges facing academic libraries during times of dynamic technology is the ability to understand the changing needs and perspectives of their users. Libraries are more concerned to help users in coping with changing technologies as their potential has significant impact on teaching, education and research activities of academic community.

Pease and Gouke (1982) examined on-line catalog and card catalog use patterns and showed that users preferred on-line catalogs to card catalogs. Matthews *et al* (1983) surveyed 28 libraries users and non-users of on-line catalogue and reported that after the introduction of the on-line catalog there was an increase in the use of library catalogs and collections. Moreover, users consulted the on-line catalog frequently, found relevant materials in their searches, were satisfied with search results, preferred on-line catalogs to card catalogs, and said on-line catalogs were easy to use without formal instruction.

Bichteler (1987) stated that library managers should provide several levels and types of instruction in using the online catalog. Printed material near the terminal may range from a simple flier, which outlines basic operations to a complete manual for more sophisticated users. However, most users prefer online assistance, as they frequently wish to begin searching immediately without taking the time to read instructions or they may be accessing the catalog from a remote location.

Lipetz and Paulson (1987) surveyed users once before and twice after the introduction of an on-line subject catalog to measure its impact on user habits in New York State Library. They found that after the on-line catalog was introduced, the volume of catalog use and the proportion of subject searches were increased.

Klobas (1990) stated that users can be useful allies when a new technology is proposed. Indeed, some users push the library to introduce new information technology. Users should therefore be kept informed about new information technology. Informed users should accept and adopt the technology more readily and more quickly than if it were completely new to them. They may even encourage the library or its parent organisation to adopt a specific new technology. To keep users informed about technological developments, a 'Technology update' could be made available to them.

Adams and Bonk (1995) conducted a four-campus survey of faculty use of electronic information technologies and resources covering all academic disciplines. Lack of knowledge about electronic resources was the most commonly cited obstacle to use of computer-based information resources by faculty.

Another study conducted by Abels, Liebscher, and Denman (1996) found that accessibility (or connectivity) plays a major role in the use of networked information by faculty at smaller academic institutions.

Martinez-Arellano (1996) studied user attitudes and behavior before and after implementation of an On-line Catalog in the Central Library of the National Autonomous University of Mexico (UNAM). The study showed that after introducing an on-line catalog in a library, the frequency of library visits was increased, the number of catalogs users was greater and that opinion about library services was better, use of the catalog was easier, and users found more information on library holdings.

According to Yacoob and Harun (1996), as the use of IT becomes an increasingly important part of daily life, users have to be educated so that optimum use and advantage of the facilities is ensured. Promoting and encouraging the use of the new library services has been one of the main responsibilities of the library staff. There is an increasing need for user education for novice users. Outreach programmes are needed to market the systems, and to teach the formulation of simple and complex boolean search strategies. Similar instruction is also needed for the use of other IT applications, such as CDROM, CD-Net and multimedia.

Budd and Connaway (1997) surveyed 1348 faculty in six different departments at eight universities across the United States to know their habits or attitudes towards the use of networked information and received 651 responses. 91.6 percent of the respondents (n=647) report that they do have access to an Internet connection at work. Over half (55.3 percent, n=644) say that they use the Internet in some way to search bibliographic databases. Almost 60 percent (n=645) have used networks to search the library catalogs of institutions other than their own. Almost half of the respondents

(46.9 percent, n=637) say that their patterns of behavior regarding collaboration have changed. About 47 percent (n=329) state that they have co-authored papers as a result of this kind of networking. Some report more substantive effects on their collaboration with colleagues. A faculty member offers, "I now have a regular research relationship with colleagues in Holland, India, Thailand, and the U.K.".

Starkweather and Wallin (1999) used two qualitative research methods- focus groups and interviews – to explore the experience and concerns of selected faculty of the University of Nevada, Las Vegas. Most participants replied that the library's computer-based information resources affected the way they conducted research. They saved time when searching electronic periodical indexes, they had increased confidence in their review of the literature by using electronic resources, and they could identify resources in remote libraries and archives. It was generally held that online access to catalogs and periodical indexes was very convenient and saved faculty time both by "speeding up" the research process and reducing trips to the library. With regard to the best method for the library to let them know what was available in the library, most participants favored brief periodic electronic mail announcements.

2.9 CONCLUSION

Today, Libraries have wide range of opportunities and variety of challenges offered by the rapid development and wide application of Information Technology (IT). IT has become an integral part of all library operations and information services. This movement of using IT in libraries has dramatically changed the ways by which data acquisition, processing and access has been carried out and information services have been provided by the libraries. As this technology provides librarians with new choices, new opportunities and new challenges, there has been a phenomenal progress in the use of IT applications in library operations and information services in the developed countries of world. IT usage in Indian libraries has also gained considerable momentum in recent years, which is going to increase at much faster rate in future. This chapter presented the reasons for IT applications in libraries and discussed the impact of IT on various aspects of library operations and information services. It also briefly reviewe the latest trends of using IT applications in libraries in different countries of the world in general and India in particular.

2.10 REFERENCES

Abels, E., Liebscher, P., & Denman, D.W. (1996). Factors that influence the use of electronic networks by science and engineering faculty at small institutions. Part 1. Queries. *Journal of the American Society for Information Science*, 47, 146-158.

Abifarin, F.P. (1993). Availability and use of information technologies in Nigerian University libraries. *Library Review*, 42(5), 4-14.

Adams, J. A. & Bonk, S. C. (1995). Electronic information technologies and resources use by university faculty and faculty preferences for related library services. *College & Research Libraries*, 56(2), 119-131.

Agalo, Joyce. (1998). *Emerging developments of Audiovisual and multimedia use in National and Academic libraries in Kenya*. Papers of 64th IFLA general conference, Amsterdam, 16-21 August,(pp.44-46).

Akeroyd, J. (1991). Launch of CD network has rapid impact. *Information* World *Review*, 59,10-11.

Ansari, M.M (1998). Automation of university libraries of Bihar: Problems and possible solutions. In CALIBER-98: Information technology applications. (Papers presented at Fifth National Convention of CALIBER-98, Bhuvaneswar, 4-5 March, (pp.283-284). Ahemadabad: INFLIBNET Centre.

Badu, Edwin Ellis. (1993). The impact of the use of microcomputers on the university of Ghana library. *Library Review* 42(5), 23-37.

Bevan, Nick (1994). Transient technology. The future of CD-ROMs in libraries. *Program*, 28(1), 1-14.

Bichteler, J. (1986). Human aspects of High Tech in special libraries', *Special Libraries*, 77(3), 121-8.

Bichteler, Julie. (1987). Technostress in libraries: Causes, effects and solutions. *The Electronic Library*, 5(5).

Biddiscombe, R (1991). Networking CD-ROMs at the University of Birmingham library. *ITs News*, 24, 27-28.

Biradar, S. K. (1995). *A report on organisation study and market research for evaluation* of technological infrastructure of government, academic and research libraries *for dissemination of information to users.* MBA dissertation submitted to the Kouali Institute of Management Studies, Karnataka University, Dharwad.

Borgman, Christine L. (1996). Automation is the answer, but what is the question? Progress and Prospects for Central and Eastern European Libraries. *Journal of Documentation,* 52(3), 252-295.

Brimsek, Tobi A. (1990). A technological assessment of the SLA membership: Summary report. *Special Libraries,* 81 (Spring 1990), 146-151.

Brindley, L.(ed). (1989). *The electronic campus.* London: British library.

Brod, C. (1984). *Technostress:The human cost of the computer revolution.* Massachusetts: Addison-Wesley.

Budd, John M. & Connaway, Lynn Silipigni. (1997). University Faculty and Networked Information: Results of a Survey. *Journal of the American Society for Information. Science.* 48(9), 843-852.

Chandran, D. & Ramesh Babu, B. (1999). Use of Information Technology in Academic and Professional College Libraries in Tirupati (AP): An opinion survey of the library staff. paper presented at 44th ILA conference held during 25-28 February, (555-560). Hyderabad.

Chaya Devi, V. (1998). Computerised informations services in university libraries of AP- A comparative study. In CALIBER-98: Information technology applications. (Papers presented at Fifth National Convention of CALIBER-98, Bhuvaneswar, 4-5 March, (pp.275-282). Ahemadabad: INFLIBNET Centre.

Chen, Ching-Chih. (1997). Multimedia technologies, (pp.206). *World Information Report* (1997/98). Paris: UNESCO.

Cleary, J. (1994). Academic libraries, networking and technology: some recent developments. *Australian Library Journal,* 43(4), 235-56. Cockrill, A. (1997).

Coping with change: issues facing British and German university libraries in the 1990s. *Journal of Librarianship and Information Science* 29(2), 77-88.

Corbin, J. (1991). Automation and non-professional staff – the neglected majority. *Serials,* 4(3), 39.

Cortez, Edwin M. (1983). Library automation and management information systems. *Journal of Library Administration,* 4(3), 21-33.

Dainoff, M.J. (1986). *Learning from office automation: Ergonomics and human impact.In Human aspects of library automation: Helping staff and patrons cope*. .(pp. 16-29). Urbana, IL: Graduate School of Library and Information Science, University of Illinois.

Daniels, Rachel J. (1995). Effects on non-professional staff of the implementation of computer-based library systems in college libraries: Some case studies. *Program*, 29(1), 1-13.

Dobb, Linda S. (1999). Four retreats and a forum: A meditation on retreats as a response to change. *Library Trends*, 47(4), 699-710.

Dyer, Hillary,; Fossey, Deborah & McKee Kathryn. (1993). The impact of automated library systems on job design and staffing structures. *Program*, 27(1), 1-16.

Dyckman, A. A. (1992). Library assistants in the year 2000. *Journal of Library administration*, 17(1), 77-90.

Ekpenyong, Georgina Dien. (1991). Prospects for new information technology in Nigerian libraries. *Library Review*, 40(5), 12-16.

Eniya, Christian O. (1991). Computerisation in Nigerian libraries: A state of the art review. *International Library Review* 23, 159-174.

Fong, W. Wilfred. (1997). Library and information technology in Southeast Asia. *Information Technology and Libraries*, 20-26

Furness, Karen L. & Graham, Margaret E. (1996). The use of information technology in special libraries in the UK. *Program*, 30(1), 23-37.

Furuta, Kenneth. (1990). The Impact of automation on professional catalogers. *Information Technology and Libraries*, September, 242-252

Ganpule, S.R & Waydande, H.S. (1994). Computerisation and aftermath in central library of IIT Bombay. (Paper presented in the seminar on library automation and it aftermath, Hyderabad, 5-6 April 1994) (PP.1-20). Hyderabad : ASRC.

Gopinath, M.A. (1995). Information Technology, knowledge processing and libraries of the future: An interlinked information service. In CALIBER-95: Information Access Through Networks. (working papers for CALIBER-95, Hyderabad, 10-12 February, 1995. (pp.129-143). Ahmadabad: INFLIBNET Centre.

Griffiths, Jose-Marie & King, Donald W. (1989). *Library systems in New York State* (pp.157-158). Rockville, Maryland, King Research Inc.

Gyeszly, S.D. (1991). Automation in Hungarian libraries. *Information Technology and Libraries*, June, 128-132.

Harbour, R. T. (1994). Managing library automation: London: ASLIB.

Haravu, L. J. (1993). Library automation and networking in India: an overview of recent developments. *Annals of Library Science and Documentation*, 40(1), 32-40.

Haravu, L. J. (1995). Strategies for the adoption of New Information technologies. In CALIBER-95: *Information Access Through Networks.* (working papers for CALIBER-95, Hyderabad, 10-12February, 1995. Ahemadabad: INFLIBNET Centre.

Haravu, L.J. 2004. Library Automation: Design, Principles And Practice. New Delhi: Allied Publishers, 262p.

Hauptman, R., & Anderson, C. L. (1994). The people speak: the dispersion and impact of technology in American libraries. *Information Technology and Libraries,* 13(4), 249-56.

Hayter, M. & Heery, M. (1989). Use of IT by senior managers in UK academic libraries. *ASLIB proceedings,* 41 June , 203-211.

Higginbotham, B.B. & Bowdoin, S. (1993). *Access vs. assets.* Chicago: American Library Association.

Himmelfarb, Gertrude. (1999). Revolution in the library. *Library Trends,* 47(4), 612-619.

Horny, K.L. (1987). Fifteen years of automation: Evolution of technical services staffing. *Library Resources and Technical Services,* 31(1), 69-76.

Hossein Farajpahlou, A. (1994). Status of automation in Iranian academic libraries. *International Information & Library Review,* 26, 107-137.

Johnson, P. (1991). *Automation and organizational change in libraries.* Boston: G.K. Hall.Kannappanavar, B.U. & Vjayakumar, M. (2001). Use of IT in University of Agricultural Science Libraries of Karnataka: A comparative study. *DESIDOC Bulletin of Information Technology* 21(1), 21-26.

Kaula, P.N. (1997). Information and Communication Technology: Impact and Challenges. *University News,* 35(35), 1-5.

Keefer, Alice., & Jimenez, Miguel.(1992). Library automation in Spain: an overview. *Program,* 26(3), 225-237.

Khan, N. A. (1995). Information technology in the university libraries of Pakistan: stresses and strains. *Pakistan Library Bulletin,* 26 (1), 1-11.

Kiesler, S., Obrosky, S. & Pratto, F. (1987). *Automating a university library: some effects on work and workers.* In Kiesler, S. and L Sproull, (Eds). Computing and change on campus (pp. 131-149). Cambridge: Cambridge University Press.

Klerk, Ann De & Euster, Joanne R. (1989). Technology and organisation metamorphoses. *Library Trends,* 37(4), 457-468.

Klobas, Jane E. (1990). Managing technological change in libraries and information services. *The Electronic library,* 8(5), 344-349.

Konnur, M. B., & Rajendra, A. R. (1994). Automated libraries: some experiences. *Herald of Library Science,* 33(1-2), 24-8.

Kumar, K. P. V. (1994). Impact of information technology on Indian society. An overview. *Herald of Library Science,* 33(1-2), 3-8.

Kumar, P.S.G. (1987). *Computerisation of Indian libraries.* Delhi: B.R. publishing corporation.344p.

Kumar, R.P. (1994). An overview of modern technologies: Applications in Indian libraries. *International Information and Library Review,* 26, 327-339.

Lakshmana Moorthy, A. (2000). *Impact of electronic media on library and information centres with a specific reference to India.* Ph.D. thesis. Karnataka University, Dharwad.

Lancaster, F. W., & Sandore, B. (1997). *Technology and management in library and information services.* Urbana-Champaign: University of Illinois. Graduate school of Library and Information Science.

Larsen, G. (1992). Library automation in European community countries: An overview. *Program,* 26(4), 361-71.

Laxman Rao, N. (1993). *Planning and Implementation of Automated Circulation System for Osmania University Library System.* Ph.D. thesis. Osmania University, Hyderabad. 327p.

Lee, Lucy Te-chu & Chuang, Tao-ming. (1994). Automated Library Systems in the National Universities and Colleges: The Taiwan Experience. *Journal of Information, Communication & Library Science,* 1(2), 24-33.

Li, Tze-chung. (1997). Technological Development in Asia: Library Automation in Taiwan. *Information Technology and Libraries,* Mar , 26-29.

Lin, Sharon C. (1988). Library automation in China. *Information Technology and Libraries,* 7(3), 230-242.

Lin, S.K. (1997). *The impact of information technology on library organizations.* Karori, Wellington: New Zealand.

Lipetz, Ben-Ami & Paulson, Peter J. (1987). A study of the impact of introducing an online subject catalog at the New York State Library. *Library Trends,* 35, 619-629.

Longley, D. & Shain, M. Macmillon. (1985). *Dictionary of Information Technology* (2nd ed.). London: Macmillan.

Luce, Richard E. (1991). Changes on the technological horizon down-under:

developments in information technology in Australia impact resource sharing. *Journal of Educational Media and Library Sciences,* 28(3), 299-314.

Luquire, W. (1983). Attitudes toward automation/innovation in academic libraries. *The Journal of Academic Librarianship,* 8, 344.

Maceviciene, V., & Tolusis, S. (1995). Library automation in the Lithuanian academic libraries. *Microcomputers for Information Management* 12(4), 267-77.

Mader, B. (1995). Library automation systems in academic libraries in Hungary. *Program,* 29(3), 285-93.

Malik, Khalid Mahmood. The status of library automation in Pakistan. *Library Review* 45(6), 36-42.

Martinez-Arellano, Filiberto F. (1996). User attitudes and behavior before and after the implementation of an On-line Catalog. *International Information & Library Review,* 28, 275-287.

Matthews, J.R., Lawrence, G. & Ferguson, D.K. (eds). (1983). *Using Online Catalogs: A Nationwide Survey.* New York: Neal-Schuman.

Mayor, Federico. (1997). Preface. *World Information Report* (1997/98).(pp.5-7). Paris: UNESCO.

McKenna, B., & Forrester, W. (1998). Library automation at the interface of the World Wide Web. *Electronic Library,* 16(3), 177-9.

Metz, Roy. (1990). The impact of electronic formats and campus networks on university libraries in the United States. *Computers in Libraries,* 10 (5), 30-31.

Ming, D. C. (1996). Assessing the impact of IT on university library services in the 21st century. *Malaysian Journal of Library & Information Science,* 1(2), 79-87.

Moore, Nick. (1997). The Information Society, *World Information Report* (1997/98) (pp.271-283). Paris: UNESCO.

Mukesh saikia (1997). Application of information technology in Tezpur University Library.In Moorthy, A.L & Mangla, P.B (Eds). *CALIBER-1997: Information Technology Applications in Academic Libraries.* (Papers presented at the Fourth

National Convention for the automation of libraries in education and research, Patiala, 6-8 March 1997), (pp.46-48). Ahmedabad: INFLIBNET Centre.

Murthy, S.S. (1999). Role of libraries in the New Millennium of Information Technology, *DESIDOC Bulletin of Information Technology,* 19 (4-5), 3-10.

Neelameghan, A. (1998). Information technology applications in enterprises: Opportunities and challenges. *Information Studies*, 4 (1), 13-32.

O'Leary, M. (1990). Local online: the genic is out of the bottle. Part 1,*Online*, 14(1), 15-18.

Pease, Sue & Gouke, Mary Noel. (1982). Patterns of use in an online catalog and a card catalog. *College and Research Libraries*, 43, 279-291.

Person, L. (1986). *Training issues in changing technology*. Chicago: ALA.

Pong, Lai Yeen (1990) Computerisation of library operations in Singapore: An overview. *International Library Review*, 22, 163-179.

Rajan, T.N. , & Satyanarayana, R. (1987). Applications of information technologies in India (Problems and perspectives). In B.M.Gupta et al. (Eds.) *Handbook of Libraries, Archives and Information Centres in India* (pp.22). New Delhi: Information Industry Pub.

Rajashekar, T.B. (1998). Virtual libraries: Internet based library and information services. In SIS-98 : *Internet based library information services* (working papers on virtual libraries, 12-14 March. Hyderabad: University of Hyderabad.

Ramaiah, L.S. (1998). Automation of University Libraries: Some Basic problems. *Images and Perceptions in Library and Information Science*.(pp. 161-67). New Delhi, Ess Ess Pub.

Rama Reddy, E; Pommal Rao, R; & Srinivasulu, P. (1997). Database creation and maintenance operations : A case study of Indira Gandhi Memorial Library. In Moorthy, A.L & Mangla, P.B (Eds). *CALIBER-1997: Information Technology Applications in Academic Libraries*. (Papers presented at the Fourth National Convention for the automation of libraries in education and research, Patiala, 6-8 March 1997), (pp.63-67).Ahmedabad: INFLIBNET Centre.

Rama Reddy, E (2000). Organization of information resources in the networked environment. In Vengan, R., Mohan, H.R. & Raghavan, K.S. (Eds.). CALIBER-2000: *Information Services in a Networked environment in India*. (Papers presented in the Seventh National Convention for the automation of libraries in education and research, Chennai, 16-18 February, 2000).(pp.3.3-3.12). Ahmedabad: INFLIBNET Centre.

Rashid, A. (1996). Library automation: an overview. *Library Science with a Slant to Documentation and Information Studies* 33(1), 45-54.

Ravichandra Rao, I.K. (1983). Library automation. *DRTC refresher seminar*, 14, Bangalore.

Ravichandra Rao, I.K. (1997). Automation of academic libraries in India: Status, Problems and Future (Theme Paper). *In CALIBER-1997: Information*

Technology Applications on Academic Libraries. (Papers presented at the Fourth National Convention for the automation of libraries in education and research, Patiala, 6-8 March 1997),(pp.1-4). Ahmedabad: INFLIBNET Centre.

Ressler, Sandy & Trefzger, Bill. (1997). Development of the NIST virtual library. *IEEE Internet computing,* Sep/Oct, 35-41.

Roffe, Pedro., Aning, Kwaku & Tesfachew, Taffere. (1995). Overview, *UNCTAD Advanced Technology Assessment System.* Issue 10 Autumn, p.v

Roose, T. (1986). Ergonomics in the Library. *Library Journal,* 111, 17, 15, 54-55.

Rowley, J.E. (1993). *Computers for libraries,* 3 (Rev. ed.). London. Library Association Publishing, 311p.

Satyanarayana, R. (1996). *Information technology and its facets.* New Delhi: Manaka publication, 64-65.

September, Peter E. (1990). Automation and academic library management: A case study. Library Review, 39(3), 6-21.

Sharma, Pandey S K. (1993). In Ravinder Kumar Chadha and S.P. Gupta (Eds.) *Library computerisation: why Information Technology and Librarianship* (pp.1-10). (Papers presented at AGLIS Annual National Convention). Jaipur.

Shaw, D. (1986). Staff opinions in library automation planning: a case study. *Special libraries,* 77(3), 140-151.

Sievert, M.E., Albritton, R. L., Roper, P., & Clayton, N. (1998). Investigating computer anxiety in an academic library. *Information Technology and Libraries,* 7(3), 243-252.

Sippings, Gwenda. (1987). Use of information technology by information services: The Aslib information technology survey 1987. *The Electronic Library,* 5(6), 354-357.

Smith, Elaine Davis. (1993). A comparison of the effects of new technology on searching habits in industrial and academic institutions. *Journal of Information Science,* 19, 57-66.

Soubra, Yehia. (1995). Trends and current situation in the diffusion and utilization of information technology. *UNCTAD Advanced Technology Assessment System.* Issue 10 Autumn, 49.

Starkweather, Wendy M. & Wallin, Camille Clark. (1999). Faculty response to library technology: Insights on attitudes. *Library Trends,* 47(4), 640-668.

Statham, A., & Bravo, E. (1990). The introduction of new technology: Health implications for workers. *Women and Health,* 16(2), 105-129.

Sujatha G. (1996). A study on resource sharing and networking of university libraries in *Andhra Pradesh (A.P.)*. Ph.D. thesis. Andhra University, Waltair.

Sung, Y. (1994). Library automation and networking in R.O.C.: review and comments. *Journal of Information, Communication, and Library Science*, 1(2), 11-18.

Sykes,P. (1986). Automation and non-professional staff at the Polytechnic of the South Bank. *Training and Education*, 3(3), 50-56.

Tang, Shaoming. (1994). A brief introduction to the development of public library service in China. *Focus on Int.l & Comparative Librarianship*, 25(2), 78-79.

Tedd, Lucy A. (1997). *An introduction to computer-based library systems*, (2nd ed.). chichester: John Wiley.

Van Borm, Julien., & van Borm, J. (1991). Library automation in Belgium in 1990. *Program* 25(3), 241-249.

Venkataramana, P & Chadrasekhar Rao, V. (1998). Impact of information technology on library operations and services. In B. Satyanarayana et al (Eds). *Information Technology: issues and trends*, v.1. (pp.184-193). New Delhi: Cosmo Publication.

Venkataramana, P. 2004. Information Technology Applications in Libraries. New Delhi: Ess Ess Publisher, 307p.

Vijaykumar, J. (1995). *Professional attitude towards library computerization: A study of university and special libraries in Andhra Pradesh (A.P.)*. Ph.D. thesis. Andhra University, Waltair.

Viswanathan, T. (1995). *Overview of computer technology unit 1. Application of information technology* (MLIS-06), (pp.5-30). New Delhi: IGNOU.

Vivekananda Jain (1998) Information Management status in the Banaras Hindu *University Library System :An Overview CALIBER-98: Information Technology Applications in Academic Libraries.* (Papers presented at the Third National Convention for the automation of libraries in education and research, Bhubhaneswar, 4-5 March 1998), (pp.291-292).Ahmedabad: INFLIBNET Centre.

Vyasamoorthy, P. (1989). Use of computers in university libraries: Some facts and thoughts to help frame a policy. In N.B.Inamdar & L.S.Ramaiah (Eds.) *National Policy on University Libraries in India: Problems and Perspectives* (pp.251-259). New Delhi, Concept Publishing.

Walckiers, M. (1992). Library automation in Europe. *IATUL Proceedings* (New Series) 1, 16-22.

Wood, Joanna. (1990). Library automation: European dimension. *Learning Resources Journal*, 6(3), 69-71.

Woods, Rollo G. (1986). Library automation in British universities. *Program,* 20(4), 359-381.

Wright, Kicth C. (1995). *Computer – related technologies in library operations.* England: Gower, 201.

Yaacob R. A., & Harun, M. H. (1996). Information technology implementations in libraries and information centres in Malaysia: Impact and pitfalls. *Electronic Library* 14(3), 233-42.

Younis, Abdul Razeq. (1990). Library automation in Jordan. *International Library Review* 22(1), 19-29.

Zhu, Qiang. (1998). Increasing the Pace of an Integral Library System in China: Moving toward the twenty-first century. *College & Research libraries,* 169-176.

3
University Libraries in India

"A University stands for humanism, for tolerance, for reason, for the adventure of ideas and for the search of truth. It stands for the onward march of the human race towards ever-higher objectives. If the Universities discharge their duties adequately then it is well with the Nation and the people". — **Jawaharlal Nehru**

3.1 INTRODUCTION

India has achieved a vast multi-faceted socio-economic development during the last 63 years of its independence. It has made a commendable progress in educational, scientific, technological, engineering, philosophical and cultural fields.

India has developed during the last 65 years a very large system of education and has created a vast body of men and women equipped with a high order of scientific and technological capabilities, robust humanist and philosophical thought and creativity (Indian National Commission for Cooperation with UNESCO, 1998).

Education plays a key role for the development of any society. Universities are the most important institutions of society for the preservation, creation and dissemination of knowledge as well as the custodians of intellectual and ethical traditions and values in society (Mehta, 1998). Universities serve teaching, educational and research needs of higher education in the country. It primarily serves postgraduate students, teachers, researchers etc. The standard of study, teaching, education and research of a university largely depends upon the quality of the service rendered by the university library.

3.2 UNIVERSITIES IN INDIA: HISTORICAL BACKGROUND

India is one of the most ancient civilizations of the world with a kaleidoscopic variety and rich cultural heritage. Universities in India were established more than two thousand years ago. Higher learning centers have existed in our country from ancient times. India was well known for Her different seats of learning in the various monasteries, math's, temples and Buddhist viharas spread across the country. These learning centers were known by different names such as *Gurukula, Parishad, Paatsala, Seminary, Madarasa* etc. The theme of higher knowledge and higher education was fashioned in India by the ancient Rishis and Sages in the Vedic age. The early Gurukul (The home of the teacher as the university) system of education flourished in the Vedic and Upanishadic periods. There were many famous centers of learning in ancient India of which the most renowned were Taxila in the 6th Century B.C., Nalanda and Vikramsila in the 4th and 5th Centuries A.D. respectively. Taxila University considered to be the first university in the world, acquired an international reputation as a centre of advanced studies. It was the most famous seat of Buddhist learning where scholars from far-off countries came to study not only Buddhism but also Medicine, Law and Military science. The University of Nalanda attracted students from China, Nepal, Tibet and Korea. Some of the other important centers of learning in Ancient India were *Vallabhi, Odantapuri, Somapuri, Jaggadal, Mithila, Kanheri* etc. With the coming of Islam, *Madarasas* were established as institutes of higher learning at Lahore,

Delhi, Rampur, Ajmer, Lucknow, Allahabad etc., During 1800s, Christian Missionaries established many educational centers like Hindoo College (now known as Presidency College), Calcutta; St. John's College, Agra; Madras Medical College, Madras; Wilson College, Bombay etc.,

3.3 ESTABLISHMENT OF MODERN UNIVERSITIES IN INDIA

The British rulers initiated modern universities in India. Indian Universities owe their origin to the Wood's Dispatch of 1854, a report on higher education prepared by Sir Charles Wood in 1854. Because of its importance, it has been rightly described as the '*magna carta*' of English education in India. As an outcome of this Report, three universities were established in Calcutta, Bombay and Madras in 1857 on the model of London University. For the next quarter of a century, no new universities were established. Later Punjab University was started in Lahore (now in Pakistan) in 1882 and University of Allahabad in 1887.

3.3.1. Indian Universities Act (1904)

Indian Universities Commission was set up in 1902 to enquire into the affairs of newly established universities and recommend suitable measures to improve the quality of higher education in India. Based on the recommendation of this Commission, the Indian Universities Act was passed in 1904 with a specific statutory provision for the universities and colleges to undertake more teaching and research activities and to maintain well-equipped libraries.

The formulation of Education Policy in India in 1913 caused the establishment of many new universities at different places in India. They include Banaras Hindu University in 1916, University of Patna in 1917, Osmania University in 1918, Aligarh Muslim University in 1920 and so on. There were 20 universities in India prior to Independence in 1947. The period of 90 years from 1857 to 1947 was the period of slow rate of development of universities in India. Dr S. R Ranganathan (1963) stated that the objective of Indian universities during pre-independence period was not for the advancement of learning and research but to conduct examinations and award degrees as a hallmark of fitness for recruitment to the civil service of the country.

3.4 DEVELOPMENT OF UNIVERSITIES IN INDIA

Education being a key factor for the growth and development of a country, Government of India appointed various commissions and committees to make recommendations for the reorganisation and improvement of the standard of higher education system and make it relevant to the changing needs of the nation after independence. The recommendations of some of the prominent commissions and committees are given below:

3.4.1. University Education Commission (1948-49)

The Government of India setup University Education Commission under the Chairmanship of Dr S.Radhakrishnan to report on university education and suggest improvements and extensions that may be desirable to suit present and future requirements of the country. The Commission reported that "Democracy depends for its very life on a high standard of general, vocational and professional education. Dissemination of learning, incessant search for new knowledge, unceasing effort to plumb the meaning of life, provision for professional education to satisfy the occupational needs of our society are the vital tasks of higher education". The Commission strongly recommended for the establishment of University Grants Commission (UGC) in India on the basis of identical body in Great Britain.

3.4.2. University Grants Commission (1956)

The University Grants Commission is a statutory organisation established by an Act of Parliament in 1956 in India. The UGC, being a national, autonomous and advisory body, is empowered by the Act to take all the necessary measures for the promotion and coordination of university education and for the determination and maintenance of standards of teaching, examination and research in universities.

The UGC formulates and directs the policies and programmes of higher education in India. In addition to its role of giving grants to universities and colleges, it also advises central and state Governments on the measures necessary for the improvement of university education.

3.4.3. Education Commission (1964-66)

In 1964, the Government of India set up another education commission under the chairmanship of Dr. D.S. Kothari to advise the Government on the national pattern of education and on the general principles and the policies for the development of education at all stages in all aspects. Education Commission set out the following functions of the universities in the modern world.

- To seek and cultivate new knowledge, to engage vigorously and fearlessly in the pursuit of truth, and to interpret old knowledge and beliefs in the light of new needs and discoveries;
- To provide the right kind of leadership in all walks of life by helping individuals to develop their potential;
- To provide society with competent men and women trained in all professions who are inclined with a sense of social purpose;
- To strive to promote equality and social justice and to reduce social and cultural differences through diffusion and education;
- To foster in the teachers and students, and through them in the society generally, the attitudes, and values needed for developing the good life in individuals and society; and
- To bring universities closer to the community through extension of knowledge and it's application for problem sclving.

3.4.4. National Policy on Education (1986)

The National Policy on Education (NPE) characterises higher education as a crucial factor for survival providing the Indian people with an opportunity to reflect on the critical, social, economic, cultural, moral and spiritual issues facing the humanity. It contributes to national development through dissemination of specialised knowledge and skills. NPE advocated a nation-wide movement for improvement of existing libraries and the establishment of new ones as well as provision of library facilities in all educational institutions.

3.5 GROWTH OF UNIVERSITIES IN INDIA

Indian Universities constitute one of the largest higher education systems in the world. Prior to Independence, the growth of universities was very slow and diversification in areas of studies was very limited. After Independence, the number of universities has increased significantly from 20 in 1947 to 523 in 2011.

According to *UGC Annual Report 2011-12,* there are 523 Universities/University Level Institutions in India as on 31.03.2011 which include 43 Central Universities, 265 State Universities, 80 State Private Universities, 5 Institutions established through State Legislation and 130 Institutions Deemed to be Universities. The above 523 Includes Agricultural, Veterinary, Medical, Engineering/Technical and Open Universities. In addition, there are 33,023. colleges affiliated to these universities. These universities and colleges together have 6,82,787 teachers and 1,69,74,883 students for under-graduate, post-graduate and research degrees in the entire country. The growth of universities in India is presented in Table 3.1.

Table 3.1: Growth of Universities in India

Year	No of Universities	Year	No of Universities
Upto 1857	3	Upto 1950	26
1900	5	1960	47
1910	7	1970	90
1920	12	1980	122
1930	15	1990	191
1940	16	2000	248
1947	20	2011	523

3.6 UNIVERSITY SYSTEM

The universities in India are basically of two types – unitary and affiliating. The unitary universities have a single campus and largely concentrate on post-graduate studies and research, though some may also have provision for undergraduate courses. e.g. AMU, BHU and JNU. Affiliating universities generally have a central campus in which schools and departments are located to impart post-graduate instruction and conduct research. These universities also have a variable number of colleges affiliated to them. Most Indian universities belong to affiliating type. In addition to the two main types, the UGC recognises a number of 'deemed universities' and 'institutions of national importance' which specialise in teaching a particular area of knowledge, have the power to award their own degrees, and enjoy the privileges and status of a university. Universities in India are established by Acts of either Parliament or State Legislature.

3.6.1. Higher Education and Coordinating Bodies

Higher education in India is coordinated by several agencies. While the university system falls within the jurisdiction of UGC, professional institutions are coordinated by different bodies. The following are a few important apex bodies at the Central and the State level, which perform different roles and functions for promoting higher education and research in the country.

- Central Advisory Board of Education (CABE)
- Indian Council of Agricultural Research (ICAR)
- Indian Council of Social Sciences Research (ICSSR)
- Council of Scientific and Industrial Research (CSIR)
- All India Council for Technical Education (AICTE)
- Association of Indian Universities (AIU)

The State Councils of Higher Education, Distance Education Council, National Council for Teacher Education, Bar-Council of India, Medical Council of India, Council of Architecture, Dental Council of

India, Pharmacy Council of India and Indian Nursing Council etc., (most of them being statutory in character) are the coordinating bodies vested with powers to regulate standards of academic performance in their respective disciplines in the country.

3.7. UNIVERSITY LIBRARIES IN INDIA

University libraries play a vital role in the development and promotion of university education in the country. Dr.Shankar Dayal Sharma, the then President of India, while inaugurating the world Book Fair at New Delhi in 1988 rightly observed that "a library is more important than that of a university because library can function without a university whereas a university cannot do without a library".

Library being a treasure house of information, not only gather, store and disseminate information but also serve as an effective agency for creation of fresh ideas and new knowledge. The goal of a university library is to provide suitable information materials useful for study, teaching and research purposes in a university. The university library functions as conservator of knowledge, ideas, teaching, research, publication, extension and service and interpretation. Libraries supplement the classroom teaching work and provide wide range of knowledge required to attain intellectual pursuits. A well-equipped library is not only necessary for all teaching and study but also essential for research. A systematically developed library collection serves as a major academic facility to the faculty as well as to the students and enable them to achieve better results in their respective fields. A good university library is indispensable for achieving academic excellence of any university.

3.7.1. Ancient Period

Libraries of the important centers of learning such as Nalanda, Vikramsila, Taxila, Vallabhi, Odantapuri, Somapuri, Jaggadal, Mithila, Kanheri etc., have existed in our country from the very ancient times. All these centres of learning had reading materials. This period may be regarded as an (age of repositories) rather than libraries. Taxila University had an excellent library with a collection of works on

Hinduism, political science, literature, medicine and philosophy. Nalanda University library was the biggest in Asia. It had a huge library known as 'Dharmaganja' consisting of three buildings called 'Ratnasagara' (sea of gems), 'Ratnadadhi' (mean of gems), 'Ratna ganjaka' (collection of gems). Ratnadadhi was said to have a huge nine-storied building. During 1800s, many colleges established by Christian Missionaries maintained good libraries with adequate collections.

3.7.2. Pre-Independence Era

The libraries of the universities established in Calcutta, Bombay and Madras in 1857 were started in 1862, 1873 and 1907 respectively. Since these universities were not the centers of learning and research but were mainly meant for holding examinations and awarding degrees, the need for well-equipped and organised library system was not felt. This situation was evident from the Report of Indian Universities Commission 1902.

The Commission was very critical of the poor state of affairs of university libraries and observed that there is not much to be said about the present university libraries. The Commission recommended that "good reference libraries should be provided in both universities and colleges in order that students may have an opportunity of forming the habit of independent and intelligent reading".

Calcutta University Commission set up in 1917 declared that maintenance of a university library with adequate and up-to-date collection is essential to a first class university. Sadler, the Chairman of this Commission emphatically said that "great libraries and great laboratories are needed to make great universities". The Commission also recommended that 'The University Librarian' ought to be a functionary of great importance ranking with University Professor in terms of salary and status and should be an ex-officio member of the Academic Council of the university".

3.8 DEVELOPMENT OF UNIVERSITY LIBRARIES IN INDIA

Realising the value of libraries in higher education, various expert committees and commissions set up by Government of India have made strong recommendations for the development of university libraries in the country.

University Education Commission set up in 1948 under the Chairmanship of Dr.S. Radhakrishnan, realising the importance of libraries in the fulfillment of the objectives of higher education, had stated that "The Library is the heart of all university's work: directly so, as regards its research work and indirectly as regards its educational work, which derives its life from research work. Scientific research needs a library as well as laboratories, while for humanities research, the library is both library and laboratory in one".

Dr C.D. Deshmukh, the first chairman of UGC, while drawing an analogy between a university and the human body remarked that "the students form the body of the university, the administration is the head, the teachers are the soul and the library is the heart".

UGC is fully conscious of the "new and intimate role of libraries in universities/colleges life in our renaissant India" and started giving liberal grants to libraries for buildings, furniture and for the purchase of books and periodicals.

Keeping in view the value and importance of a well-organised and well-equipped library, the UGC played an extraordinary developmental role by providing adequate financial assistance for collection development, acquisition of books and journals, purchase of furniture and equipments, construction of new library buildings and various important schemes, which helped the university libraries to make rapid progress during the last five decades in the country.

3.8.1. UGC Committee for University and College Libraries (1957)

UGC appointed a library committee in 1957, under the chairmanship of Dr S. R. Ranganathan to advice on the matters relating to the proper functioning and management of college and university libraries in the country.

The Committee systematically surveyed the academic libraries and was very much disappointed to find poor facilities, service and budget of university libraries. The Committee submitted a comprehensive report in 1959 making concrete recommendations on various aspects of iibrary viz. library grant, purchase of books, cultivating reading habits, facilities for inter library loan, photocopying, reference and documentation services, building a microfilm collection, open access system, preparation of union catalogue of books and serials to facilitate cooperation among libraries, library personnel, library building and furniture etc. One of the important recommendations is that the status and the salary of the library staff should be equal to that of the teaching and research staff. The UGC accepted the Committee's recommendations as norms for the development and promotion of university libraries in the country.

The Education Commission (1964-66) reiterated the importance of libraries in higher education in its Report as"Nothing could be more damaging to a growing department than to neglect its library or to give it a low priority. No new university, college or department should be opened without taking into account its library needs in terms of books, journals, space etc."

The Commission laid stress on the proper development of university library system and recommended that a library should:

- provide resources necessary for research in all fields of special interest to the university;
- aid the university teacher in keeping abreast of developments in his field;
- provide library facilities and services necessary for the success of all formal programmes of instruction;
- open the doors to the wide world of books that lie beyond the borders of one's own field of specialisation; and
- to bring books, students, scholars together under conditions which encourage reading for pleasure, self discovery, personal growth and the sharpening of intellectual curiosity.

3.8.2. National Policy on University Libraries:

According to National Policy on University Libraries as proposed by Association of Indian Universities (AIU), the objectives of university libraries are:

- To support the teaching and research programme of the university.
- To develop collections by acquiring necessary reading materials to meet the present and future needs of its users.
- To organise its collections, operations and services so as to provide for the reading materials and information needs of its users in anticipation and on demand.
- Networking and resource sharing among university libraries should be practiced by each institution towards utilisation of all resources.
- To introduce, if necessary, technological innovation like computer/word processing etc., to facilitate users to get prompt service.
- To provide facilities like reprography, inter library loan, translation and documentation to assist users.
- To promote library user education related to technological innovation so that the academic librarian will no longer remain a craftsman but serves educationists through technological means;
- Towards achieving the above goals, to get adequate financing, staff, storage and other facilities, and
- Maximise efficiency of services with reference to inputs/ expenditure so as to make library services cost effective.

3.8.3. Committee on National Network System for Universities/ Libraries (1988)

The UGC setup a Committee on National Network System under the chairmanship of Prof. Yashpal in 1988 to suggest measures for networking of libraries and information centers in universities, deemed universities, institutions of national importance, UGC information centers, R&D institutions and colleges. This committee constituted, a working group, which prepared a project report for the establishment and development of an Information and Library Network, in short called as INFLIBNET, in the country during the Eighth Five Year Plan (1990-95) period. The detailed information on INFLIBNET is given in the later part of this Chapter.

3.9 UNIVERSITY LIBRARIES: PROBLEMS AND CHALLENGES

Dr S. R. Ranganathan stated that the books, staff and the reader - the trinity of librarianship are the basic ingredients for the working of any library - the university library.

Wilson and Tauber (1956) stressed that, (i) resources for instruction, research and extension, (ii) a competent library staff, (iii) organisation of materials for use, (iv) adequate space and equipment; (v) integration of the library with administrative and educational policies, (vi) integration of the library with community, state, regional, national and international library resources, (vii) adequate financial support, and (viii) a workable policy of library government, are essential and fundamental to the successful operation and development of the university library system of a country.

According to Srivastava and Verma (1980), the successful operation and functioning of a library is based on the premise that it should have adequate resources to support training and research, fully trained and qualified staff capable of organising the information contents in the most scientific and helpful order, and the readers who come to use the library and its resources.

The most basic requirement for running a library is finance. Adequate finance is essential for successful functioning of a university library. Although, the need for adequate funds for university libraries has been recommended by various expert committees and commissions, it has not been duly followed and implemented in practice in India. University libraries in India have not been provided sufficient funds to acquire information resources to meet the growing information needs of their users. Moreover, library budgets are decreasing every year and cost of documents is increasing day by day. These factors have great impact on the quality and quantity of collection development in university libraries. Without adequate funds, it is becoming very difficult for university libraries to provide efficient services to its users.

Srivastava and Verma (1980) stated, looking back to the history and development of university library system of the country, that university libraries in India have lagged far behind since very beginning and even today, they have not been able to develop a sound system owing to reasons that are not far to seek.

R.L.Mittal (1989) observed that the growth and development of university libraries in India after Independence has been slow, uneven and haphazard in almost all respects. No doubt, the number of universities has increased much since independence. The main reason for this state of affairs is that we have not been able to spare adequate funds for the development of the university libraries and the expenditure has been much below the norms laid down by various commissions and committees. The services provided by most of the universities are conventional and are still in the under developed stages.

Inspite of the support of UGC in developing university libraries, the situation has not improved much in the desired manner. Even today, university libraries in India are facing many challenges due to the following factors:

- Decreasing library budgets
- High inflation rate and rising cost of documents
- Increasing number of students and information seekers
- Increasing demand for current, quick and more specific information
- Information explosion

- Information technology revolution
- High cost of adoption of modern technology
- Evolution of multiple forms of electronic information resources

In view of the above, the university libraries have to examine various options and explore new avenues to face these challenges. To cope up with the growing problem of shrinking library budgets, it has become inevitable for university libraries to actively participate and promote cooperation and resource sharing with other libraries. The effective co-operation and resource sharing can be achieved only through networking of various libraries, which necessitates the introduction of modern technologies into the university libraries.

3.10 NEED FOR LIBRARY COMPUTERISATION AND NETWORKING

University libraries in India, realising the importance of library automation, are making significant efforts to computerise their operations in order to provide better services to their users. Introduction of modern technologies into university libraries enable them to easily participate in networking and resource sharing and gain access to various electronic channels and wide range of sources of information in order to provide better services to their users more effectively and in less time and cost.

Haravu (1989) stated that automation of university libraries in India helps not only to improve effectiveness and efficiency of operations but also to offer new and improved services. The other important reasons for automation include sheer volume of transactions, routine nature of operations, useful management information and performing certain works better with computers than manual means.

Laxman Rao (1993:57) stated that in the existing university library environment of facing variety of problems, probably, the management has only one alternative to improve services within the available resources i.e., computerisation. The computerisation of library operations may contribute to easy handling and successful achievement of the library objectives.

Amjad Ali (1995) stated that coumputerisation of the university libraries is a must due to shrinking budgets, escalating cost of publications, information explosion and increasing capabilities of IT. IT helps libraries not only to cope with this difficult situation but also to utilise the collections optimally and to offer better services. But in Indian universities, its potential has not been utilized properly. The university libraries must have a definite plan of computerisation to face the challenge of computer as the coming generations will depend more on it, otherwise this gap in library profession will adversely affect the overall process of education.

Networking gained a momentum in the country in the recent years due to rapid developments in computer, communication and micro electronic technology. This is evident from the establishment of many library networks viz. Delhi Library Network (DELNET) in 1992, Calcutta Library Network (CALIBNET) in 1992, Madras Library Network (MALIBNET) in 1993, Ahemedabad Library Network (ADINET) in 1993, Bombay Library Network (BONET) in 1994, Mysore Library Network (MyLIBNET) in 1994, Pune Library Network (PUNET) in 1995 etc. in the country. Some of these networks have been providing variety of services.

UGC launched a national network viz. Information and Library Network (INFLIBNET) in 1991 for networking all libraries of higher education and R&D institutions in the country.

3.11 INFORMATION AND LIBRARY NETWORK (INFLIBNET)

Information and Library Network (INFLIBNET) Centre is an autonomous Inter-University Centre of the *University Grants Commission (UGC)* of India in 1991 at Ahmedabad. NFLIBNET is involved in modernizing university libraries in India and connecting them with other information centres in the country through a nation-wide high speed data network using the state-of-art technologies for the optimum utilisation of information resources in the country.

3.11.1. Objectives

The primary objectives of INFLIBNET are:

- To promote and establish communication facilities to improve capability in information transfer and access that provide support to scholarship learning, research and academic pursuit through cooperation and involvement of agencies concerned.
- To establish a computer communication network for linking libraries and information centres in universities deemed to be universities, colleges, UGC information centres, institutions of national importance and R & D institutions, etc. avoiding duplication of efforts.

i. to promote and implement computerization of operations and services in the libraries and information centres of the country, following a uniform standard;

ii. to evolve standards and uniform guidelines in techniques, methods, procedures, computer hardware and software, services and promote their adoption in actual practice by all libraries, in order to facilitate pooling, sharing and exchange of information towards optimal use of resources and facilities:

iii. to evolve a national network interconnecting various libraries and information centres in the country and to improve capability in information handling and service;

iv to provide reliable access to document collection of libraries by creating on-line union catalogue of serials, theses/ dissertations, books, monographs and non-book materials in various libraries in India:

v. to provide access to bibliographic information sources with citations, abstracts, etc. through indigenously created databases of the Sectoral Information Centres of NISSAT, UGC Information Centres, City Networks etc;

vi. to develop new methods and techniques for archival of valuable information available in the form of digital images using high density storage media;

vii. to optimize information resource utilization through shared cataloguing, inter-library loan service, catalogue production, collection development and thus avoiding duplication in acquisition to the extent possible;

viii. to enable the users to have access to information regarding serials, theses, books etc through the facilities of INFLIBNET and union catalogue of documents;

ix. to create databases of projects, institutions, specialists, etc. for providing on-line information service;

x. to encourage co-operation among libraries, documentation centres and information centres in the country for sharing resources; and

xi. to train and develop human resources in the field of computerized library operations and networking to establish, manage and sustain INFLIBNET.

- To facilitate academic communication amongst scientists, engineers, social scientists, academics, faculties, researchers and students through electronic mail, file transfer, computer/audio/video conferencing, etc
- To undertake system design and studies in the field of communications, computer networking, information handling and data management;
- To establish appropriate control and monitoring system for the communication network and organize maintenance;
- To collaborate with institutions, libraries, information centres and other organizations in India and abroad in the field relevant to the objectives of the Centre;
- To promote R&D and develop necessary facilities and create

technical positions for realizing the objectives of the Centre;

- To generate revenue by providing consultancies and information services; and
- To do all other such things as may be necessary, incidental or conducive to the attainment of all or any of the above objectives.

3.11.2. Functional Groups

Database Management and R & D: The major objective of the group is creation of union catalogue of different type of materials which is major source of information to the users as well as to the library community. It is collaborative effort of INFLIBNET and participating libraries to improve access to the resources held in university libraries in India. It started with union catalogue of Books, Serials Holdings, Current Serials, Theses, Experts and Research Projects. The participating libraries are regularly contributing the records for merging their local holdings in to INFLIBNET union catalogue and the numbers of records are continuously growing.

The Database group has developed suitable software, search interface for managing and updating large number of bibliographic records. The following databases are available for online access round the clock.

Books database : The books database is the major source of bibliographic descriptions for use in research and collections development. The union catalogue of books currently contains 8.2 million bibliographic records from 108 universities and the number is growing constantly.

Serials database : This union database of serial covers the bibliographic information of current serials and serial holdings of the university libraries. It has approximately over 54,000 journal titles contributed by 200 institutions which are regularly updated.

Theses database : The theses database provides access to over 214000 records of doctoral dissertations submitted in 240 Indian universities.

Experts Database : Experts database provides the academic and research profile of the senior level faculty members working in Indian Universities, Colleges and other R&D organizations. It provides comprehensive information about 37000 experts, their background, skills, and accomplishments.

Research Projects : The Research Project Database contains details of the completed and ongoing funded projects, carried out by faculty members at universities in India. Currently it contains information on more than 10,000 research projects funded by agencies such as UGC, ICAR, ICMR, and DST.

Networking and Quality Control : This group has been created for promoting R & D activities in area of Networking and Quality management. Major responsibility of this group is to manage, maintain and timely update the campus wide Network and UGC INFONET. One of the major objective of this group is to coordinate with UGC-NETWORK, the wide area network connecting all academic institutions under University Grants Commission for setting/managing data centre for various databases of INFLIBNET, Indian universities, Information Centres.

UGC Infonet Management : "UGC-INFONET" linking more than 149 universities across the country.

Software Research & Development : To objective of this group is to develop software for academic community of India, Major focus areas are library automation and other supporting tools for library automation. This group is also involved in supporting all other activities of the centre by providing adequate software help time to time. The mission of this group is to provide technological support to all activities of the centre with software developments using latest technologies and available development tools.

3.11.3. Human Resource Development

CALIBER : Convention on Automation of Libraries in Education and Research

INFLIBNET Centre has been organising CALIBER every year in

different parts of the country in collaboration with different universities. CALIBER is acronym for Convention on Automation of Libraries in Education and Research Institutions. This Convention provides a unique forum to the library professionals, information providers and users involved in automation and networking of libraries to come together and interact on the subjects of mutual interest.

PLANNER: Promotion of Library Automation and Networking in North Eastern Region

PLANNER stands for "Promotion of Library Automation and Networking in North Eastern Region". INFLIBNET has been organizing this event in collaboration with Universities and other Academic institutions located in North East of India. This convention provides a unique forum to the library professionals, information providers and users involved in automation and networking of libraries to come together and interact on the subjects of mutual interest in the region.

3.11.4. New Initiatives

Open Source Software : Open source software are computer programs in which the source code is made available to the general public for use and /or modification from its original design free of charge, i.e. open. Open source programs are typically created as a collaborative effort in which programmers improve upon the code and share the changes within the community. There are a number of open source software in the field of library and information science that are available free of cost.

Institutional Repositories : Institutional Repositories (IRs) have emerged as one of the routes of open access scholarly publishing owing to the phenomenon called serials crisis which refers to the exponential and continuing increase in subscription cost of scholarly journals.IR is a digital repository of the research output of an institution. It is a service that an institution offers to its students, faculty and researchers for the management and dissemination of digital materials created by them. An institutional repository could include following research materials:

- Published material (e.g. journal articles, book chapters and conference papers);
- Unpublished / grey research material (e.g. pre-prints, working papers, theses and dissertations, technical reports, project reports and learning material); and
- Supporting research material (e.g. data sets, models, and simulations).

Access Management R & D : Access management variably called, access control, terms and conditions, licensing conditions. Digital Rights Management (DRM) refers to control of access to digital collections. Digital Rights Management (DRM) is a system of solutions created or designed as a means to prevent unauthorized access, duplication and illegal distribution of copyrighted digital media. Most publishers of online digital contents supports IP filtering and password authentication to their electronic resources. However, there are several other technologies and protocols that are in vogue for authenticating users to access and operate upon digital materials irrespective of their log-in location. Such technologies include Web proxies, Shibboleth, Referring URL, Kerberos, etc. The Centre would work on all access management technologies, especially using open source software, with an aim to help universities to adopt authentication technologies to facilitate access to e-resources to the off-campus community.

Open Access R & D

Electronic Submission of Theses and Dissertations (ETD): Theses and dissertations are known to be the rich and unique source of information. The Centre has proposed to the UGC to develop a "Regulatory Framework" with an aim to evolve a mechanism to improve the quality, accessibility and availability of Indian theses in full-text and to implement uniform standards for creating metadata of doctoral theses and a system for collecting and collating this standardized data.

The pilot project, initially proposed for 50 universities, would be extended to all universities and institutions of higher learning across the country with INFLIBNET acting as executing agency and as a harvesting service with an aim to provide a unified index to all submissions made in distributed repositories across universities. The project will ultimately be a part of the Networked Digital Library of Theses and Dissertations (NDLTD), an international initiative from the Virginiatech University.

Web Services R & D : Organization of vast information present on the Centre's website and making the website a resource gateway and a knowledge hub, to the user community is one of the main objectives of the INFLIBNET Centre. The web development group setup in promoting the access to the information in the field of research and academic pursuit by using latest web technologies is working towards in implementing this objective. The major areas of work undertaken by this group are to select, organise and present the quality resources of the Centre in a meaningful way that will be useful for the user community.

3.11.5. E-Resource Management

UGC-INFONET Digital Library Consortium

The UGC-Infonet Digital Library Consortium was formally launched in December, 2003 by Honourable Dr. A P J Abdul Kalam, the President of India soon after providing the Internet connectivity to the universities in the year 2003 under the UGC-Infonet programme. The Consortium proved to be a recipe to university libraries which have been discontinuing subscription of scholarly journals because of "Serials Crisis". The term "serials crisis" refers to exponential and continuing increase in subscription cost of scholarly journals. The crisis is a result of rise in cost of journals much faster than the rate of inflation, increase in number of journals and the paucity of funds available to the libraries

The Consortium provides current as well as archival access to more than 5000 core and peer-reviewed journals and nine bibliographic databases from 23 publishers and aggregators in different disciplines. The programme has been implemented in phased manner. In the first phase that began in 2004, access to e-resources was provided to 50 universities who had Internet connectivity under the UGC-Infonet Connectivity programme of the UGC. In the second phase, 50 more universities were added to the programme in the year 2005. It has now extended to 155 out of 171 that come under the purview of UGC, have been provided differential access to subscribed e-resources. These e-resources covers almost all subject disciplines including arts, humanities, social sciences, physical sciences, chemical Sciences, life sciences, computer sciences, mathematics and statistics, etc in three different phases. The programme is wholly funded by the UGC and executed by the INFLIBNET Centre, Ahmedabad.

The benefit of subscription to e-resources would also be extended to the colleges, to begin with the College for Potential with Excellence (CPE). The Consortium also has to launched its "Associate Membership Programme" wherein private universities and other research organizations would be welcomed to join the Consortium for selected e-resources.

3.11.6. Services

Document Delivery through JCCC : INLIBNET has initiated interlibrary loans and document delivery services from the comprehensive collection of subscribed journals under JCCC@UGC-INFONET. ILL is also known as Inter-Library Lending. INFLIBNET has designated 22 libraries to fulfill ILL request from the users, affiliated to 149 universities covered under UGC. The ILL libraries together subscribe for 2000 plus journals that is not available through consortia. Universities can request for articles from the journal holdings of those libraries wherever they find useful articles in JCCC search, that are not available in that library.

SOUL Support : The SOUL Software developed by the Centre is one of the most popular Library Management Software having maximum number of installations in the libraries of academic and research institutions across the country. The advanced feature of software attracts for increasing demand of the software. SOUL has installed more than 1688 libraries in country.

Print Archival : Besides receiving access to e-resources on complementary basis under the UGC-Infonet Digital Library Consortium, the Centre maintains a separate Archival Library consisting of print journals received as a part of the agreement with the participating publishers of the UGC Infonet Digital Library Consortium. Under the agreement, the publishers are requested to submit a copy of all the issues of the journals. This archival library is open to all users interested in using these print resources for their study / research.

Publications

The INFLIBNET Centre publishes following publications:

- Annual Report
- INFLIBNET Newsletter
- INFLIBNET Directory
- Guidelines for Data Capturing: a manual
- SOUL Guidelines for Data Capturing: a user manual
- MARC21 Code List for Field Identification
- Field List for Name and Subject Authority Database
- Fields for Indian Manuscript Database Creation
- Bibliographic Standards
- Data Input Sheet for Retro Conversion
- Information Brochures on INFLIBNET Centre, UGC-Infonet, UGC-Infonet Digital Library Consortium

National Library and Information Services Infrastructure for Scholarly Content (N-LIST)

The Project entitled "National Library and Information Services

Infrastructure for Scholarly Content (N-LIST)", being jointly executed by the UGC-INFONET Digital Library Consortium, INFLIBNET Centre and the INDEST-AICTE Consortium, IIT Delhi provides for

- Cross-subscription to e-resources subscribed by the two Consortia, i.e. subscription to INDEST-AICTE resources for universities and UGCINFONET resources for technical institutions; and
- Access to selected e-resources to colleges. The N-LIST project provides access to e-resources to students, researchers and faculty from colleges and other beneficiary institutions through server(s) installed at the INFLIBNET Centre.

Current Status : As on Aug 27 2012, a total number of 2755 colleges have registered themselves with the N-LIST programme including 2520 Govt. / Govt.-aided colleges covered under the section 12 B/2F of UGC Act as well as Non-Aided colleges . Log-in ID and password for accessing e-resources has been sent to the authorized users from these 2520 colleges. All e-resources subscribed for colleges under the N-LIST Project are now accessible to these 2520 colleges through the N-LIST website (http://nlist.inflibnet.ac.in)

Shodhganga : The Shodhganga@INFLIBNET Centre provides a platform for research students to deposit their Ph.D. theses and make it available to the entire scholarly community in open access. The repository has the ability to capture, index, store, disseminate and preserve ETDs submitted by the researchers. Theses and dissertations are known to be the rich and unique source of information. As per the UGC Regulation on M.Phil/Ph.D, the responsibility of hosting, maintaining and making the digital repository of Indian Electronic Theses and Dissertation accessible to all institutions and universities is assigned to the INFLIBNET Centre.

INFOPORTAL : INFLIBNET Subject Gateway for Indian Electronic-Resources

The INFLIBNET Centre promotes open access to Indian scholarly content through the InfoPort: A Subject Gateway for Indian

Electronic-Resources. While Centre uses and promotes Intute, a well-known subject gateway developed by MIMAS, UK, the InfoPort is designed and developed to serve as a comprehensive gateway to all Indian scholarly content. The gateway open-ups the Indian scholarly content scattered over the Internet through an integrated interface that support search, browse and multiple listing. The InfoPort selectively catalogues online resources of Indian origin on diversified subjects available in open access through an elaborate process of testing and evaluation. The Centre proposes to collaborate with librarians and scholars in college and universities in the process of identification and selection of resources.

3.12. CENTRAL UNIVERSITIES IN INDIA

The Central Legislature in 1857 passed acts for the establishment of universities at Calcutta, Bombay and Madras. The universities which were established later in British India viz. Panjab (1882), Allahabad (1887), Banaras (1916), Patna (1917) and Aligarh (1920) could also be regarded as Central, as the power to legislate for these universities was exclusively vested in the Center at that time, and their incorporation was by Acts of the Central Legislature. In 1922, Delhi University was established in the Capital, under the direct control of the Centre. With the enactment of the Government of India Act of 1935, these three universities (Banaras Hindu University, Aligarh Muslim University and Delhi University) were included in the Union List I, and thus they remained as Central Universities. With the promulgation of the Constitution in 1950, they were listed in entry 63 of Union List (UGC, 1984).

In 1951, Parliament passed an Act, which declared 'Visva Bharati' as an Institution of National Importance, and function as a unitary, teaching and residential university. Subsequently, three more central universities were established by Acts of Parliament viz. Jawaharlal Nehru University (1969), North Eastern Hill University (1973) and the University of Hyderabad (1974). The Jawaharlal Nehru University was established to endeavour to promote the principles for which Nehru stood in his lifetime. North Eastern Hill University was set up to meet the educational needs of the region and the University of Hyderabad was set up as result of the Six-Point Formula agreed to for the State of Andhra Pradesh (UGC, 1984).

3.12.1. Banaras Hindu University Inquiry Committee (1969)

Banaras Hindu University Inquiry Committee, in its Report, in 1969, enunciated the objectives and the role of Central Universities as follows:

"Central Universities should not be regarded as central merely because the Central Government finances them. They should have distinctive character of their own. The central universities should seek to supplement and not always duplicate the facilities and programmes of the State Universities".

The objectives of Central Universities are:

- To function effectively and vigorously on an all India basis.
- To build up a corporate intellectual life in the country.
- To strengthen national integration.
- To provide courses which need facilities in terms of staff and equipment ordinarily beyond the reach of State Universities or for which the demand would be too small.
- To contribute towards removal of imbalance from the academic life of our country.
- To take suitable action to help deserving students from educationally backward areas.

3.12.2. UGC Committee to Enquire into the Working of Central Universities (1984)

The University Grants Commission appointed a Committee in January1982 to enquire into the Working of the Central Universities and submitted its report in1984. The Committee agreed with the objectives made by BHU Enquiry Committee (1969) regarding the role and responsibilities of central universities. It is of the view that "Central universities should have an all-India character to be reflected in admissions, appointments and the nature of their courses and programmes, and they should cultivate excellence in all spheres of their activity, particularly in the view of the large financial inputs available to them. Central universities having been established by Acts of Parliament have to be provided funds exclusively by the Central Government through the UGC. Their funding on the whole is more satisfactory than that of the State Universities; hence their over all academic performance has to be better".

The Committee recommends that the objectives for the Central Universities may be framed along the following lines:

1. The Central Universities as institutions of national importance will endeavour to serve the purposes of human resource development and national advancement by providing a wide variety of educational programmes to suit the needs and aptitudes of the scholars with due regard to the manpower needs of the country.

2. The universities will endeavour to raise the quality of scholarship by all possible means and in particular by selection of students and scholars on merit on a national basis, by designing such educational programmes which would cultivate knowledge, reflection, creativity, scientific temper and good judgment, by adopting modern methodologies of instruction and evaluation. They will strive to cultivate humane values as also the spirit of national integration and social justice.

3. The universities will endeavour to develop deeper understanding of natural and social environment among students and motivate them to serve the community by making projects, studies and activities related to local and regional development as integral part of the relevant courses.

4. The universities will pursue excellence in the sphere of research and encourage research on problems connected with social,

economic and cultural development. For implementing relevant courses and research programmes, the universities will endeavour to establish suitable linkages with other institutions and agencies in the region.

3.13 PROFILES OF CENTRAL UNIVERSITIES

At present there are 16 central universities established in different parts of the country. They are:

1. Banaras Hindu University (BHU) (1916)
2. Aligarh Muslim University (AMU) (1920)
3. University Of Delhi (UOD) (1922)
4. Visva-Bharati (VB) (1951)
5. Jawaharlal Nehru University (1969)
6. North-Eastern Hill University (NEHU) (1973)
7. University Of Hyderabad (UOH) (1974)
8. Indira Gandhi National Open University (IGNOU) (1985)
9. Pondicherry University (PU) (1985)
10. Jamia Millia Islamia (JMI) (1988)
11. Assam University (AU) (1994)
12. Babasaheb Bhimrao Ambedkar University (BBAU) (1994)
13. Nagaland University (NU) (1994)
14. Tezpur University (TU) (1994)
15. Mahatma Gandhi Antarrashtriya Hindi Vishwavidyala (MGAHV) (1997)
16. Maulana Azad National Urdu University (MANUU) (1998)

The year of establishment of each university and its jurisdiction are presented in Table 3.2. Their locations in different parts of the country are shown in Map 3.1. Some of these were started afresh as

Central Universities while others were elevated later on and granted the status of Central Universities. There were three central universities established before Independence. The first and the oldest central university established in India was BHU in 1916 followed by AMU in 1920 and UOD in 1922. After Independence, 13 central universities were established during the last 50 years at an average rate of one university per four years. Although only one university was established during 1950s and 1960s, subsequently the trend changed to two per decade in 1970s, three in 1980s and substantial rise in 1990s by six i.e., at an average rate of one university per two years. The main sources of data presented in the profiles of each central university are universities Handbook 2000, brouchers and annual reports of concerned universities. A brief profile of each central university is given below:

Table 3.2: Establishment of Central universities in India and their Jurisdiction

S. No	Name of University	Year of establishment	Location	State/ Union Territory	Jurisdiction
1	BHU	1916	Varanasi	Utter Pradesh	Nation wide
2	AMU	1920	Aligarh	Utter Pradesh	Nation wide
3	UOD	1922	Delhi	Delhi	Nation wide
4	VB	1951	Santiniketan	West Bengal	Nation wide
5	JNU	1969	New Delhi	Delhi	Nation wide
6	NEHU	1971	Shillong	Meghalaya	Meghalaya, Nagaland & Mizoram
7	UOH	1974	Hyderabad	Andhra Pradesh	Nation wide
8	IGNOU	1985	New Delhi	Delhi	Nation wide
9	PU	1985	Pondicherry	Pondicherry	Pondicherry, Andaman, Nicobar & Lakshadweep Islands

10	JMI	1988	New Delhi	Delhi	Nation wide
11	AU	1994	Silchar	Assam	Five districts of South Assam
12	BBAU	1994	Lucknow	Uttar Pradesh	Nation wide
13	NU	1994	Lumami	Nagaland	Nagaland
14	TU	1994	Tezpur	Assam	Assam
15	MGAHV	1997	Wardha	Maharastra	Nation wide
16	MANUU	1998	Hyderabad	Andhra pradesh	Nation wide

The first central university established after Independence was VB in 1951 and the recent one was MANUU in 1998. They impart education on a wide range of general, special, technical and professional disciplines catering the educational needs of students across the Nation. The courses range from Diploma, Degree to Doctorate level. Though they differ substantially in their age, size and location etc., they all serve students, faculty and staff members.

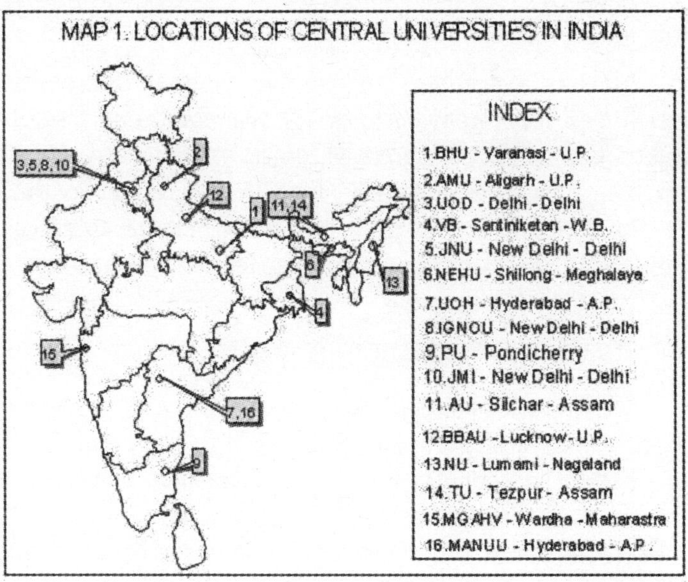

Map 3.1: India Map Showing Locations of 16 Central Universities

3.13.1. Banaras Hindu University (BHU) (1916)

The proposal to establish Hindu University at Banaras was first made at a meeting held in 1904 under the presidentship of H. H. Maharaj Prabhu Narayan Singh of Banaras.

The Banaras Hindu University Society was registered in 1911, and the Central Hindu College was handed over to the Society. The Hindu University Act (Act XVI of 1915) got the assent of the Governor General of India who laid the foundation stone of the university on February 4, 1916. The university began functioning from October 1, 1917. The university may also fund special centers and laboratories for research in humanities, science and technology, education, medicine and other subjects and spheres of learning and knowledge. The university has three institutes, 14 faculties, four affiliated colleges under its jurisdiction.

3.13.2. Aligarh Muslim University (AMU) (1920)

The Aligarh Muslim University is a residential academic institution, which was established in 1920.

AMU is a premier well-known Central University of International repute having a variety of modern and traditional faculties. It draws students from all corners of the country as well as from foreign countries, especially Africa, West Asia and South-East Asia. The University is open to all irrespective of caste, creed, colour or sex. The University has 11 faculties, 80 teaching departments and nine institutions (AMU, 2000).

3.13.3. University of Delhi (UOD) (1922)

The University of Delhi was incorporated as a unitary, teaching and residential university by an Act of the Central Legislature in 1922. The original conception of a unitary and teaching university had, however, to be given up gradually in favor of a federal university. Subject to the control and co-coordinating influence of the university, the colleges remained as autonomous teaching units, working in co-operation with each other and with the university. This envisaged the establishment of a federal university with its constituent colleges situated on the campus. Out of 66 colleges, 12 are located on the university campus. Ten colleges conduct classes in evening for U G students. The Delhi University Amendment Act of 1952 has made the university a teaching and affiliating university.

The University of Delhi is one of the best universities of the country. It has two campuses (North and South) with 14 faculties, 20 specialised centers, 86 post-graduate departments and 78 colleges. The University was authorised to affiliate a college in Bhutan.

3.13.4. Visva-Bharati (VB) (1951)

Visva-Bharati grew out of Santiniketan, founded in 1863 by Maharshi Debendaranath Tagore. In 1901, an Asram Vidyalaya was started at Santiniketan by Rabindranath Tagore. Since 1921 Santiniketan has been the seat of Visva-Bharati, which became a University by Act XXIX (1951) of the Parliament. The Act was amended successively in 1961, 1971 and 1984. The jurisdiction of the University embraces an area known as Santiniketan and Sriniketan (11.5sq miles) in the district of Birbhum in West Bengal. There are seven Constituent Colleges under Visva-Bharati.

3.13.5. Jawaharlal Nehru University (JNU) (1969)

The Jawaharlal Nehru University was established in 1969 in the memory of Jawaharlal Nehru. The first Schedule to the Act sets the objects of the University. "The University shall endeavour to promote the study of the principles for which Jawaharlal Nehru worked during his life-time; national integration, social justice, secularism, democratic way of life, international understanding and scientific approach to the problems of society. The objects of the University are:

- foster the composite culture of India and establish such departments or institutions as may be required for the study and development of the languages, arts and culture of India,
- take special measures to facilitate students and teachers from

all over India to join the university and participate in its academic programmes,

- promote in the students and teachers an awareness and understanding of the social needs of the country and prepare them for fulfilling such rules,
- make special provision for integrated courses in humanities, science and technology in the educational programmes of the university,
- take appropriate measures for promoting interdisciplinary studies in the university,
- establish such departments or institutions as may be necessary for the study of languages, literature and life of foreign countries with a view to inculcating in the students a world perspective and international understanding, and
- provide facilities for students and teachers from other countries to participate in the academic programmes and life of the university (JNU, 1989).

The jurisdiction of the University extends to all over the country. It has the power to establish, maintain, recognise and incorporate or associate with institutions of higher learning.

3.13.6. North-Eastern Hill University (NEHU) (1973)

The University was founded by the North-Eastern Hill University Act No. 24 of 1973 passed by the President of India on July 19, 1973 and started functioning from August 3, 1973. Section 4 of the Act of this University listed its objectives as follows:

"The objects of the University shall be to disseminate and advance knowledge by providing instructional and research facilities in such branches of learning as it may deem fit; to pay special attention to the improvement of the social and economic conditions and welfare of the people of the hill areas of the North Eastern region and, in particular, their intellectual, academic and cultural advancement".

Its jurisdiction extends to the States of Meghalaya, Nagaland and Union Territory of Mizoram. The university has two campuses - one at Shillong (Meghalaya) and the other at Aizwal (Mizoram).

3.13.7. University of Hyderabad (UOH) (1974)

The University of Hyderabad was established by Act No.39 of 1974 passed by the Parliament on October 2, 1974. The objects of the University as envisaged in the Act are: "to disseminate and advance knowledge by providing instructional and research facilities in such branches of learning as it may deem fit and by the example of its corporate life, and in particular, to make special provisions for integrated courses in humanities and science in the educational programmes of the University and to take appropriate measures for promoting interdisciplinary studies and research in the University".

The University has various Schools in faculties of Mathematics & Computer/Information Sciences, Physics, Chemistry, Life Sciences, Humanities, Social Sciences, Management Studies and Sarojini Naidu School of Performing Arts, Fine Arts & Communication.

3.13.8. Indira Gandhi National Open University (IGNOU) (1985)

Indira Gandhi National Open University was established in 1985 by an Act No. 50, of the Parliament to democratise higher education. The Jurisdiction of university extends to whole of India. The aim was to provide cost-effective, quality education to large sections of our population including those living in remote and far flung areas. The university has been a pioneer in Distance Education.

Today, it serves the educational aspirations of over 4 million students in India and 36 other countries through 21 Schools of Studies and a network of 67 regional centres, around 3,000 learner support centres and 67 overseas centres. The University offers about 490 certificate, diploma, degree and doctoral programmes, with a strength of nearly 420 faculty members and academic staff at the headquarters and regional centres and about 36,000 academic counsellors from conventional institutions of higher learning, professional organisations, and industry among others (IGNOU 2012).

The mandate of the University is to:

- Provide access to higher education to all segments of the society;
- Offer high-quality, innovative and need-based programmes at different levels, to all those who require them;
- Reach out to the disadvantaged by offering programmes in all parts of the country at affordable costs; and
- Promote, coordinate and regulate the standards of education offered through open and distance learning in the country.
- To achieve the twin objectives of widening access for all sections of society and providing continual professional development and training to all sectors of the economy, the University uses a variety of media and latest technology in imparting education. This is reflected in the formulated vision of IGNOU, keeping its objectives in focus, which reads:

IGNOU has four million students with extremely varied profiles, spread throughout the length and breadth of the country. The University serves through a network of 67 Regional (5 of which are Army command centers) and 3000 Study Centers spread all over India. As an open university, IGNOU has come a long way since 1985, having crossed national boundaries providing higher education as well as assisting other developing countries.

3.13.9. Pondicherry University (PU) (1985)

The Pondicherry University was established on 16 October 1985 by an Act of Parliament. It is a teaching cum affiliating central university. The jurisdiction of the University extends over the union territory of Pondicherry, Andaman and Nicobar and Lakshadweep islands. It has 20 affiliated institutions.

3.13.10. Jamia Millia Islamia (JMI) (1988)

Jamia Millia Islamia was founded at Aligarh in 1920. Jamia became one of the few institutions of national importance that were based on the spirit of Mahatama Gandhi's constructive programme in the sphere of education.

UGC gave Jamia 'Deemed University' status in 1962 and Central University status in 1988. In view of the historic origin of Jamia and its distinctive character, the survival and progress of the University is a tribute to the national, secular and liberal genius of the country. Today the Jamia imparts an integrated education right from nursery stage to the postgraduate level.

3.13.11. Assam University (AU) (1994)

The Assam University Act No XIII of 1989 was enforced by the Govt. of India by a Notification on 15 January 1994. The objective of the University is to disseminate and advance knowledge by providing instructional and research facilities and pay special attention to the improvement of social and economic condition and welfare of the people of the state.Assam University is a teaching-cum-affiliating university.

3.13.12. Babasaheb Bhimrao Ambedkar University (BBAU) (1994)

The Babasaheb Bhimrao Ambedkar University, Lucknow was originally set up as a state university in April 1989 to provide for postgraduate teaching and research in the emerging areas as a fitting tribute to Dr. Bhimrao Ambedkar, the Father of Indian Constitution. On the request of the State Government, the Central Government Passed Babasaheb Bhimrao Ambedkar University Act awarding the status of central university by Parliament in August 1994.

The University endeavours to promote advancement of knowledge by providing instructional and research facilities in science and frontier areas of technology and other allied disciplines; to offer appropriate courses for development of socially and economically depressed sections of people including agricultural technology and rural crafts; to promote the study of the principles for which Babasaheb Bhimrao Ambedkar worked during his life time namely national integration, social justice, democratic way of life, study of constitutions of the world and to take appropriate measures for promoting innovations in teaching-learning processes in interdisciplinary studies and research.

3.13.13. Nagaland University (NU) (1994)

Nagaland University (teaching and affiliating) was setup in 1989 through Act of Parliament (No 35 of 1989) with its headquarters at Lumami in the State of Nagaland. The University became functional on 6 September 1994 as per the notification of the Ministry of Human Resource Development, New Delhi. The Colleges located in Nagaland, which were earlier affiliated with North-Eastern Hill University, were transferred to Nagaland University. The Postgraduate / Research Departments (History & Archaeology, Commerce, Education, English, Linguistics and Geology) of NEHU at Kohima are now the institutions of Nagaland University.

The University endeavours to the advancement of knowledge by providing instruction and research facilities; make provisions for integrated courses in social sciences, agricultural and forestry and other allied disciplines. It has a School of Agricultural Sciences & Rural Development at Medziphema and 34 affiliated colleges spread across the state.

3.13.14. Tezpur University (TU) (1994)

Tezpur University was established by an Act of Parliament (Act No.45, 1993) in the year 1994. The jurisdiction of University extends to the whole of the state of Assam.

The objects of this unitary type central university as envisaged in the statutes are that it shall:

- strive to offer employment oriented and interdisciplinary courses, mostly at post graduate level, to meet the local and regional aspirations and the development of the state of Assam;
- offer courses and promote research in areas which are of special and direct relevance to the region and in the emerging areas in science and technology;
- promote national integration and study of the rich cultural

heritage of the region and in particular, the diverse ethnic, linguistic and cultural of the state;

- utilise distance education technique and modern communication technologies to provide access to higher education for large segment of the population, and in particular the disadvantaged group such as those living in remote and rural areas; to up grade the professional knowledge and skill of in-service personnel, in particular school teachers, medical personnel and extension staff, and to provide opportunities for life long learning for adults; and
- provide an innovative system of university level education flexible in regard to methods and space of learning and encourage excellence in new fields of knowledge (TU, 2000).

3.13.15. Mahatma Gandhi Antarrashtriya Hindi Vishwavidyala (MGAHV) (1997)

Mahatma Gandhi Antarrashtriya Hindi Vishwavidyala (MGAHV) has been incorporated as residential and teaching university for the promotion and development of Hindi language and literature, through an Act (No.3 of 1997) of Parliament which received assent of the President of India on January 8, 1997. The headquarters of the University are at Wardha with its jurisdiction extending to whole of India.

The objects of the University are:

- to promote and develop Hindi language and literature in general and, for that purpose, to provide for instructional and research facilities in the relevant branches of learning;
- to provide for active pursuit of comparative studies and research in Hindi and other Indian languages;
- to create facilities for development and dissemination of relevant information in the country and abroad;
- to offer programmes of research, education and training in areas like translation, interpretation and linguistics for

improving the functional effectiveness of Hindi;

- to reach out to Hindi scholars and groups interested in Hindi abroad and to associate them in teaching and research and to popularize Hindi through distance education system.

3.13.16. Maulana Azad National Urdu University (MANUU) (1998)

The Maulana Azad National Urdu University was established by an Act of Parliament at Hyderabad in 1998 (Act No.2 of 1997, dated 8.1.1997) (MANUU, 2000). The important and salient features of the Act are to (i) Promote and develop Urdu language, (ii) Provide vocational and technical education through the Urdu medium, (iii) Provide education through conventional teaching and distance education system, and (iv) Provide focus on women's education.

3.14 CENTRAL UNIVERSITY LIBRARIES

Libraries form an important integral part of central university education system in India. Basically, the main function of a university library is to provide suitable information materials useful for study, teaching, research and education purposes in a university. The information pertaining to the establishment of CU Libraries, the availability of separate buildings and their names are presented in Table 3.3. The table shows that out of 13 universities furnished information, eight started libraries in the same year, two within one year and the remaining two universities with in a period of two years. Regarding separate building and name for libraries, out of 13 universities, 12 have separate buildings exclusively for library and five universities have even separate names for their libraries.

These facts clearly indicate that central universities have given due recognition and importance in setting up of their libraries subsequently.

Table 3.3: Central University Libraries in India

S. No	Name of Uni.	Year of establishment Uni.	Library	Timelag	Wether Library has separate Building	Name (If so, pl. specify)
1	BHU	1916	1916	0	Y	Sayajirao Gaekward Library
2	MU	1920	1920	0	Y	Maulana Azad Library
3	UOD	1922	1922	0	Y	N
4	VB	1951	1951	0	Y	N
5	JNU	1969	1969	0	Y	N
6	NEHU	1971	-	-	Y	N
7	UOH	1974	1976	2	Y	Indira Gandhi Memorial Library
8	IGNOU	1985	1986	1	Y	N
9	PU	1985	1986	1	Y	Anand Rangapillai Library
10	MI	1988	1988	0	Y	Dr. Zakir Hussain Library
11	AU	1994	1994	0	Y	N
12	BBAU	1994	1998	2	N	N
13	NU	1994	-	-	Y	N
14	TU	1994	-	-	Y	N
15	GAH	1997	-	-	-	N
16	MANUU	1998	1998	0	N	N

3.15 SUMMARY

India has a rich heritage of higher learning centers from ancient times. The most renowned centers viz. *Taxila, Nalanda and Vikramshila* offered courses in advanced studies and attracted students from other countries. Universities in India were existed more than two thousand years ago. Modern universities in India owe their origin to the Wood's Dispatch of 1854. Britishers setup the first three universities in 1857 in Calcutta, Bombay and Madras on the model of

London University.

After Independence, Government of India took keen interest and set up various Commissions and Committees to reorganize and improve the standard of higher education in the country.

UGC established in 1956 has been playing a key role for the promotion and coordination of university education and for the determination and maintenance of standards of teaching, examination and research in universities in the country. Universities in India are established by Acts of either Parliament or State Legislature.

After independence, UGC's University Education Commissions Committees made strong recommendations which have significantly contributed for the improvement of library conditions in universities. However, university libraries in India were not given due importance commensurate to their expected role in university education.

Consequently, university libraries in India are facing many problems and challenges due to various factors. In order to face these problems and challenges, it has become inevitable for university libraries to computerise their operations and to participate in networking and resource sharing with other libraries. UGC launched INFLIBNET in 1991 to network library and information centers in universities, institutions of national importance and R&D institutions in the country for effective sharing of information resources, facilities and services to the optimum utilization. In order to achieve these objectives, INFLIBNET has undertaken a number of activities and projects for development of library automation and networking of university libraries in the country.

As university libraries come under great pressure to provide improved services with less resource, an alternative strategy is to modernise their library operations and services through the use of IT. There is a strong need to use IT applications in all library operations in order to facilitate networking and resource sharing and to provide efficient information services to users. Therefore, university libraries must ensure that they are sensitive to the changes taking place not only in IT but also in society and prepare themselves to serve the academic community with a dynamic role, which is required in the future challenging educational environment.

3.16 REFERENCES

Aligarh Muslim University (2000). *Guide to admissions 2000-2001.* Aligarh: AMU.

Amjad Ali. (1995). Computerising university libraries. *University News,* May 1, 9-11.

Anand, A.K. (1987). Academic libraries in India. *COMLA Newsletter,* (56) June 87, 12,16.0.

Calcutta University Commission *1917-19* (1919). *Report*. IV. Education Commission (1964-66) (1971). *Report.* New Delhi: NCERT.

Haravu, L.J. (1989). Managing university library resources and services: The role of automation. In *National Policy on University Libraries in India: Problems and Perspectives* (Pp. 237-250). New Delhi: Concept Publishing.

Indian National Commission for Cooperation with UNESCO. (1998). Higher education in India: Vision and Action (country paper). *UNESCO world conference on Higher education in the Twenty-first century,* 5-6, October (pp. 7). Paris. New Delhi Office.

Indian Universities Commission(1903). *Report.* Simla, Central Printing office.

Indira Gandhi National Open University (2012). *Profile 2012.* New Delhi:IGNOU. http://www.ignou.ac.in/ignou/aboutignou/profile/2 (accessed on 4.9.2012).

INFLIBNET Newsletter 6(1), 12-13. URL http://www.inflibnet.ac.in (accessed on 4.9.2012).

INFLIBNET Centre (2012). URL http://www.inflibnet.ac.in (accessed on 4.9.2012).

INFLIBNET Centre. (1999). *Progress report of the Review Committee meeting,* 17-18, February, Nagpur (pp.10). Ahmedabad: INFLIBNET Centre. (mimeographed).

INFLIBNET Centre. (2000). *INFLIBNET:* A profile. In *Souvenir of CALIBER-2000:* Seventh National Convention on Information Services in a Networked Environment in India, 16-18 February. (pp. 20-38).Chennai: University of Madras.

INFLIBNET Centre. (2000). *Progress Report of the Review Committee* meeting, 16-18, February, Chennai. Ahmedabad: INFLIBNET Centre, 15p (mimeographed).

INFLIBNET Centre. (2000). *Directory of University Libraries funded under INFLIBNET programme*. Ahmedabad: INFLIBNET Centre, 20p (mimeographed). Jawaharlal Nehru University. (1989). *20th Anniversary Booklet* (9-10). New Delhi: JNU.

Laxman Rao, N. (1993). *Planning and implementation of Automated circulation system for Osmania University library system*. Ph.D. thesis in library science submitted to Osmania University, Hyderabad. 327p.

Maulana Azad National Urdu University. (2000). *MANUU: A profile*. Hyderabad: MANUU.

Mehta, V.R. (1998). From the Desk of the Vice-Chancellor. In Aparna Basu (Ed.). *University of Delhi 1922-1997: Platinum Jubilee* (pp. 1). Delhi: University of Delhi.

Mittal, R.L. (1989). National policy for University libraries in India. In N.B. Inamdar & L.S. Ramaiah (Eds.) (pp. 30-45). *National policy for university libraries in India: problems and prospects*. New Delhi: Concept.

National policy on university libraries. (1986). *Report of AIU Committee* (mimeographed).

Ranganathan, S. R. (1963). University libraries: Then and now. *Library Herald* 6, 62.

Srivastava, Shyam Nath & Varma, Subhash Chandra. (1980). *University libraries in India: Their organisation and administration* (pp.1-30). New Delhi: Sterling. Tejpur University. *Prospectus 2000-2001* (pp.1).

Tejpur: TU.University Education Commission *(1948-49)*. (1950). *Report*. New Delhi: Ministry of Education.

University Grants Commission (India). (1965). *University and College libraries containing the Report of the Library Committee and proceedings of the seminar*. New Delhi: UGC.

University Grants Commission (1984). *Report of the Committee to enquire into the working of the Central Universities*(pp.185). New Delhi: UGC.

University Grants Commission (1988). *Development of an Information and Library Network Report of the Inter Agency Working Group*. New Delhi: UGC.

University Grants Commission. (2012). *Annual Report 2011-2012*. New Delhi: UGC.

University Grants Commission. (2000). *Annual Report 1999-2000*. New Delhi: UGC.

University of Hyderabad. (2001). *Prospectus 2001-2002* (pp.1-2, 52-53). Hyderabad: UOH.

Wilson, Louis Round & Tauber, Maurice F. (1956). *The University library* .(pp.19). New York: Columbia Univ. Press.

4
Use of Information Technology in Central University Libraries in India

4.1 INTRODUCTION

The World is amidst information explosion, IT revolution and Network evolution leading to an emergence of global information society. In this society, the production of goods as well as services is becoming more and more information-based. The generation, demand, consumption and importance of information has increased tremendously in recent years due to the use of modern technologies. Information is growing exponentially not only in paper form but also in various electronic forms such as magnetic tapes, floppy disks, optical disks, networks etc. Pritchett (1994) reported that there has been more information produced in the last 30 years than during the previous 5,000 years and that the information supply available to us doubles every 5 years.

The management of massive volume of information and its proliferation into many forms has created the problems of storage, processing, retrieval and dissemination in libraries. The evolution of modern technologies has greatly improved the capabilities of managing this explosive growth of information effectively. Libraries have tried to overcome the problems of information management by adopting modern computer and communication technology.

The use of IT has become imperative for the efficient management of modern libraries. The rapid revolutionary developments in ICT have great potential in increasing the efficiency of house-keeping operations and effectiveness of information services in libraries. If the libraries have to manage their operations efficiently and to develop effective information services, they have to make most effective use of new technologies of many kinds. Use of IT solutions in libraries is no longer a matter of choice but a matter of survival in global information society.

IT applications in library and information system have made remarkable progress in developed countries of the world, due to the use of modern technologies. Rapid technological advancements, have enabled these libraries to computerise their operations and information services successfully. Besides performing library operations efficiently and improving services effectively, libraries are able to evolve effective computer networks towards sharing and optimum utilisation of their resources, facilities and services. The library networks in USA are in the most advanced level of development. The three foremost bibliographic utilities and networks in USA are Online Computer Library Center (OCLC), Research Libraries and Information Network (RLIN), Washington Library Network (WLN) and JANET in UK.

In the similar lines, UGC launched Information and Library Network (INFLIBNET) in India in 1991 to network library and information centers in universities, institutions of national importance and R&D institutions in the country for effective sharing and utilisation of information resources, facilities and services. (INFLIBNET Center, 2001).

Libraries have been using IT in general and computer technology in particular, to automate a wide range of administrative and technical processes, develop databases, build resource sharing networks and provide better information services to their users. The use of IT for better management of information within libraries has grown significantly in recent years. This wide spread use of IT in libraries has created a profound impact on all aspects of the present library environment. There have been no systematic studies conducted to investigate the use of IT in university libraries in India. With the result, no clear insights are available as to how this new technology has been perceived, introduced and used in the library environment. Therefore, this study has been proposed as a pioneering attempt in this direction. There are 16 Central Universities established by Acts of Parliament. They receive funds from Government of India through UGC. The present research aims to study the use of IT in Central University Libraries in India.

4.1.1. Objectives

This study has been designed with a view to achieve the following objectives:

- To find out the status of Information Technology (IT) used in Central University (CU) Libraries in India.
- To examine planning approaches adopted for IT implementation in CU Libraries
- To find out the constraints faced in IT implementation in CU Libraries
- To find out the extent of use of IT applications to various library operations and services in CU Libraries
- To explore the perceived positive and negative effects of using IT in CU Libraries.

- To find out the impact of using IT on library operations and services as perceived by staff and users.

4.1.2. Scope

There are 16 central universities established by Acts of Parliament in India. In view of the sound resources of central universities, it was presumed that CU Libraries must be actively involved in using IT in their operations and services. Hence this study has been proposed to cover all the CU Libraries in India. The reasons for choosing CU Libraries are:

- They represent a homogeneous group of university libraries.
- These universities ensure a national coverage, as they are located in different parts of the country.
- They are better off in terms of all resources such as financial, human, infrastructure facilities etc.

The list of Central Universities established in India are

1. Aligarh Muslim University (AMU), Aligarh
2. Assam University (AU), Silchar
3. Babasaheb Bhimrao Ambedkar University (BBAU), Lucknow
4. Banaras Hindu University (BHU), Varanasi
5. University of Delhi (UOD), Delhi
6. University of Hyderabad (UOH), Hyderabad
7. Indira Gandhi National Open University (IGNOU), New Delhi
8. Jamia Millia Islamia (JMI), New Delhi
9. Jawaharlal Nehru University (JNU), New Delhi
10. Mahatma Gandhi Antarrastreeya Hindi Viswavidyalaya (MGAHV)
11. Maulana Azad National Urdu University (MANUU), Hyderabad
12. Nagaland University (NU), Kohima

13. North-Eastern Hill University (NEHU), Shillong
14. Pondicherry University (PU), Pondicherry
15. Tezpur University (TU), Tezpur
16. Visva Bharati (VB), Shanti Niketan,West Bengal

4.1.3. Methodology

Survey research method has been adopted for the present study covering all the 16 CU Libraries in India.

i. Data Collection

The data required for this study has been collected from both primary and secondary sources. Primary data was collected through three different questionnaires supplemented by personal interview, discussions and interactions with library staff and users as well as personal observation of automated operations in different CU Libraries. Secondary sources of data used include journal articles, books, committee's reports, annual reports, official records and other published documents.

ii. Contents of the Questionnaires

This study has been carried out in phases through three different questionnaires designed separately for university librarians, library staff and users respectively. Prior to gathering the primary data for the research study, questionnaires were pilot tested. The purpose of pilot study was to test the validity of the questionnaire both as a data collection instrument and a statistical measurement device. The pilot testing helped to refine the questionnaire.

The first questionnaire was designed to gather data about the status of use of IT in CU Libraries in India. It is divided into five sections. Each section contains questions and sub-questions covering major aspects related to IT applications in libraries. The first section intends to gather data about library background, collection, users, staff, budget and source of funds. The second section covers infrastructure, hardware, software, library automation objectives, constraints and practices in IT implementation process. Third section gathers data on computerised library operations, databases created, portion of catalogue converted and methods followed for retrospective conversion of catalogue. Fourth section is on automated information services, types of databases used for information retrieval services and number of computers provided to users. Fifth section covers database formats, database sources used for catalogue conversion, access to networks, and future plans of computerisation. Finally, additional comments were invited on the IT implementation process in their libraries.

iii. Distribution of Questionnaires'

University Libraries : The questionnaires were mailed by registered post to all the 14 CU Librarians in September 1998 except MGAHV and MANUU, which were established recently in 1997 and 1998 respectively. AIU's *Directory of University Institutions in India (1998)* was used as a basis for addresses. Subsequently, another copy of the questionnaire was distributed personally to some CU Librarians during CALIBER Convention at Nagpur in February 1999. The questionnaire was followed later by a few follow-up letters and telephone calls. The Researcher has visited the libraries of AMU, UOD, UOH, IGNOU, JMI and JNU personally and interacted with the library staff members and supplemented the information. All the 14 duly filled-in questionnaires were received with a response rate of 100%. This questionnaire covers first four objectives of the study.

University Libraries' Staff : After receiving responses to the first questionnaire from the CU Librarians, the second questionnaire was designed to gather data about library staff perceptions on the impact of using IT on various aspects of the library. The questionnaire was distributed to 100 library staff members who are involved in library automation activities in eight CU Libraries where IT is being actively used. The staff members were served questionnaires based on the information furnished in the responses of the first questionnaire by their respective university librarians. The questionnaire was divided into five sections. The first section aims to gather data on respondents' background, involvement in IT related courses, training, conferences and technologies accessible to respondents, time spent on computers, computer experience etc in their libraries. While second section covers the impact of IT on overall library, third section on library house-keeping operations, fourth section on information services and fifth section on library staff. Finally comments were invited from respondents to give their opinions about their experiences of using IT in their respective library environments. Respondents were asked to answer most of the questions using a five point Likert Scale with five being Strongly Agree (SA) and one being Strongly Disagree (SD).

University of Hyderabad Library Users : The University of Hyderabad Library has the distinction of being the first university library in the country to have fully automated all its house-keeping operations. Therefore, the researcher has proposed to make an in-depth study to assess the impact of using IT on library services from library users. He has chosen UOH library as a case and selected a sample of 413 out of 2207 users using stratified random sampling technique. The third questionnaire was designed with four sections. The first section intends to gather data on users' background and technological facilities accessible to them in the library. While second section covers the impact of using IT on library, third section on library services and fourth section on the assessment of user satisfaction. Finally, users were requested to state the problems and give their comments relating to the use of IT facilities/services in the library. The questionnaire was distributed to 413 library users of different categories including faculty members, Ph.D, and M.Phil scholars and PG students of UOH during February and May 2000. The details of all the three questionnaires distributed and responses received are presented in Table 4.1.

Table 4.1 : Survey Sample Size and Response

S. No.	*Sample Name*	*No. of Questionnaires Distributed*	*Received*	*Percent*
1	University Librarians	14	14	100
2	Library Staff members	100	64	64
3	Library Users	413	315	76

iv. Likert Scale

Likert Scale is applied to a complete set of statements about an operation or a service. To implement this scale, the researcher constructed a series of statements on various operations and services to obtain perceptions of staff and users after using IT. Some of these statements are favorable and some are unfavorable. The scoring of the statements in a five-point scale are Strongly Agree (SA) = 5, Agree (A) = 4, Undecided (U) = 3, Disagree (D) = 2, Strongly Disagree (SD) = 1. In this scoring method, the most positive attitude is represented by the highest score. When the scores for all responses are averaged, the scores that are closest to 5 are the ones that represent the most positive attitude.

There are many close-ended statements presented on the Likert Scale. The respondent's checks off the most appropriate response or marks a particular point on scale of values according to the degree to which the statement is considered positive or negative. The maximum possible score for any statement is 5. The data collected are manipulated by statistical package and calculated Means, Standard Deviation, and other measures.

Likert Scale has been used by a number of studies conducted in library and information science literature to survey and assess the library staff and users' attitudes, perceptions, views opinions and reactions towards technological implementation in different libraries around the world. Some of these include: (i) An attitudinal study of academic library professionals in United States by Olsgaard (1984). (ii) A study on the use of microcomputers in university libraries in

USA by Mustafa (1985). (iii) Users reactions to second Online Public Access Catalogue in University of Central Florida, Orlando by Scharf and Ward (1989). (iv) Attitudes of academic library professionals towards computer-based systems in Taiwan by Su (1993). (v) The people speak the dispersion and impact of technology in American Libraries by Hauptman and Anderson (1994) and (vi) A study of information technology adoption in Hongkong by Ng Tye and Chau (1995).

(v) *Analysis of Data*

For the convenience of data processing and analysis work, the data collected through questionnaire have been coded using a coding structure in which the statements of the questionnaire are referred with coded variables as Q (representing question) followed by main question number and serial number of an aspect/statement/service. For example, the first aspect i.e., efficiency given in Question no. 12 is coded as Q.12.1.

The data collected were tabulated and analysed statistically using appropriate descriptive and inferential techniques included in the Statistical Package for Social Sciences (SPSS). The descriptive statistics including frequency distribution, percentage, mean, standard deviation etc. were used to provide a general picture of the current status of IT used in the CU Libraries India. The tables containing frequencies, percentages and means are provided in Chapter 4 and 5. The inferential statistical techniques viz. cross tabulation and Chi-Square test were used to point out the association between the attributes. To facilitate data analysis, the necessary numerical indices and measurement scales were used.

To test the dependency of the attributes, further statistical analysis of cross tabulations and Chi-Square test was performed on the data. This analysis included the six independent attributes viz., gender, library science qualification, training courses attended, involvement in IT implementation, in-house training given to staff, percentage of time staff spend working at computer per day etc. used in the questionnaire to measure the staff and user perceptions on the impact of using IT on library operations, information services and to explore association between them. Cross tabulations are computed for all possible pairs of attributes. The level of significance chosen was .05. The tables having statistically significant results are provided in Appendix 3.

4.1.4. Significance of the Study

The researcher has taken up the present study, which would be useful in the following aspects:

1. This study would provide library professionals with a broad idea about the status of library computerisation work currently taking place in CU Libraries in India.
2. The knowledge and awareness of the potentiality, benefits and implications of using IT CU Libraries would help in designing appropriate strategic plans for effective implementation of IT and to minimise the problems in future.
3. This study would also provide library managers, professionals, automation planners and policy makers with some clear insights about the benefits of using IT. This would also affect their perceptions of planning library automation and enables them to take appropriate decisions in this regard.
4. Decisions made by these librarians and their automation practices usually have significant impact on other libraries in their respective regions in the country.

4.1.5. Limitations of the Study

The major limitation of the present study is the time dimension of the current status of use of IT in CU Libraries. There are rapid developments in all components of IT at breath-taking speed. Managements have also now realised and seriously concerned about making use of new technologies in their libraries. The data, figures and the developments related to the use of IT in CU Libraries, reported in the study have to be taken only in the current perspective. Therefore, this study covers the status of using IT upto a particular point of time and has no control over new implementations and future developments that take place subsequently in the libraries surveyed.

4.1.6, Presentation of Data

This chapter presents the analysis of data gathered through the first questionnaire designed for the study. There were, at the time of the survey, 16 central universities established in different parts of the country. Out of 16, the questionnaires were sent to 14 Central University (CU) libraries as the two universities viz. Mahatma Gandhi Antarrastriya Hindi Viswavidyala and Moulana Azad National Urdu University were established recently in 1997 and 1998 respectively which are in the process of developing infrastructural facilities, academic programmes and libraries. The data analysis is based on the questionnaire responses of 14 libraries as shown in Table 4.2 representing central university library system in the country. The group of CU Libraries surveyed ranged widely in terms of age, size, stock, budget, number of users etc. The abbreviated form of the names of central universities used in this study represent their respective university libraries.

Table 4.2: Survey Response by Central University Libraries

S. No	Description	No. of Universities
1	Total No of Central Universities	16
2	No of Questionnaires sent	14
3	No of CU Libraries responded	14
4	Percentage of Response	100

4.2. LIBRARY COLLECTION IN CU LIBRARIES

Library collection forms a sound foundation for providing efficient services to the users. The details of collection of CU Libraries are presented in Table 4.3. Delhi University Library System (DULS) is an integrated network of 30 libraries including five divisional libraries, four faculty libraries, four special libraries, 13 departmental libraries and four zonal libraries, which are maintained at the expense of UOD. The Aligarh Muslim University Library System is a centralised one consisting of a main library viz. Moulana Azad Library, four college libraries, 50 department / institutes libraries and 14 libraries of the halls of residence. These libraries are simply extensions of the central library located at different places in the campus for the convenience of teachers and students. They function under the full administrative and technical control of university library.

Table 4.3: Collection of Central University Libraries in India

S. No	Name of University	Books	Back volumes of periodicals	Theses	Audio-Visual Materials	CDROM data bases	Others
1	AMU	9,80,000	20,000	8,448	---	---	---
2	AU	32,357	6	---	---	---	2,000
3	BBAU	1,000	---	---	---	---	---
4	BHU	7,67,383	1,01,756	8,684	---	---	7,201
5	UOD	14,00,000	---	14,500	4,175	30	---
6	UOH	1,82,000	69,000	2,800	---	25	---
7	IGNOU	73,291	5,077	25	---	91	---
8	JNU	3,07,058	1,48,552	---	6,311	---	---
9	JMI	2,50,000	6,000	600	300	---	---
10	NU	25,204	10,000	200	---	---	---
11	NEHU	1,61,737	36,764	3,500	200	30	
12	PU	1,00,000	5,000	1,329	---	8	1,976
13	TU	8,800	250	---	60	21	---
14	VB	3,59,601	60,771	550	---	---	23,225
Total		46,48,431	4,63,176	40,636	11,046	205	34,402

As can be seen from the Table 4.3 that DULS has the largest collection of 14 lakh books including back volumes of periodicals followed by AMU with 9,80,000 books and BHU with 7,67,383 books. On the other hand, BBAU has the smallest number of 1000 books. BHU, UOD, UOH, and NEHU have good collections of more than 3,000 theses in each library, while JNU has a good collection of AV materials. UOH, IGNOU, NEHU and TU have also acquired CDROM databases. Regarding back volumes of periodicals, JNU Library has the largest number of 1,48,552 volumes followed by BHU with 1,01,756 and UOH with 69,00 volumes.

4.3. CURRENT PERIODICALS IN CU LIBRARIES

Current periodicals are the most important channels for communication of latest research results and information to the users. In current periodicals presented in table 4.4, DULS subscribes to the largest number of 3000 current periodicals followed by BHU with 1,301 and JNU with 1000 periodicals. It is worth noting that TU has reported having 85 periodicals in floppy disc and 21 in CDROM discs followed by PU with eight and one respectively.

Table 4.4: Current Periodicals in CU Libraries

S. No	Name of University	Indian	Foreign	Gift/ Exchange	Total
1	AMU	632	455	---	1,087
2	AU	84	19	2	105
3	BBAU	---	---	---	---
4	BHU	---	---	595	1,301
5	UOD	---	---	---	3,000
6	UOH	70	650	20	740
7	IGNOU	215	296	13	524
8	JNU	795	---	205	1,000
9	JMI	---	---	---	500
10	NU	27	60	40	127
11	NEHU	366	316	126	808
12	PU	---	---	20	384
13	TU	56	6	---	62
14	VB	256	130	145	531
	Total	2,501	1,932	1,166	10,169

4.4. LIBRARY USERS IN CU LIBRARIES

Users are most important people to be served by any library. Library users consist of faculty members, students and administrative staff of a university. The details of each category of users of CU Libraries are presented in Table4.5. Out of 14 CU Libraries surveyed, one library did not indicate user figures. The remaining 13 universities have a total of 76,157 users representing 11, 281 (14.8%) faculty, 9,980 (13.1%) research scholars, 32,466 (42.6%) PG students, 11,759 (15.5%) administrative staff and 10,671 (14%) others are including students of undergraduate, distance education courses etc.

Table 4.5: Library Users in CU Libraries

S. No	Name of University	Faculty Members	Research Scholars	PG. Students	Administrative staff	Others	Total	Average visitors*
1	AMU	450	300	950	805	110	2,615	---
2	AU	130	60	1,700	250	---	2,140	300
3	BBAU	14	3	150	20	---	187	20
4	BHU	1,222	1,180	10,409	5,575	309	18,695	---
5	UOD	7,000	4,300	12,000	---	---	23,300	2,500
6	UOH	260	860	1,158	1,000	3,200	6,478	500
7	IGNOU	373	---	---	810	---	1,183	156
8	JNU	462	1,696	1,525	612	46	4,341	600
9	JMI	400	911	1,750	1,112	4,015	8,188	---
10	NU	37	10	144	50	200	441	150
11	NEHU	373	400	1,100	350	200	2,423	428
12	PU	---	---	---	---	---	---	500
13	TU	135	10	320	125	15	605	40
14	VB	425	250	1,260	1,050	2,576	5,561	225
Total		11,281	9,980	32,466	11,759	10,671	76,157	5,425
Percentage		14.8	13.1	42.6	15.5	14	100	---

*Average no. of users visiting library per day

The DULS has the largest number of 23,300 users followed by BHU with 18,695 and JMI with 8,188 users. Regarding the average number of users visiting library per day, DULS is on the top of all with 2500 followed by JNU with 600 and UOH and PU with 500 each. The total number of users visiting these libraries per day is 5,425 and the average is 452 users per university.

4.5. LIBRARY STAFF IN CU LIBRARIES

Human resources play a prominent role for the successful management of any library. The details of human resources available in CU Libraries are presented in Table 4.6. The table demonstrates that there are 1,214 staff members working in 14 CU Libraries. Out of 14 responded libraries, DULS has the largest number of 400 staff members followed by JNU with 160 and NEHU with 85.

Of the 1,214 library staff, there are 12 (1%) university librarians, 30 (2.5%) deputy librarians, 94 (7.7%) assistant librarians (including documentation officers and two information scientists), 248 (20.4%) professional assistants, 415 (34.2%) library assistants and remaining 415 (34.2%) includes semi-professional and other supporting staff. The data analysis reveals that the CU Libraries are managed by a good team of professional and non-professional staff.

Table 4.6: Library Staff in CU Libraries

S. No	Name of University	University Librarian	Deputy Librarians	Assistant Librarians	Professional Assistants	Library Assistants	Others	Total
1	AMU	1	4	12	65	125	25	232
2	AU	1	0	1	5	4	10	21
3	BBAU	1	---	1	2	---	2	6
4	BHU	1	1	9	5	35	---	51
5	UOD	1	10	24	78	162	125	40
6	UOH	1	2	5	8	16	40	72
7	IGNOU	1	---	2	3	4	10	20

8	JNU	1	4	18	31	16	90	160
9	JMI	1	3	3	11	8	35	61
10	NU	---	---	1	---	2	11	14
11	NEHU	1	1	4	10	34	35	85
12	PU	1	1	4	7	---	10	23
13	TU	1	---	1	1	1	6	10
14	VB	—	4	9	22	8	16	59
	Total	12	30	94	248	415	415	1,214
	Percentage	1	2.5	7.7	20.4	34.2	34.2	100

The supervisory staff drawing UGC scales in the cadres of ULs, DLs and ALs constitute 11.2% of total staff. More than half of the library staff comprising professional assistants and library assistants belongs to middle level staff. The remaining one third of staff include semi-professional and supporting staff.

4.6. LIBRARY BUDGET IN CU LIBRARIES

Finance is the life blood of any organisation. Annual budget is an important indicator of financial commitment of any library. CU Libraries spend significant amount for acquisition of books, subscription of periodicals and implementation of IT. The details of the budget of CU Libraries are presented in Table 4.7. The table shows that DULS's budget for acquisition of books and periodicals during 1997-98 was four crore rupees followed by JNU with Rs. 1.38 crores and UOH with Rs. 1.18 crores.

Nine CU Libraries reported IT budget figures, have spent Rs.677.87 lakhs for IT during three years from 1995-96, 1996-97 and 1997-98. PU reported to have spent Rs. 35.6 lakhs for databases during 1995-98. According to *INFLBNET Directory (2000),* all the CU Libraries shown in Table 4.5 were provided funds except BBAU. In addition, UGC provided special grants to some CU Libraries. This clearly shows that CU Libraries in general, are spending significant amounts on IT and are in a better position in using new technologies.

The situation may further be improved, as libraries are likely to invest more in IT in future.

Further analysis reveals that out of total amount, a lion's share has gone for IT hardware and less amount was spared for software. IT maintenance and training were allotted very meager amounts. This confirms the findings of several earlier studies, which reported that inadequate funds were allocated for training staff in the use of IT.

Table 4.7: Library Budget (in lakhs) in CU Libraries

S. No	Name of University	Books			Periodicals			Information Technology		
		1995 -96	1996 -97	1997 -98	1995 -96	1996 -97	1997 -98	1995 -96	1996 -97	1997 -98
1	AMU	—	—	—	70.00	77.00	77.00	10.00	--	--
2	AU	99.00	60.00	20.00	0.20	0.20	3.00	--	--	--
3	BBAU	--	--	10.00	--	--	--	--	--	--
4	BHU	--	--	--	--	97.00	104.00	--	--	--
5	UOD	--	--	400.00	--	--	--	*100.00	*100.00	--
6	UOH	20.00	20.00	25.00	77.00	83.00	93.00	20.05	1.45	2.43
7	IGNOU	35.00	27.50	60.00	13.00	20.00	20.00	--	10.00	15.00
8	JNU	12.55	10.85	18.11	120.00	120.00	120.00	--	--	--
9	JI	14.43	31.23	9.94	--	--	--	--	*200.00	--
10	NU	8.25	13.00	33.00	5.00	5.00	7.00	--	--	--
11	NEHU	10.00	10.00	10.00	60.00	60.00	60.00	*100.00	--	--
12	PU	7.31	27.46	--	22.20	22.14	--	--	8.84	0.60
13	TU	--	--	--	3.00	5.00	5.00	2.50	3.00	4.00
14	VB	10.84	17.80	20.75	28.08	28.76	44.00	--	*100.00	--

*UGC special grant

4.7. IT INFRASTRUCTURAL FACILITIES IN CU LIBRARIES

IT Infrastructural facilities form a sound basis for effective

Table 4.8: IT Infrastructural Facilities in CU Libraries

S. No	Name of University	Tele phone	Fax	E mail	Internet	Web site	Home Page	Xerox	Bar-code	Sca-nner	Multi media	Online search	Micro-film	Micro fische	Slide Proje	TV	VCR	OHP
1	AMU	Y	N	Y	Y	N	N	Y	N	N	N	N	Y	N	Y	N	N	N
2	AU	Y	Y	N	N	N	N	Y	N	Y	N	N	N	N	N	N	N	N
3	BBAU	Y	N	Y	N	N	N	N	N	N	N	N	N	N	N	N	N	N
4	BHU	Y	N	Y	N	N	N	Y	N	N	N	N	N	N	N	N	N	N
5	UOD	Y	Y	Y	Y	N	N	Y	N	Y	Y	Y	Y	Y	N	Y	Y	Y
6	UOH	Y	Y	Y	Y	Y	Y	Y	Y	Y	Y	Y	N	N	Y	N	N	Y
7	IGNOU	Y	N	Y	Y	N	N	Y	Y	Y	Y	Y	Y	Y	N	Y	Y	N
8	JNU	Y	N	Y	Y	N	N	Y	Y	Y	N	Y	Y	Y	N	N	N	N
9	JMI	Y	Y	Y	Y	N	N	Y	N	N	N	N	N	N	Y	Y	N	N
10	NU	N	N	N	N	N	N	N	N	N	N	N	N	N	N	N	N	N
11	NEHU	Y	Y	Y	N	N	N	Y	N	N	N	N	Y	Y	Y	Y	Y	N
12	PU	Y	Y	Y	Y	Y	Y	Y	N	Y	Y	Y	N	N	N	Y	Y	Y
13	TU	Y	N	Y	N	N	N	Y	N	N	N	N	N	N	N	N	N	N
14	VB	Y	Y	Y	N	N	N	Y	N	N	N	N	N	N	N	N	N	N
Total		14	7	13	7	2	2	12	3	6	5	5	5	4	3	5	4	3
%age		100	50	93	50	14	14	86	21	43	35	35	35	28	21	35	28	21

Y= Yes; N=No;

communication both within and outside the library. The data gathered from questionnaire responses regarding the IT infrastructural facilities available in CU Libraries is presented in Table 4.8. This table shows that all the 14 (100%) libraries surveyed have telephone, 12 (86%) have xerox and e-mail, seven (50%) have fax, Internet and six (43%) have scanners. In addition to the items mentioned in the Table 4.7, UOH has V-SAT, voice input devices and film projector, IGNOU has video conferencing, PU has V-SAT and VB has telex facilities. Since most of the CU Libraries have the basic IT infrastructural facilities, they would facilitate the introduction and use of IT in these libraries.

4.8. PLANNING APPROACHES TO IT IMPLEMENTATION IN CU LIBRARIES

Strategic planning is a key to the successful library automation implementation. Therefore, this section is intended to cover the kind of planning approaches and policy considerations taken into account by CU Libraries to support the introduction and use of IT. In order to identify planning approaches to library automation, the survey included questions about what are the important objectives of library automation, who has participated in planning, what steps they have taken for implementation and, what are the important factors considered in choosing software.

Each of these questions contained a variable number of choices and the respondents were asked to priorities them beginning with one in the order of importance. All these numbered responses were totaled and averaged to get Mean scores. These scores were used as a basis for assigning ranks to the choices. The mean score closer to one is the most important one and the rest are in the decreasing order of their importance.

4.8.1. Objectives of Library Automation in CU Libraries

In order to identify the goals for library automation, university librarians were offered 10 choices plus "any other" and asked to prioritise each choice in the order of their importance (one is the most important). The result is presented in Table 4.9. The most important objectives of library automation rated by respondents are: to improve access to collection, to improve the quality of existing services and to reduce routine and time consuming clerical works. The other objectives are shown in the table according to their descending order of their rank. The least regarded objectives are to improve prestige and visibility of our library and to reduce the number of staff required. It clearly shows that libraries are more concerned to improve user services.

Table 4.9: Objectives of Library Automation in CU Libraries

Rank*	Mean	N	Objective
1	1.7	13	To improve access to our collection
2	2.8	13	To improve the quality of existing services
3	3.8	13	To reduce routine and time consuming clerical works
4	4.8	13	To improve the speed of cataloguing, technical processing and putting items on shelves faster
5	4.9	13	To offer improved range of services.
6	5.2	13	To improve co-operation and resource sharing among libraries
7	6.2	12	To easily participate and utilise national and international computer networks
8	7.8	12	To provide more current and comprehensive reporting of library information to managers
9	7.9	12	To reduce the number of library staff required
10	9.6	12	To improve prestige and visibility of our library

Rank ordered by mean score; N = No. of libraries

Of all the automation objectives, improving access to collection received the highest rank, as it is the primary objective of any library. This confirms the findings of Borgman (1996) who surveyed library automation progress in six Central and Eastern European countries.

4.8.2. Persons involved in Library Automation Planning in CU Libraries

The success of library automation largely depends upon the persons involved in its planning and implementation. Respondents were, therefore, asked to rank the persons in the order of their involvement in automation planning and implementation process. They were offered five choices plus 'any other' and asked to rate them using one as the most important. Table 4.10 indicates the range of staff involved in the automation planning and implementation process. The first position goes to the head of the library i.e., university librarian, followed by deputy librarian with second rank and assistant librarian with third rank. The other persons participated include information scientist and other professional staff.

Table 4.10: Persons involved in Library Automation Planning in CU Libraries

Rank*	Mean	No. of libraries	Designation
1	1.4	11	University Librarian
2	2.0	6	Deputy Librarian
3	2.6	11	Asst. Librarian
4	3.1	10	Computer specialist
5	3.7	3	I/C of Automation program
6	4.3	6	Any other: other professionals

* Rank ordered by mean score

4.8.3. Steps Taken for Library Automation Implementation in CU Libraries

The basic knowledge of technology is essential for successful planning and implementation of library automation. There are a variety of ways to gain knowledge of using IT in libraries. Regarding the steps taken for library automation implementation, the respondents were offered six choices plus 'any other' and asked to rank them in the order of their usefulness using one as the most important.

Table 4.11 shows the steps taken for library automation implementation. The highly rated steps are: sending staff for training courses, visits to automated libraries and consultation with other librarians. This indicates that training has been identified as the most important step as it is a crucial to the successful library automation implementation.

Table 4.11 : Steps Taken for Library Automation Implementation in CU Libraries

Rank*	Mean	N	Steps
1	2.4	11	Sending staff for training courses
2	2.7	12	Visits to automated libraries
3	2.9	12	Consultation with other librarians
4	3.5	11	Attending meetings on library automation
5	3.8	11	Read library automation literature
6	5.8	4	Hired a consultant on library automation

* Rank ordered by mean score; N = No. of libraries

4.8.4. Factors in Selecting Library Automation Software in CU Libraries

Software package plays a key role for the success of library automation. There are a number of factors, which influence the selection of a particular package. To identify the important factors considered influential in selection of library automation software, respondents were offered eight factors plus 'any other' and asked to rank them. Table 4.12 shows the important factors in selecting a library automation software package.

The first three ranked factors are:

- The software that is the easiest for library staff and users to use,
- Supports the cataloging record format most used in the country

and is in use at other libraries in the country.

- The other reason indicated by one library is that the software is integrated and comprehensive.

This shows that the user-friendliness has been accorded as the major factor for selection of software in CU Libraries.

Table 4.12 : Important Factors in Selecting Library Automation Software in CU Libraries

Rank*	Mean	N	Factor
1	2.4	12	The Software is the easiest for library staff and users to use
2	2.6	11	The Software supports cataloging record format most used in the country
3	3.53	10	The Software is in use at other libraries in the country
4	3.6	9	The Software has the best features for connecting library to other computer networks
5	4.6	9	The Software company offers the best training for library staff
6	4.7	7	The Software is the least expensive overall
7	5.8	6	The Software is rated as the best in competitive bidding process
8	5.9	7	The Software has been endorsed for general use in our country by the appropriate agency.

* Rank ordered by mean score; N = No. of libraries

4.9. CONSTRAINTS IN LIBRARY AUTOMATION IN CU LIBRARIES

Library automation is an expensive, complex and continuous process involving various constraints faced in its implementation. In order to identify various constraints faced in library automation implementation by CU Libraries, the respondents were offered 10 problems plus 'any other' and asked to rank each problem in the order of their severity using one as the most important. Table 4.13 indicates the ranked order of the number of constraints faced in library automation. The highly ranked constraints were inadequate financial resources, lack of well-accepted standard software package and non-availability of IT trained personnel. The problem of inadequate funds has been confirmed in the studies reported by Burton (1987), Hauptman and Anderson (1994) and R.P. kumar (1994). The least ranked problem was non-availability of consultancy services followed by resistance of library staff.

Table 4.13: Constraints in Library Automation Implementation in CU Libraries

Rank*	Mean	N	Constraint
1	2.2	11	Inadequate financial resources
2	3.6	9	Lack of well accepted standard software package
3	3.7	10	Non availability of IT trained personnel
4	4.8	10	Lack of official / policy guidelines
5	5.0	6	Non availability of less expensive software
6	5.3	8	Low priority of libraries
7	5.4	7	Unawareness of potential benefits of IT
8	5.7	9	Inadequate management support
9	6.5	8	Non availability of consultancy services
10	7.4	7	Resistance of Library Staff

* Rank ordered by mean score; N = No. of libraries

4.10. COMPUTERS USED IN CU LIBRARIES

The number of computers used in a library serves as an indicator of the level of library automation implementation. To identify the types of computers being used by the CU Libraries, the respondents were requested to indicate the computer facilities available and also the number of computers used in their libraries. The data analysis indicates that most of the respondents except two indicated using some sort of computers and the result is presented in Table 4.14. When these were analysed according to size, most of CU Libraries are using Personal Computers while Mini Computer is used only in UOH and none had Mainframe Computer.

Regarding the use of Personal Computers, out of 14, the largest number i.e., 11 (79%) libraries found using computers, two are in the process of procurement and one did not report the number of computers available in the library. These 11 libraries have a total of 169 Personal Computers ranging from one to 53 with an average of 15 PCs per CU Library. There are altogether 30 terminals in five libraries providing OPAC service. In addition, the table demonstrates that eight (57%) libraries have computer network and five (36%) libraries have CD network too.

Table 4.14: Computers Used in CU Libraries

S. No	Name of University	Mini Computer	No of Personal Computers	CD Drives	OPAC terminals	Computer Network	CD Network
1	AMU	N	11	---	N	N	N
2	AU	N	1	1	N	N	N
3	BBAU	N	1	---	---	N	N
4	BHU	N	11	1	---	N	N
5	UOD	N	53	---	10	Y	N
6	UOH	Y	25	25	8	Y	Y
7	IGNOU	N	3	---	2	Y	Y
8	JNU	N	18	5	6	Y	Y
9	JMI	Y	13	---	---	Y	---
10	NU	---	---	---	---	---	---
11	NEHU	N	Y*	---	---	Y	Y
12	PU	N	21	11	4	Y	Y
13	TU	N	5	---	---	Y	N
14	VB	N	---	---	---	N	N
	Total	2	169	43	30	8	5
	Percentage	14	---	---	---	57	36

Y= Yes; N=No; Y*= Number not mentioned.

4.11. SOFTWARE PACKAGES USED IN CU LIBRARIES

Another measure of IT utilisation is studied with respect to application software packages used in CU Libraries. Responses indicate that 13 (93%) libraries use different operating systems, word processors, application software and programming languages. The result of the analysis of responses is presented in Table 4.15.

Regarding operating systems, 13 (93%) libraries are using both MS-DOS and Windows and nine (64%) are using UNIX. With regard to word processors, 12 (86%) libraries use MS-Word, 11 (79%) WordStar, and five (35%) use Word Perfect.

The application software indicated as being in use for creating and maintaining internal databases are dBase III plus, CDS/ISIS and commercial library software packages. CDS/ISIS (freely distributed by UNESCO) is the most widely used software by many libraries. Almost 12 (86%) libraries are using CDS/ISIS, eight (57%) LIBSYS (a commercial software package), five (35%) dBase III plus/IV and four (28%) libraries use ILMS/SOUL developed by INFLIBNET of UGC. This finding confirms the results of the surveys reported by INFLIBNET Centre (2000) and Lakshmana moorthy (2000).

In addition, DULS uses Troodon and IGNOU uses Foxplus. Regarding programming languages, four CU Libraries use C, two each Basic and Pascal.

4.12. COMPUTERISED LIBRARY OPERATIONS IN CU LIBRARIES

The mere availability of IT in a library is not enough, unless these technologies are put to use for solving problems of work environment. In order to obtain a benchmark on the progress of implementing automated systems for housekeeping operations, the survey offered a list of functions and asked the respondents to mark the computerized operations in their libraries.

Table 4.16 lists the housekeeping operations computerised in CU Libraries. Although, the question asked for a list of operations currently in use, responses appear to include planned as well as current

Table 4.15: Software Used in CU Libraries

S. No	Name of University	Operating systems			Word processors				Library Softwares				
		MS DOS	UNIX	Win dows	Word Perfect	Word Star	MS Word	Dbase III+/IV	LIB SYS	Basis plus	CDS/ ISIS	ILMS/ SOUL	Others
1	AMU	Y	N	Y	Y	Y	Y	N	N	N	Y	—-	—-
2	AU	Y	N	Y	N	Y	Y	N	N	N	Y	N	N
3	BBAU	Y	N	Y	N	Y	Y	Y	N	N	Y	Y	N
4	BHU	Y	Y	Y	N	Y	Y	N	N	N	Y	Y	N
5	UOD	Y	N	Y	Y	Y	Y	N	N	N	Y	N	Troodon
6	UOH	Y	Y	Y	Y	Y	Y	Y	Y	N	N	N	N
7	IGNOU	Y	Y	Y	Y	Y	Y	Y	Y	N	Y	N	FoxPlus
8	JNU	Y	Y	Y	N	Y	Y	N	Y	Y	Y	N	N
9	JMI	Y	Y	Y	N	N	Y	N	Y	N	Y	N	N
10	NU	—-	—-	—-	—-	—-	—-	—-	—-	—-	—-	—-	—-
11	NEHU	Y	Y	Y	Y	Y	N	Y	Y	N	Y	N	N
12	PU	Y	Y	Y	N	Y	Y	N	Y	N	Y	Y	N
13	TU	Y	Y	Y	N	Y	Y	N	Y	N	Y	Y	N
14	VB	Y	Y	Y	Y	Y	Y	Y	Y	N	Y	N	N
	Total	13	9	13	5	11	12	5	8	1	12	4	—-
Percentage		93	64	93	35	79	86	35	57	7	86	28	—-

Y= Yes; N=No;

operations. Table 4.16 shows that the most widely used library operations reported by 12 (86%) libraries are word processing followed by 11 (79%) in-house database creation, 10 (71%) cataloguing and nine (64%) retrospective conversion, eight (57%) serials control, seven (50%) acquisition and OPAC. The other applications in descending order are budgeting, management information, circulation and statistical reports. In addition to these, the other services provided are publications by DULS, network access by UOH and indexing and abstracting service by IGNOU etc. The data analysis reveals that the majority of libraries surveyed use IT to various operations.

Of all the operations, word processing widely used in CU Libraries. This finding agrees with Mustafa (1985) who made a study on the use of microcomputers in 114 university libraries in USA.

4.12.1. Library Automation Implementation in CU Libraries

There are different methods for library automation. Regarding the method followed for library automation implementation, the results are presented in Table 4.17. As can be seen from the table that eight (57%) libraries have adopted a single function approach in a phased manner in developing their computerised systems and two have stated for simultaneous implementation. Half of the libraries have integrated all modules of library operations. Overall it is observed that CU Libraries are in favour of integrated approach in a phased manner. In the order of automating library functions, out of four responded libraries, three have accorded first priority to cataloguing.

Respondents were asked to indicate the operations they maintain in parallel both automated and manual systems, six (43%) libraries indicated cataloguing and serials control followed by circulation by five (35%) and acquisition by four (28%). From this it is observed that CU Libraries will maintain both manual and automated systems parallelly for a specified period of time until the reliability of the new system is established.

Table 4.16: Computerised Library Operations in CU Libraries

S. No	Name of University	Word Processing	In house Database	Acquisition	Cataloguing	OPAC	RECON	Circulation	Serials Control	Budgeting	Statistical Reports	Management Information
1	AMU	Y	Y	—-	—-	—-	—-	—-	N	—-	—-	—-
2	AU	Y	N	N	Y	N	Y	N	Y	N	N	N
3	BBAU	Y	Y	Y	Y	Y	N	N	Y	Y	Y	Y
4	BHU	Y	Y	N	N	N	Y	N	N	N	N	N
5	UOD	Y	Y	Y	Y	Y	Y	N	Y	N	N	Y
6	UOH	Y	Y	Y	Y	Y	Y	Y	Y	Y	Y	Y
7	IGNOU	Y	Y	Y	Y	Y	Y	Y	Y	Y	N	N
8	JNU	Y	Y	Y	Y	Y	Y	N	Y	N	N	N
9	JMI	Y	Y	N	Y	N	N	N	N	N	N	N
10	NU	—-	—-	—-	—-	—-	—-	—-	—-	—-	—-	—-
11	NEHU	Y	Y	N	Y	N	Y	N	N	N	N	N
12	PU	Y	Y	Y	Y	Y	Y	N	Y	Y	Y	Y
13	TU	Y	Y	Y	Y	Y	Y	Y	Y	N	N	N
14	VB	N	N	N	N	N	N	N	N	N	N	N
	Total	12	11	7	10	7	9	3	8	4	3	4
	Percentage	86	79	50	71	50	64	21	57	28	21	28

Y= Yes; N=No;

Table 4.17: Library Automation Implementation in CU Libraries

S. No	Name of University	In Phases	Simulta-neously	Integrated	Automation order
1	AMU	Y	---	---	---
2	AU	---	---	---	---
3	BBAU	N	Y	N	---
4	BHU	Y	N	N	---
5	UOD	Y	N	Y	---
6	UOH	Y	N	Y	Catg., Acqn., Sl.Cntl., Tech&Circ.
7	IGNOU	N	Y	Y	---
8	JNU	Y	N	Y	Catg, Doc,Serls, Membship, Acqn.
9	JMI	Y	N	Y	---
10	NU	---	---	---	---
11	NEHU	N	N	N	---
12	PU	Y	N	Y	ReCon.. Acqn., Sl.Cntl.,OPAC
13	TU	Y	N	Y	Catg., Circ., Sl.Cntl ., Acqn.
14	VB	N	N	N	---
	Total	8	2	7	---
Percentage		57	14	50	---

Y= Yes; N=No;

4.13. DEVELOPMENT OF DATABASES IN CU LIBRARIES

Creation of databases of books, serials and theses is a pre-requisite for on-line library operations and networking. As an indicator of automation, respondents were asked to indicate the databases they created for public use such as books, serials and theses along with the number of records in each database. The results are presented in Table 4.18. As can be seen from the table that many CU Libraries have made considerable progress in database activity as most of them have created one or more local databases. However, databases are not developed corresponding to their huge volume of collections.

Out of 14 libraries, 11(79%) have created database for books, eight (57%) theses, six (43%) serials and the rest are in the process. As compared to the number of documents viz. books, back volumes of periodicals and theses given in Table 4.3, it indicates that 11.4% books, 16.7% back volumes of periodicals and 82% theses are entered into the databases. Although CU Libraries have developed databases covering most of theses, they are yet to enter major portions of collection in respect of books and back volumes of periodicals.

NEHU initiated library computerization in 1986 followed by UOH, IGNOU and JNU in 1989. The remaining CU Libraries started computerization after 1995 and made significant progress during last five years, which may be more faster in the next couple of years.

Table 4.18: Development of Databases in CU Libraries

S.No	Name of University	Year of starting computerisation	Number of records		
			Books	Back Vols. of journals	Theses
1	AMU	1998	40,000	---	4,701
2	AU	1997	---	---	---
3	BBAU	1998	1,007	---	---
4	BHU	1996	305	2,010	8,500
5	UOD	1998	80,000	3,000	14,500
6	UOH	1989	1,82,000	69,000	2,800
7	IGNOU	1989	65,000	1,000	25
8	JNU	1989	95,940	1,880	1,195
9	JMI	1996	10,000	---	600
10	NU	---	---	---	---
11	NEHU	1986	20,000	---	---

12	PU	1995	70,000	600	1,000
13	TU	1995	5,500	50	--
14	VB	1998	--	--	--
Total records		5,29, 752	77,540	33,321	
Total collection as per Table 4.2		46,48,431	4,63,176	40,636	
Percentage		11.4	16.7	82.0	

The most remarkable fact is that the UOH has developed a database for complete collection over 1,82,000 records of books and 69,000 back volumes of serials followed by JNU with 95,940 records, DULS with 80,000, PU with 70,000 and IGNOU with 65,000 records in books database.

4.14. BIBLIOGRAPHIC STANDARDS FOLLOWED IN CU LIBRARIES

Standardisation is essential in the field of computersation for compatibility, exchange, economy in cost, efforts and sharing of resources. The ISO has brought out some standards for mechanization and automation in documentation. Sharing resources in an automated environment requires agreement on standards among the participants especially for the content and structure of records to be exchanged or merged. Exchange of catalogue records is based on several related international standards for record description and structure (Borgman, 1996).

Standards for record content and structure are to be followed for successful development and use of databases and to facilitate sharing of resources. To find out the bibliographic standards followed in CU Libraries, respondents were offered choice of formats and asked to indicate the formats used in their libraries. The result of the analysis of data is presented in Table 4.19.

From the table, it is found that eight (57%) libraries are using CCF, followed by one (7%) each using ISO 2709, MARC, MARC compatible, local format and LIBSYS format. This finding conforms the results reported by INFLIBNET Centre (2000).

Regarding sources used for retrospective conversion of catalogue, many stated that they have converted their records by their own staff only and not used any electronic database sources.

The trend is different in Western countries, where libraries make maximum use of external CD-ROM and network databases for conversion of their records into machine readable form. The reason for this could be that the libraries in the West follow standards, which would facilitate easy downloading of data.

Table 4.19: Bibliographic Standards followed in CU Libraries

S. No	Name of University	Formats					
		MARC	UNI MARC	MARC compatible	CCF	ISO 2709	Others
1	AMU	N	N	N	Y	N	N
2	AU	N	N	N	Y	N	N
3	BBAU	N	N	N	N	N	local
4	BHU	N	N	N	Y	N	N
5	UOD	N	N	N	Y	N	N
6	UOH	N	N	Y	N	N	N
7	IGNOU	N	N	N	N	N	Libsys
8	JNU	N	N	N	Y	Y	N
9	JMI	N	N	N	Y	N	N
10	NU	---	---	---	---	---	---
11	NEHU	Y	N	N	N	N	N
12	PU	N	N	N	Y	N	N
13	TU	N	N	N	Y	N	N
14	VB	N	N	N	N	N	N
Total	1	---	1	8	1	1	
Percentage		7	---	7	57	7	7

Y= Yes; N=No

4.15. RETROSPECTIVE CONVERSION (RECON) OF CATALOGUE IN CU LIBRARIES

In order to know the extent, the library catalogue converted into machine-readable form, respondents were offered choices and asked them to indicate how much of their catalogue has been converted into machine-readable form. The result is summarised in Table 4.20. As can be seen from the table, that only four libraries have converted all of their records and the rest are at various stages of progress.

Retrospective conversion of a catalogue is a complex task, which requires not only a lot of efforts and time but also huge financial and human resources. This is more so with CU Libraries because of their large size holdings. Therefore, the retrospective conversion of catalogue work is progressing steadily in CU Libraries.

Respondents were also asked to indicate which method they followed for retrospective conversion of their catalogue. As can we seen from the Table 4.19 that six libraries have done with existing staff, two each with temporary staff and contract basis.

Table 4.20: Retrospective Conversion of Catalogue in CU Libraries

S. No	Name of University	Portion of library catalogue converted						Method followed		
		Last 1-2yr	Last 3-5yr	Last 6-10yr	All Con verted	Some Portion	None	Contr-act	temp. staff	Existing staff
1	AMU	Y	N	N	N	N	N	N	N	Y
2	AU	N	N	N	N	N	Y	N	Y	Y
3	BBAU	N	N	N	Y	N	N	N	N	N
4	BHU	N	N	N	N	Y	N	N	N	N
5	UOD	Y	N	N	N	N	N	N	Y	Y
6	UOH	N	N	N	Y	N	N	N	N	Y
7	IGNOU	N	N	N	Y	N	N	Y	N	N
8	JNU	N	N	Y	N	N	N	N	N	Y
9	JMI	Y	N	N	N	N	N	Y	N	N

10	NU	---	---	---	---	---	---	---	---	---
11	NEHU	N	Y	N	N	N	N	N	N	Y
12	PU	N	N	N	Y	N	N	N	N	Y
13	TU	N	N	N	N	Y	N	N	N	Y
14	VB	N	N	N	N	N	N	N	N	N
	Total	3	1	1	4	2	3	2	2	6
Percentage		21	7	7	28	14	21	14	14	43

Y= Yes; N=No

4.16. COMPUTERIZED LIBRARY INFORMATION SERVICES IN CU LIBRARIES

To measure the degree of automation in information services, the survey included questions about the computerised information services offered by each library. The result is present in Table 4.21. This table shows that seven libraries provide accession list, six internet service, five each reference service, and CD-ROM service, four each online service, ILL, and CAS etc. The range of services offered by these libraries varied from three to seven.

Table 4.21: Computerised Library Information Services in CU Libraries

S. No	Name of University	Accession List	Reference Service	CDROM service	Per.Cont pgs.	CAS	Online Service	Internet search	ILL	SDI Service	Indexing
1	AMU	N	N	N	N	N	N	N	N	N	N
2	AU	N	N	N	N	N	N	N	N	N	N
3	BBAU	N	N	N	N	N	N	N	N	N	N
4	BHU	N	N	N	N	N	N	N	N	N	N
5	UOD	Y	Y	Y	N	N	N	Y	N	N	N
6	UOH	Y	Y	Y	Y	Y	Y	Y	Y	Y	N
7	IGNOU	Y	Y	Y	N	Y	N	Y	Y	Y	Y

8	JNU	N	Y	Y	N	N	Y	Y	Y	N	Y
9	JMI	Y	N	N	N	Y	N	Y	N	N	N
10	NU	—-	—-	—-	—-	—-	—-	—-	—-	—-	—-
11	NEHU	Y	N	N	N	N	N	N	N	N	N
12	PU	Y	Y	Y	Y	Y	Y	Y	Y	Y	Y
13	TU	Y	N	N	N	N	Y	N	N	N	N
14	VB	N	N	N	N	N	N	N	N	N	N
	Total	7	5	5	2	4	4	6	4	3	3
	Percentage	50	35	35	14	28	28	43	28	21	21

Y= Yes; N=No;

4.16.1. Databases Used in CU Libraries

Databases form sound foundation for providing efficient information services in a library. Respondents were asked to indicate type of databases used in their libraries for providing information retrieval services to users. The summary of analysis of databases used is presented in Table 4.22.

Table 4.22: Databases Used in CU Libraries

S. No	Name of University	In-house database	CD-ROM database	INFLIBNET database	On-line database	Others
1	AMU	N	N	N	N	N
2	AU	N	N	N	N	N
3	BBAU	N	N	N	N	N
4	BHU	N	N	N	N	N
5	UOD	Y	Y	N	Y	DELNET
6	UOH	Y	Y	Y	Y	N
7	IGNOU	Y	Y	N	N	DELNET
8	JNU	Y	Y	Y	Y	N
9	JMI	Y	N	N	Y	N

10	NU	---	---	---	---	---
11	NEHU	N	Y	N	N	N
12	PU	Y	Y	Y	N	COPSAT(NCSI)
13	TU	N	N	N	N	N
14	VB	N	N	N	N	N
	Total	6	6	3	4	3
Percentage		43	43	21	28	21

Y= Yes; N=N

The table shows that six libraries each use internal databases and CD-ROM databases followed by four, online databases and three, INFLIBNET databases.

4.17. COMPUTERISED FACILITIES OFFERED TO USERS IN CU LIBRARIES

User is the kingpin of the library. So the main purpose of computersiation is to provide better facilities and services to users. The survey has asked to indicate the number of computers made available to users to use online catalogues, online and CD-ROM databases and Internet within the library. Table 4.23 indicates the availability of computers and facilities accessable by the end-users. As can be seen from the table that six libraries have provided computers for end users. The total number of computers provided by four libraries is 17 ranging from two to eight.

Regarding facilities accessable by end-users within the library, five libraries provide access to OPAC, four each CD-ROM search service, electronic mail and Internet.

Table 4.23: Computerised Facilities Offered to Users in CU Libraries

S. No	Name of University	Computers provided for users	No of computers	OPAC	CD-ROM search	E-mail	Internet	On-line search
1	AMU	N	---	N	N	N	N	N
2	AU	N	---	N	N	N	N	N
3	BBAU	N	---	N	N	N	N	N
4	BHU	N	---	N	N	N	N	N
5	UOD	N	---	N	N	N	N	N
6	UOH	Y	8	Y	Y	N	Y	Y
7	IGNOU	Y	2	Y	Y	Y	Y	N
8	JNU	Y	3	Y	Y	Y	Y	Y
9	JMI	N	N	N	N	N	N	N
10	NU	---	---	---	---	---	---	---
11	NEHU	Y	N	N	N	N	N	N
12	PU	Y	4	Y	Y	Y	Y	N
13	TU	Y	---	Y	N	Y	N	N
14	VB	N	---	N	N	N	N	N
	Total	6	17	5	4	4	4	2
Percentage		43	---	35	28	28	28	14

Y= Yes; N=No;

4.18. NETWORKING AND RESOURCE SHARING IN CU LIBRARIES

One of the major objectives of computerisation is to facilitate networking and resource sharing. In order to assess the progress made by CU Libraries towards networking and resource sharing, respondents were asked to indicate their accessibility as well as level of participation in networks.

Table 4.24: Networking and Resource Sharing in CU Libraries

S.No	Name of University	Accessibility to Networks INFLIBNET	ERNET	NICNET	INET	Others	Participation MAN	LAN
1	AMU	N	N	N	N	N	N	N
2	AU	N	N	N	N	N	N	N
3	BBRAU	N	N	N	N	N	N	N
4	BHU	N	Y	N	Y	N	N	Y
5	UOD	N	N	N	N	DELNET	Y	N
6	UOH	Y	Y	N	Y	N	Y	Y
7	IGNOU	N	N	N	N	DELNET	Y	Y
8	JNU	Y	N	Y	N	DELNET	Y	Y
9	JMI	N	N	Y	N	N	Y	Y
10	NU	---	---	---	---	---	---	---
11	NEHU	N	N	N	N	N	N	N
12	PU	Y	Y	Y	Y	N	N	Y
13	TU	Y	N	N	N	N	N	Y
14	VB	Y	Y	N	N	N	N	Y
	Total	5	4	3	3	3	5	8
Percentage		35	28	21	21	21	35	57

Y= Yes; N=No

The result of responses is presented in Table4.24. The table shows that five libraries have access to INFLIBNET, four ERNET, three NICNET, DELNET and INET each. Regarding participation in networks, seven libraries participate in LAN while five in MAN.

4.19. FUTURE PLANS OF CU LIBRARIES

Finally, the respondents were asked an open-ended question soliciting the details of their future plans of using IT in their libraries. Most of the CU Libraries have indicated their enthusiastic future plans of using IT extensively for computersiation. These future plans ranged widely from initial level of introducing IT, computerisation of one or more new functions, integration of all operations, development and participation in networks and resource sharing and provision of Internet services to the advanced level of developing digital libraries.

4.20. CONCLUSION

Use of IT in libraries has become inevitable in an era of information explosion, shrinking library budgets, the emergence of a wide range of new technologies and rising users expectations. Effective use of IT in libraries helps in performing their operations and services most efficiently. In India, many libraries have been adopting IT applications to library operations for providing efficient services and participating in networks for sharing resources. Implementation of IT to library operations is a complex and continuous process. It requires imaginative, intelligent planning and huge investment of financial as well as human resources. Libraries intending to use IT have to plan systematically well in advance for successful implementation to derive maximum benefits and minimise problems. To keep pace with the technological developments, libraries need to re-define and re-evaluate their roles and make consistent and systematic efforts to make use of the new technologies in order to satisfy variety of complex information needs of users. The role of the libraries in future would be heavily involved in adopting modern technologies and repackaging of information to provide need-based, value-added services to their users.

The Survey has provided a useful summary of current state-of-the art of using IT in CU Libraries in India. The survey confirmed that IT has deeply embedded in the management of information in university libraries. It has become a powerful tool in the management of routine library operations and services. The analysis has shown that the use of technology in CU Libraries is increasing steadily and significantly. The level of response shown to the present survey indicated that CU Libraries continue to be more interested in using IT in future. The respondents clearly indicated an awareness of current developments concerned with automated library systems even in those libraries where IT has not been used much.

The results of the analysis of the data obtained from the questionnaires served to survey the use of IT in CU Libraries in India has been summarised below.

1. Out of 16 CU Libraries, 14 were surveyed on the use of IT and received duly filled-in questionnaires from all the 14 (100%) libraries. The remaining two CU Libraries viz. MGAHV and MANUU were not included in the survey as they were established recently in 1997 and 1998 respectively.

2. All the 14 CU Libraries have a huge collection of about 46,48,431 books, 4,63,176 back volumes of periodicals, 40,636 theses, 11,046 audio-visual materials and 34,402 others. In electronic form, six libraries reported having 205 CD-ROM databases. The sizes of collection of CU Libraries vary widely from 1000 (in BBAU) to 14 lakhs (in DULS).

3. CU Libraries subscribe to 10,169 periodicals. Only four CU Libraries viz. AMU, BHU, UOD and JNU subscribe to more than 1000 periodicals while five subscribe more than 500 and the remaining libraries subscribe less than 500 periodicals.

4. The user community of CU Libraries comprises 42.6% P.G. Students, 14.8% Faculty, 13.1% Research scholars, 15.5% Administrative staff and 14% others including students of under graduate and distance learners.

5. CU Libraries have a total of 1,214 staff members comprising 11.2% supervisory cadres, 54.6% middle level professionals and 34.2% other staff including semi-professional and supporting staff.

6. The annual books budget of CU Libraries is ranging from seven lakhs to 60 lakhs. DULS consisting 30 libraries has spent about 4 crore rupees for both books and periodicals during the year 1997-98. IGNOU has spent 60 lakh rupees while NU, UOH, VB and AU have spent more than 20 lakhs for books during

the year 1997-98. The highest amount of budget spent for periodicals was Rs.1.2 crores by JNU, followed by BHU with Rs.1.04 crores and UOH with Rs.0.93 crores. The other CU Libraries are spending in the range of five to Rs.77 lakhs each for periodical subscriptions. Nine CU Libraries reported IT budget figures, have spent Rs.677.87 lakhs for IT only during three years from 1995-96, 1996-97 and 1997-98.

7. With regard to infrastructural facilities used in CU Libraries, telephone, fax, internet, email, Xerox, TV and multimedia are the common facilities used. Two CU Libraries viz., UOH and PU have their websites, homepages and V-SAT.

8. Regarding the objectives of library automation the top goals of CU Libraries are to: improve access to their collection, improve the quality of existing services and reduce routine and time consuming clerical operations.

9. Library Automation planning is done by both library professionals and computer personnel. However UL, DL and AL are rated as the key persons involved in planning library automation in CU Libraries.

10. To cope up with the implementation of technological changes, the important steps recognized by CU Libraries include sending staff for training courses, visits to automated libraries and consultations with the other librarians.

11. CU Libraries have considered the user-friendliness as the most important factor in selecting the software for library automation followed by supporting the cataloguing format and successful use in other libraries.

12. The three most important constraints faced in IT implementation in CU Libraries include inadequate financial resources, lack of standard and well accepted software package and lack of IT trained personnel.

13. Most of the CU Libraries are using personal computers for library automation while only UOH library has minicomputer

and none had mainframe computer. UOD, UOH, JNU and PU are using large number of computers ranging from 18 to 53.

14. Regarding software usage in CU Libraries, MS-DOS, Windows and UNIX are the most common operating systems while WordStar, Word processing and MS-word are the widely used word processors. dBase III+ / IV is used by five libraries. The programming languages viz. Basic, Pascal and C are also used by very few libraries. The major library application software used in CU Libraries include CDS/ISIS, LIBSYS, BASIS/ TECHLIBplus, ILMS/SOUL etc., CDS/ISIS promoted by NISSAT is used by almost all CU Libraries. LIBSYS is used in eight libraries, followed by ILMS/SOUL in five libraries and BASIS/ TECHLIBplus and Troodon in one library.

15. More than half of CU Libraries reported database creation, acquisition, cataloguing, OPAC, retrospective conversion etc. are computerized operations. Word processing is used for office automation by most of the libraries while budgeting and management information are the other areas reported by some CU Libraries. Regarding method of implementation, more than half of CU Libraries adopt computerisation in phases in an integrated way. Some libraries are maintaining cataloguing, circulation and serial control operations parallally both in manual as well as in copmuterised system.

16. About half of CU Libraries have created databases for books, back volumes of periodicals, theses etc. altogether ranging from 10,000 to 2.5 lakh records while others are in the process of development. One university library viz. UOH has completed the creation of database for the total collection of more than 2.5 lakh volumes. CU Libraries are using mainly CCF format. More than one third of CU Libraries have made some progress in retrospective conversion of their catalogue into electronic form mostly through manual data entry by staff rather than using CD-ROM databases and networks.

17. Nearly half of CU Libraries have been offering computerised information services such as accession list, CD-ROM and internet search service while, reference service, CAS, SDI and Indexing service are offered by a few libraries. Nearly half of CU Libraries use CD-ROM databases and internal databases for information retrieval services while a few use INFLIBNET databases and online databases including DELNET.

18. Nearly half of CU Libraries provide access to computers ranging from two to eight to the end-users. These computers are used for OPAC, Online, CDROM search, Email and Internet search services.

19. Regarding accessibility to various networks, five CU Libraries have accessibility to INFLIBNET followed by four libraries ERNET, three libraries NICNET, DELNET each and two INET. Nearly half of CU Libraries participate in LAN while five participate in MAN.

4.21. REFERENCES

Abifarin, F.P. (1993). Availability and use of Information technologies in Nigerian University Libraries. *Library Review* 42(5), 1993, 4-14.

Borgman, Christine L. (1996). Automation is the answer, but what is the question? Progress and Prospects for Central and Eastern European Libraries. *Journal of Documentation*, 52(3), 252-295.

Burton Paul F. (1987). *Microcomputer Applications in Academic Libraries II [Library and Information Research Report 60]*. British Library Research and Development Department.

Hauptman, R. & Anderson, C. L. (1994). The people speak: the dispersion and impact of technology in American libraries. *Information Technology and Libraries*, 13(4), 249-56.

INFLIBNET Center. (2000). *Progress Report of Review Committee meeting* on 15th Feb, Ahemadabad.15p. (mimeographed)

INFLIBNET Center. (2001). INFLIBNET Center: A Profile. In *Souvenir* of CALIBER 2001: Eighth National Convention on creation and management of Digital Resources 15-16 March 2001. (PP. 7-15). Pune: University of Pune.

Kumar, R.P. (1994). An overview of modern technologies: Applications in Indian libraries. *International Information and Library Review*, 26, 327-339.

Lakshmana Moorthy, A. (2000). *Impact of Electronic Media on Library and Information Centres with a specific reference to India.* Ph.D. thesis. Karnataka University, Dharwad.

Mustafa, Suleiman Hussain. (1985). *Micro computer-based information storage and retrieval: An exploratory study on the use of Microcomputers in university libraries.* Ph.D. Thesis. University of Pittsburgh, Pittsburgh.

Ng Tye, Eugena M. W & Chau, Patrik Y.K. (1995). A study of information technology adoption in Hong Kong. *Journal of Information Science*, 21(1), 11-19.

Olsgaard, J.N. (1984). *The relationship between administrative style and the use of computer-based systems: an attitudinal study of academic library professionals.* Ph.D. dissertation, University of Illinois, Urbana-Champaign.

Pritchett, Price (1994). New Habits for a Radically Changing World. Pritchett & Associates, Dallas

Rowley, Jennifer E. (1988). *The Basics of information technology.* London: Cline Bingley.

Saffady, William. (1989). Library automation: an overview. *Library Trends*, 37(3),269-81.

Scharf, Meg., & Ward, Jeannette. (1989). Side-by-side: Users react to a second Online Public Access Catalog. *Library Trends*, 37(4), 402-13.

5

Impact of Information Technology on Central University Libraries in India

5.1 INTRODUCTION

Information Technology has profound impact on library operations, information resources, information services, and staff competences and users expectations. IT has radically transformed the way of functioning and management of modern libraries. It has greatly enhanced the capabilities of libraries to improve the efficiency of their operations and offer innovative and intelligent information services to their users. It has dramatically changed the way the information is gathered, processed, organized, stored, retrieved and delivered in libraries.

The analysis of data, regarding the use of IT in Central University

(CU) Libraries in India presented in Chapter 4 indicated that UOH has computerized all library operations and the other seven CU Libraries viz. UOD, IGNOU, JMI, JNU, NEHU, PU, and TU are actively involved in IT implementation process while the remaining are at various stages of progress. Therefore, the study was further extended to the above stated group of eight CU Libraries to study the impact of using IT through the perceptions of the library staff working in these libraries and also the users of UOH Library where all operations are computerized and services are offered.

This Chapter reports the results of the analysis of data gathered through the second and third questionnaires designed for library staff of Central University Libraries and users of University of Hyderabad respectively in order to assess their perceptions on the impact of using IT on library house-keeping operations and information services. Each of the questionnaires has two major parts. The first part covers respondents' background information and the second part contains statements of effects of using IT. The respondents' were asked to answer on a five-point Likert Scale with five being 'Strongly Agree (SA)' and one being 'Strongly Disagree (SD)' which is discussed in detail in section 4.1.3. The statistical analysis tables containing frequencies, percentages, rank etc are presented in this chapter.

Table 5.1: Survey Response by Library Staff

S. No	Name of University	Number of Questionnaires Sent	Received	Percentage of response
1	UOD	10	5	50
2	UOH	35	30	86
3	IGNOU	8	5	63
4	JMI	5	2	40
5	JNU	17	10	59
6	NEHU	15	10	67
7	PU	6	—	—
8	TU	4	2	50
Total	100	64	64	

One hundred questionnaires were sent to the staff of eight CU Libraries that are known to have been actively involved in using IT and received duly filled-in questionnaires from 64 (64%) respondents. The details of responses are presented in Table 5.1. The survey on staff of CU Libraries intends to cover the impact of using IT on library house-keeping operations and information services.

5.2 LIBRARY STAFF BACKGROUND INFORMATION

The characteristics such as gender, age, education, designation, experience, involvement in IT related activities, IT facilities, training etc. of respondents have been studied and the detailed analysis are presented below.

5.2.1. Gender Distribution of Respondents

The gender details of the respondents presented in Table 5.2 show that out of 64 respondents, 47 (73.4%) are men and 17 (26.6%) women.

Table 5.2: Gender Distribution of Respondents

S. No	Gender	No. Of Respondents	Percent
1	Male	47	73.4
2	Female	17	26.6
	Total	64	100.0

5.2.2. Age of Respondents

The respondents were classified into four categories according to their age and presented in Table 5.3. According to the table, the age of three (4.7%) respondents was less than or equal to 30 years, 16 (25%) between 31 and 40, 33 (51.6%) between 41 and 50 and 12 (18.7%) more than 50 years. The average age of respondents was 44.4 years.

Table 5.3: Age of Respondents

S. No	Age range	No. of respondents	Percent
1	Less than or equal to 30 years	3	4.7
2	Between 31and 40 years	16	25.0
3	Between 41and 50 years	33	51.6
4	More than 50 years	12	18.7
	Total	64	100.0

5.2.3 Educational Background of Respondents

The educational background of 64 respondents is presented in Table 5.4. The general education reveals that 21 (32.8%) respondents have Bachelors Degree, 37 (57.8%) Masters degree and three (4.7%) have Doctoral Degree. With regard to library science, 21 (32.8%) have B.L.I.Sc. 38 (59.4%) M.L.I.Sc. and three (4.7%) have Doctoral degree. In computer science, three (4.7%) respondents have PGDLAN followed by two (3.1%) with PGDCA and 59 (92.2%) have not reported any formal course on computer applications. Altogether nearly 8% of the respondents pursued courses on computer applications.

From the above, it is observed that more than 50% of respondents are highly qualified having two masters degrees both in general education as well as in library science. This clearly indicates that the responded universities have highly qualified personnel working in their libraries, which would facilitate the use of IT in their libraries.

Table 5.4: Educational Background of Respondents

S.No	Course name	General education		Library Science	
		No. of respondents	%	No. of respondents	%
1	Degree	21	32.8	21	32.8
2	Masters Degree	37	57.8	38	59.4
3	Ph.D.	3	4.7	3	4.7
4	No answer	3	4.7	2	3.1
5	Total	64	100	64	100

5.2.4. Designation of Respondents

The details of designation-wise distribution of respondents are summarized in Table 5.5. As can be seen from the table that there are 19 (29.7%) Professional Assistants, followed by 15 (23.4%) Assistant Librarians and 12 (18.8%) Junior Professional Assistants. This clearly shows that all levels of staff members are being participated in implementation of technologies with overall domination by middle level staff. As staff participation boosts their morale and motivation, the trend of involving all levels of staff enables effective implementation of IT.

Table 5.5: Designation of Respondents

S. No	Designation	No. of Respondents	Percent	Cumulative%
1	Librarian	3	4.7	4.7
2	Deputy Librarian	3	4.7	9.4
3	Assistant Librarian	15	23.4	32.8
4	Sr. Professional Assistant	4	6.2	39.0
5	Professional Assistant	19	29.7	68.7
6	Jr. Professional Assistant	12	18.8	87.5
7	Library Assistant	8	12.5	100.0
	Total	64	100.0	

5.2.5. Work Areas of Respondents

The numerical breakdown of respondents by the area in which they work is presented in Table 5.6. Out of 64 respondents, 18 (28.1%) are working in Technical Section followed by Acquisition, Computers and Circulation with eight (12.5%) each. This finding shows that IT had a greater effect on Technical Section (especially cataloguing activity) as compared to other sections.

Table 5.6: Work Areas of Respondents

S. No	Work Area	No. of respondents	Percent
1	Library	7	10.9
2	Acquisition	8	12.5
3	Technical processing	18	28.1
4	Serials control	6	9.4
5	Circulation	8	12.5
6	Computers	8	12.5
7	Other Sections	4	6.3
8	No answer	5	7.8
	Total	64	100.0

5.2.6. Experience of Respondents

An analysis of the respondents' work experience is presented in Table 5.7. Regarding the total length of library service, 29 (45.3%) respondents have experience between 21 and 30 years, followed by 23 (35.9%) between 11-20 years and nine (14.1%) have less than or equal to 10 years of experience. The average work experience of respondents is 19.42 years.

With regard to experience in the present library, 28 (43.8%) respondents have experience between 21 and 30 years followed by 26 (40.6%) between 11 – 20 years and 10 (15.6%) have less than or equal to 10 years of service. The average experience in the present library is 17.52 years.

The above finding shows that almost half of respondents belong to senior staff having an experience ranging between 21 and 30 years. Further analysis reveal that majority of respondents have been working in the same university since the beginning of their career.

Table 5.7: Experience of Respondents

S.No	Experience range (years)	Total Experience		Experience in present library	
		No of respondents	%	No of respondents	%
1	Less than or equal to 10	9	14.1	10	15.6
2	Between 11and 20	23	35.9	26	40.6
3	Between 21and 30	29	45.3	28	43.8
4	More than 30 years	3	4.7	—	--
	Total	64	100	64	100

5.2.7. Participation in IT Activities

Respondents were asked to indicate the number of IT related training courses and seminars they attended and papers presented / published both before and after IT implementation. The result of analysis is presented in Table 5.8. Regarding the number of training courses attended, only 11 (17.2%) respondents attended training courses ranging from one to five before IT implementation while 25 (39.1%) attended courses ranging from one to seven after IT implementation, showing a significant increase of more than double. The duration of training courses vary from one to five weeks with a majority of them being one and two week courses. Of all the respondents, only six (9.4%) respondents attended seminars ranging from one to four before IT implementation, while 20 (31.3%) attended seminars after IT implementation which shows more than three-fold increase.

There is a tremendous growth in the number of papers presented/published by respondents after IT implementation. While one (1.6%) respondent presented/published paper before IT implementation, 16 (25%) had papers ranging from one to 10 after IT implementation showing rapid increase of 16 times. It is worth mentioning that one respondent published highest number of 10 papers after he/she started using technologies in work place. This clearly shows the growing awareness and interest among the library personnel about the use of IT in libraries. On the whole, only 18 (28.2%) respondents attended training courses/conferences and published papers before IT implementation, while 61 (95.3%) have attended training courses/conferences and published papers after IT implementation showing a significant increase of more than three times.

Table 5.8: Participation in IT Activities

S. No	IT related activities	Before IT Implementation		After IT Implementation	
		No. of respondents	%	No of respondents	%
1	Training courses attended	11	17.2	25	39.1
2	Conferences/Seminars attended	6	9.4	20	31.3
3	Papers presented/published	1	1.6	16	25.0
	Total	18	28.2	61	95.4

5.2.8. Involvement in IT Implementation

The data regarding the level of staff involvement in IT implementation and the extent to which it helped them to improve their performance is collected and presented in Table 5.9. Of all the respondents, 46 (71.9%) were involved in IT implementation. With regard to the effect of staff involvement on their performance, all the 46 involved accepted that IT had improved their performance.

A number of studies in library science literature have demonstrated the favourable effects and success owing to the involvement of all levels of employees in the automation process. This finding is in conformity with the results of studies reported by Olsgard (1984), Dakshinamurthy (1985) and Jones (1989 & 1998). As staff involvement in IT implementation boosts their morale and motivation, all the staff concerned should be involved for successful IT implementation.

Table 5.9: Involvement in IT Implementation

S. No	Involved in IT implementation	No. of respondents	Percent
1	Yes	46	71.9
2	No	15	23.4
3	Not responded	3	4.7
	Total	64	100.0

5.2.9. IT Training of Respondents

The need for training in the new technologies has been emphasized in a number of studies conducted on library staff. Respondents were asked to indicate whether they were given training in the use of IT in their library. The data analysis is presented in Table 5.10. According to the table, out of 64 respondents, 38 (59.4%) indicated that they have received training while 23 (35.9%) were not.

Regarding the assessment of quality of training, the respondents indicated variations in the quality of training received in their libraries. Out of 38 trained, one (2.6%) stated that the training he/she received was extensive, 12 (31.6%) adequate, six (15.8%) inadequate and the largest number of 19 (50%) respondents indicated the need for more training. This finding is in conformity with the studies done by Ganga Dakshinamurti (1985) and Jones (1989). These findings show that not only more number of staff members need to be trained but also the mode, module and quality of training course need to be thoroughly revised and improved to suit the different learning styles of individuals so as to improve the effectiveness of training programmes in libraries.

Table 5.10 : IT Training of Respondents

S. No	Training given	No. of Respondents	Percent
1	Yes	38	59.4
2	No	23	35.9
3	Not responded	3	4.7
	Total	64	100.0

Table 5.11 : Assessment of IT Training by Respondents

S. No	Assessment	No. of Respondents	Percent
1	Extensive	1	2.6
2	Adequate	12	31.6
3	Inadequate	6	15.8
4	Need more training	19	50.0
	Total	38	100.0

5.2.10. IT Facilities of Respondents

Respondents were asked to indicate the IT facilities accessible to them in their section. The result of data analysis is presented in Table 5.12. The table shows that 61 (95.3%) respondents have access to the computer in their work place, followed by printer with 38 (59.4%), LAN with 34 (53.1%) and Internet with 32 (50%). This finding showed that most of the respondents have access to the computer in their work place, which enable them to learn and improve their performance. It also demonstrates the respondents' working knowledge and experience on computers, which would support the validity and reliability of the responses reported in the questionnaire.

Table 5.12 : IT Facilities of Respondents

S. No	IT Facilities	Computer		Printer		LAN		Internet	
		N	%	N	%	N	%	N	%
1	Available	61	95.3	38	59.4	34	53.1	32	50
2	Not available	3	4.7	26	40.6	30	46.9	32	50
	Total	64	100	64	100	64	100	64	100

N= Number of respondents

5.2.11. Time Spent on Computer at Work Place by Respondents

Consequent upon the use of IT, the respondents are expected to spend a part of their time daily on computers in performing routine works in their libraries. The results are presented in Table 5.13. Of the 64 respondents, 22 (34.4%) indicated that they spend between 51 – 75 % of their time on computer at workplace, followed by 21 (32.8%) between 0 – 25%, 14 (21.9%) between 26 to 50% and three (4.7%) between 76 – 100% of their time. This finding shows that overall library staff spends less than half of their time on computerised operations and are yet to make extensive use of available technological facilities.

Table 5.13 : Time Spent on Computer at Work Place by Respondents

S.No	Percentage of time spent on computer	No. of respondents	Percent
1	0 – 25	21	32.8
2	26 – 50	14	21.9
3	51 – 75	22	34.4
4	76 – 100	3	4.7
5	Not responded	4	6.3
	Total	64	100.0

5.2.12. IT Enthusiasm of Respondents

To the question, which was asked to know how far library staff are enthusiastic in working with computers, a majority of 53 (82.8%) respondents indicated that they are computer enthusiasts while nine (14.1%) are not. This clearly shows that the respondents have significant interest in using technology, which facilitate easier ana successful implementation of technology in the libraries.

Table 5.14: IT Enthusiasm of Respondents

S. No	Enthusiast	No. of respondents	Percent
1	Yes	53	82.8
2	No	9	14.1
3	Not responded	2	3.1
	Total	64	100.0

5.2.13. IT Experience of Respondents

The number of years of computer experience can be considered as the length of time the respondents have been using IT. It has been found that the experience has a strong effect on the attitudes and perceptions of people in the success of IT adoption in libraries. Therefore, the years of computer experience is used as the indicator to measure the level of its impact on respondents' perceptions. The details of years of IT work experience is presented in Table 5.15.

Out of 64 respondents, 11 did not report the period, 27 had less than or equal to five years of IT work experience, 22 between six and 10 years and four had more than 10 years of IT experience. This finding shows that, all the respondents reported to have IT work experience ranging from one to 14 years.

Table 5.15: IT Experience of Respondents

S. No	IT Experience range	No of respondents	Percent
1	Less than or equal to 5 years	27	42.2
2	Between 6and 10 years	22	34.4
3	More than 10 years	4	6.2
4	Not responded	11	17.2
	Total	64	100

5.3 IMPACT OF IT ON LIBRARY

IT has immense impact on various aspects of the library. In order to assess the perceptions on the impact of using IT in library, respondents were asked to rate the improvement in ten aspects listed in the questionnaire. A five point scale ranging from '5=Very much improved' to '1=Deteriorated' has been used. Most respondents acknowledged varied levels of improvement in all the aspects. The average scores on the ten aspects were high ranging from 4.10 to 3.67. The result is summarised in Table 5.16.

The highly improved aspects of using IT are: efficiency,

effectiveness and user satisfaction. The other aspects are presented in the decreasing order of their rank in Table 5.16.

Table 5.16: Impact of IT on Library

Rank	Aspects	Q .No	Mean	VI	MI	LI	NI	D
1	Efficiency (Doing faster more things)	Q12.1	4.10	20	31	8	3	—
2	Effectiveness (Doing more right things)	Q12.2	3.98	14	38	6	3	1
3	Users' satisfaction	Q12.9	3.94	15	34	9	2	2
4	Work environment	Q12.8	3.85	12	35	10	4	1
5	Innovation (new ways of work/service)	Q12.6	3.81	9	38	9	6	—
6	Productivity	Q12.4	3.80	8	38	10	5	—
7	Services	Q12.5	3.79	10	37	8	6	1
8	Utilization (Resources/ services usage)	Q12.7	3.74	12	29	15	5	1
9	Cost effectiveness (Doing more with same cost)	Q12.3	3.67	6	35	13	4	1
10	Status	Q12.10	3.67	7	32	17	5	—

VI=Very much Improved (5); MI=Much Improved (4); LI=Little Improved (3); NI=Not Improved (2); D=Deteriorated (1);

Further, the cross tabulation results of chi-square test indicated that :

- Staff spending around 50% of their time working on computer perceived that the efficiency, productivity and services are much improved.
- Staffs involved in IT implementation are more positive towards improvement in the effectiveness, productivity, services and utilization of library.

- Staff attended more number of training courses reported that cost-effectiveness is much improved in the library.
- Staff involved in IT implementation, attended more training courses and spending around half of their time working on computer per day at work place, have more positive perceptions on the impact of using IT in library.

5.3.1. Effects of Using IT in Library

There are many positive effects of using IT in library. This section is intended to know the perceptions about the effects of using IT in CU Libraries in India. Respondents were therefore asked to assess the effects (positive and negative) of using IT in their libraries in five-point Likert Scale from 'strongly agree' to 'strongly disagree'. The result of data analysis of the positive effects are presented in Table 5.17a and negative effects in Table 5.17b.

Table 5.17a: Effects (Positive) of Using IT in Library

Rank	Statements	Q. No	Mean	SA	A	U	D	SD
1	Facilitated networking and resource sharing	Q13.7	4.05	14	41	4	2	1
2	Eliminated duplication of efforts	Q13.13	3.97	9	36	4	2	1
3	Improved the speed of operations	Q13.2	3.97	14	40	1	6	1
4	Improved standardization	Q13.17	3.95	9	45	5	2	1
5	Enabled rapid communication	Q13.18	3.94	8	44	8	2	–
6	Provide comprehensive management information support	Q13.8	3.92	9	43	5	3	1
7	Improved accuracy, consistency and reduced errors	Q13.3	3.89	11	41	2	5	2

Rank	Statements	Q. No	Mean	SA	A	U	D	SD
8	Enabled to streamline complex tasks and simplify procedures	Q13.25	3.85	4	49	6	2	1
9	Improved the efficiency of correspondence & secretarial work	Q13.28	3.85	7	45	5	4	1
10	Developed integrated library management system	Q13.29	3.84	6	46	6	2	2
11	Improved collection development / management	Q13.6	3.84	8	42	6	3	2
12	Enabled to generate variety of statistical reports	Q13.15	3.81	12	35	7	7	1
13	Enabled enormous savings in time and efforts	Q13.11	3.77	8	39	8	4	2
14	Perform tasks which cannot be done by manual system	Q13.20	3.76	8	42	4	5	3
15	Improved capability to handle increased work load	Q13.26	3.75	3	49	3	3	3
16	Improved control over operations	Q13.10	3.74	5	42	8	5	1
17	Reduced physical work/activity/movement	Q13.23	3.72	8	40	2	10	1
18	Improved management attitude	Q13.21	3.66	4	40	12	5	1
19	Facilitated effective utilization of funds	Q13.12	3.61	4	38	9	6	2
20	Reduced delays and backlogs in work	Q13.27	3.57	3	45	1	8	4
21	Enabled to market library services	Q13.16	3.52	6	28	22	4	2

Rank	Statements	Q. No	Mean	SA	A	U	D	SD
22	Enabled non-professional staff to perform professional tasks	Q13.22	3.32	3	34	10	10	5
23	Reduced unit costs of operations	Q13.5	3.25	4	30	7	13	5
24	Reduced the need for more staff	Q13.1	2.97	6	21	8	17	9

SA = Strongly Agree (5); A=Agree (4); U= Undecided (3); D= Disagree (2); SD = Strongly Disagree (1);

A look at the Table 5.17a shows that most of the respondents acknowledged the positive effects of using IT in their libraries. The average scores of most of the effects were high ranging from 4.05 to 2.97. The most positive aspects of using IT in library are:

- Facilitated networking and resource sharing
- Eliminated duplication of efforts and
- Improved speed of operations.

The other effects are listed in the table in descending order of their rank. These findings agree with those of Abifarin (1993), Lancaster (1997), Kumar (1987) and Haravu (1995).

Further, the cross tabulation results of chi-square test indicated that

- Staff spending between 50-75% of their time working at computer per day agreed with enormous savings in time & efforts, enable to market library services, and improved management attitude.
- Staff involved in IT implementation would agree with improved the speed of operations, performing tasks which cannot be done by manual system and development of integrated library management system.
- Majority of staff spending around 50% of their time working

on computer disagree with the negative effect of frequent systems breakdown/failure.

- Staff trained in the use of IT agree with frequent system breakdown/failure and frequent virus problems.

Respondents perceived that positive effects outweighed the negative effects of using IT in library. The average score of all the negative effects were much lower than those of positive effects ranging from 3.55 to 2.58. The result is presented in the Table 5.17b. The low scores indicated that they are not much serious problems. As shown in the table, the identified negative effects of using IT are: increased expenditure on systems maintenance; reduced inter-personal communication and increased violation of copyright act.

Table 5.17b: Effects (Negative) of Using IT in Library

Rank	Statements	Q. No	Mean	SA	A	U	D	SD
1	Increased expenditure on systems maintenance	Q13.9	3.55	6	35	10	9	2
2	Reduced inter-personal communication	Q13.4	3.18	5	27	6	20	3
3	Increased violation of Copyright Act	Q13.30	2.93	4	11	26	17	3
4	Frequent systems break down	Q13.19	2.84	3	21	6	27	5
5	Frequent virus problem (corruption of files)	Q13.24	2.63	3	10	14	31	4
6	Required to perform too-many steps to complete a single task	Q13.14	2.58	1	15	8	33	5

SA = Strongly Agree (5); A=Agree (4); U= Undecided (3); D= Disagree (2); SD = Strongly Disagree (1);

5.4 IMPACT OF USING IT ON HOUSEKEEPING OPERATIONS

It has tremendous impact on various house-keeping operations of a library. A series of statements were designed and listed in the questionnaire to solicit respondents', perceptions about the effects of using IT on various housekeeping operations of the library such as acquisition, classification, cataloguing, circulation, serials control, networking and management information etc. Respondents were asked to rate the statements of effects on each of these operations in a five-point Likert Scale from strongly agree to strongly disagree.

5.4.1. Acquisition

Acquisition is concerned with procurement of books to be provided to users. One of the complicated activities in acquisition is funds, which get through various sources, allocates under various divisions and spends through several agencies. Keeping track of all these manually is very difficult process. Computerisation helps in maintaining these funds accurately and systematically. This process involves various clerical, routine, repetitive and labour intensive activities, which are quite time consuming in manual system. Computerised acquisition not only helps in performing these activities most efficiently but also offers several other benefits. Respondents were, therefore, asked to rate each of these benefits listed in the questionnaire in a five point Likert Scale from Strongly Agree to Strongly Disagree.

The average scores of the 15 statements of acquisition are high ranging from 4.13 to 3.50 which are presented in Table 5.18.

The highly rated statements are:

- Enabled faster pre-order duplicate checking,
- Facilitate easy preparation of purchase orders and
- Enabled to keep updated vendor database.

The top most time consuming and important activity in acquisition process is checking the availability of the approved books in the existing collection in order to avoid procuring duplicate materials. This is more so especially in university libraries, which contain large collections. This activity has become not only quite easier but also became much faster saving a lot of time and energy with the help of computers. Therefore, the respondents gave utmost importance to this activity and rated as highly benefited activity of computerized acquisition system.

Table 5.18: Acquisition

Rank	Statements	Q. No	Mean	SA	A	U	D	SD
1	Enabled faster pre-order duplicate checking	Q14.3	4.13	12	40	3	1	-
2	Facilitate easy preparation of purchase orders	Q14.4	4.05	8	44	3	1	-
3	Enabled to keep updated vendor database	Q14.9	4.02	6	46	3	1	-
4	Enabled to maintain up-to-date fund utilization account	Q14.8	4.00	7	44	4	-	1
5	Facilitate to send timely reminder and order cancellation letters	Q14.6	4.00	9	41	3	3	-
6	Enabled accurate and up-to-date record of orders	Q14.1	3.98	4	47	5	-	-
7	Facilitate easy accessioning and invoice processing	Q14.10	3.96	7	41	5	2	-
8	Enabled easy preparation of subject-wise list of orders	Q14.7	3.91	4	45	4	1	1
9	Facilitate electronic ordering	Q14.5	3.84	7	38	6	5	-
10	Enabled automatic generation of accession list/register	Q14.11	3.79	6	37	9	3	1

Rank	Statements	Q. No	Mean	SA	A	U	D	SD
11	Facilitate to send letters for adjustment of advances	Q14.13	3.78	3	41	8	2	1
12	Facilitate easy book selection	Q14.2	3.73	3	46	6	6	-
13	Facilitate preparation of vendor performance report	Q14.15	3.73	3	40	9	3	1
14	Facilitated prompt notifications to users	Q14.12	3.71	1	43	7	5	-
15	Facilitate to send letters to bank for foreign exchange drafts	Q14.14	3.50	2	33	13	7	1

SA = Strongly Agree (5); A=Agree (4); U= Undecided (3); D= Disagree (2); SD = Strongly Disagree (1);

5.4.2. Classification

Computerisation helps in classifying the documents acquired for the library. The analysis of data is presented in Table 5.19. According to respondents, the three benefited activities in classification are: enabled easy checking of previously assigned call numbers, enabled to save time by avoiding frequent consultation of schemes and enabled easy construction of call numbers. As the expert systems for classification schemes are in the process of development, they may be of great use in assigning call numbers to the documents in automated environment.

Table 5.19: Classification

Rank	Statements	Q. No	Mean	SA	A	U	D	SD
1	Enabled easy checking of previously assigned call numbers	Q15.1	3.97	14	38	3	2	3
2	Enabled to save time by avoiding frequent consultation of schemes	Q15.2	3.78	9	36	11	1	3

Rank	Statements	Q. No	Mean	SA	A	U	D	SD
3	Enabled easy construction of call numbers	Q15.3	3.68	8	35	10	4	3

SA = Strongly Agree (5); A=Agree (4); U= Undecided (3); D= Disagree (2); SD = Strongly Disagree (1);

5.4.3. Cataloguing

Cataloguing is one of the most important functions performed to provide information about documents in the library. The time consuming work involved in catalogue production is tremendously reduced by the use of computers. Computerisation offered many benefits in cataloguing. Respondents were offered ten benefits in cataloguing and asked to rate each in five point Likert Scale from strongly agree to strongly disagree. The result of data analysis is presented in Table 5.20.

The highly rated benefits in cataloguing are:

- Speed in cataloguing and updation
- Many access points and in-depth subject cataloguing and
- Enabled multiple users to access simultaneously from remote locations.

Table 5.20: Cataloguing

Rank	Statements	Q. No	Mean	SA	A	U	D	SD
1	Enabled speed in cataloguing and updation	Q16.3	4.05	13	44	1	-	3
2	Enabled many access points and in-depth subject cataloguing	Q16.5	3.98	9	43	5	1	1
3	Enabled multiple users to access simultaneously from remote locations	Q16.6	3.95	11	36	10	2	-
4	Enabled to import and export of data	Q16.9	3.95	6	44	9	-	-

Rank	Statements	Q. No	Mean	SA	A	U	D	SD
5	Enabled easy cataloguing	Q16.1	3.92	12	41	1	5	2
6	Enabled more efficient and better cataloguing	Q16.2	3.88	11	41	1	4	3
7	Enabled to compile union catalogues	Q16.8	3.85	5	43	8	3	-
8	Enabled many by-products from the machine-readable records.	Q16.4	3.82	10	39	6	3	3
9	Enabled to generate thesaurus/authority files	Q16.10	3.73	5	37	13	4	-
10	Enabled to eliminate the need to maintain card catalogue	Q16.7	3.51	6	32	9	10	2

SA = Strongly Agree (5); A=Agree (4); U= Undecided (3); D= Disagree (2); SD = Strongly Disagree (1)

5.4.4. Circulation

Circulation process in a conventional system is a very lengthy and consumes much of staff time in performing repetitive works. Computer-based circulation system offers various benefits. Respondents were asked to rate 15 benefits of using IT in circulation as listed in the questionnaire. The result is presented in Table 5.21. According to the table.

The highly recognised benefits are:

- Improved accuracy and control over circulation activities,
- Facilitate easy renewal and reservation of items and
- Facilitate to send timely recall notices and reminder letters.

Table 5.21: Circulation

Rank	Statements	Q. No	Mean	SA	A	U	D	SD
1	Improved accuracy and control over circulation activities	Q17.2	4.07	9	46	5	-	-
2	Facilitate easy renewal and reservation of items	Q17.3	4.02	6	50	3	1	-
3	Facilitate to send timely recall notices and reminder letters	Q17.7	4.00	7	46	5	1	-
4	Enabled accurate circulation reports by time-period (day, week etc.,)	Q17.12	3.98	7	44	6	1	-
5	Enable instant display of status of item on loan, reserve or at bindery	Q17.4	3.97	8	44	6	2	-
6	Enabled speedy charging and discharging	Q17.1	3.90	6	46	4	4	-
7	Facilitate faster provision of details of loaned items & due-dates on request	Q17.5	3.90	9	39	8	2	1
8	Enabled automatic notification on return of reserved item to the user	Q17.8	3.88	7	41	8	3	-
9	Facilitate to handle different loan periods for different categories of users and material types	Q17.6	3.88	7	41	6	4	-
10	Enabled easy preparation of collection usage statistics	Q17.11	3.86	6	41	8	3	-
11	Enabled automatic computation of fines and printing fine receipts	Q17.10	3.84	4	44	7	3	-
12	Facilitate to answer comprehensive on-	Q17.13	3.83	7	38	11	3	-

Rank	Statements	Q. No	Mean	SA	A	U	D	SD
	line enquiries							
13	Enabled automatic blocking of circulation privileges for defaulters	Q17.9	3.79	6	38	10	4	-
14	Enabled to achieve better fulfillment rate of ILL requests	Q17.15	3.78	6	39	9	5	-
15	Facilitate to send timely mailing letters to remote users	Q17.14	3.67	6	32	15	5	-

SA = Strongly Agree (5); A=Agree (4); U= Undecided (3); D= Disagree (2); SD = Strongly Disagree (1)

5.4.5. Serials Control

The continuing nature of serial subscriptions creates problems and makes it a complex process requiring a separate control system. Computerisation offers various benefits in periodicals subscription and subsequent monitoring of the receipt of individual issues. Respondents were offered 15 benefits of using IT in serial control and asked to rate each benefit in a five point scale from strongly agree to strongly disagree. The summary of the result is presented in Table 5.22.

The highly rated benefits in computerised serials control are:

- Facilitate easy generation of subscription and renewal orders,
- Enabled accurate and up-to-date record of subscriptions and holdings and
- Facilitate faster recording the receipt of journal issues of varied periodicities.

Table 5.22: Serials Control

Rank	Statements	Q. No	Mean	SA	A	U	D	SD
1	Facilitate easy generation of subscription and renewal orders	Q18.2	4.06	8	39	5	-	-
2	Enabled accurate and up-to-date record of subscriptions and holdings	Q18.1	4.04	7	40	5	—	-
3	Facilitate faster recording the receipt of journal issues of varied periodicities	Q18.3	4.02	10	35	5	2	-
4	Facilitate to list automatically missing issues and print reminder letters	Q18.4	4.02	9	36	6	1	-
5	Facilitate to prepare lists of completed volumes and binding orders	Q18.7	4.02	8	39	5	1	-
6	Facilitate preparation of list of periodicals subscribed and received	Q18.11	4.02	6	42	3	1	-
7	Facilitate to maintain up-to-date fund utilization account	Q18.6	4.00	8	37	6	1	-
8	Facilitate estimation of the budget for the next year.	Q18.12	3.98	6	40	5	1	-
9	Facilitate up-to-date supplier performance report	Q18.10	3.88	7	34	9	2	-
10	Facilitate to generate variety of reports	Q18.15	3.88	4	40	7	-	1
11	Facilitate to prepare routing lists of serials.	Q18.5	3.85	6	34	10	2	-
12	Facilitate to answer on-line queries about the status of serials	Q18.9	3.85	7	34	7	4	-

Rank	Statements	Q. No	Mean	SA	A	U	D	SD
13	Facilitate accessioning of bound volumes and their holdings updation	Q18.8	3.81	7	33	9	4	-
14	Facilitate compilation of union catalogues	Q18.13	3.67	5	33	8	4	2
15	Facilitate cooperative acquisition of periodicals	Q18.14	3.65	4	32	11	4	1

SA = Strongly Agree (5); A=Agree (4); U= Undecided (3); D= Disagree (2); SD = Strongly Disagree (1);

5.4.6. Networking and Resource Sharing

One of the important objectives of library computerization is networking for effective sharing of resources facilities and services. Library automation provides not only a sound foundation for effective networking but also provides numerous other benefits for sharing of resources. Therefore, respondents were offered 5 benefits and asked to rate them in a five point scale from strongly agree to strongly disagree. The result of data analysis is presented in Table 5.20.

Table 5.23: Networking and Resource Sharing

Rank	Statements	Q. No	Mean	SA	A	U	D	SD
1	Facilitate better exchange and sharing of resources.	Q19.3	4.09	12	38	5	1	-
2	Enabled to participate in resource sharing library networks	Q19.2	4.07	11	39	5	1	-
3	Facilitate the establishment of library networks	Q19.1	4.07	10	42	2	2	-
4	Facilitate optimum utilization of resources	Q19.5	4.02	10	41	2	2	1
5	Enabled to promote co-ordination and co-operative activities.	Q19.4	3.88	8	38	5	5	-

SA = Strongly Agree (5); A=Agree (4); U= Undecided (3); D= Disagree (2); SD = Strongly Disagree (1);

The top three benefits ranked by respondents are:

- Facilitate better exchange and sharing of resources
- Enabled to participate in resource sharing library networks and
- Facilitate the establishment of library networks.

5.4.7. Management Information

Management needs accurate and reliable information for making appropriate and effective decisions. The generation of such critical, accurate and up-to-date information through manual system is not only difficult, expensive and time consuming but also may not be accurate and comprehensive. Computerisation offers several benefits in providing variety of information to the management for taking effective decisions. The result of data analysis is presented in Table 5.20. The respondents rated the important benefits as facilitate better presentation of proposals and reports, enabled easy monitoring and evaluation of operations and facilitated easy preparation of binding lists.

Table 5.24: Management Information

Rank	Statements	Q. No	Mean	SA	A	U	D	SD
1	Facilitate better presentation of proposals and reports	Q20.1	3.98	3	49	4	-	-
2	Enabled easy monitoring and evaluation of operations	Q20.3	3.93	4	46	4	2	-
3	Facilitated easy preparation of binding lists	Q20.4	3.89	4	44	6	2	-
4	Facilitate better quality in decision making	Q20.2	3.88	5	40	10	1	-
5	Facilitate easy stock inventory/verification	Q20.5	3.73	4	38	10	3	1

SA = Strongly Agree (5); A=Agree (4); U= Undecided (3); D= Disagree (2); SD = Strongly Disagree (1);

5.5 IMPACT OF IT ON LIBRARY INFORMATION SERVICES

Information services refer to total array of services, products and facilities offered by libraries. IT offers tremendous opportunities for libraries not only to improve the quality of existing services but also to provide information services to users. Respondents were asked to rate 15 benefits of using IT in information services. The summary of the result is presented in Table 5.25.

The highly rated benefits are:

- Enabled more complex and more specific searches by combination of search terms,
- Greatly improved accessibility through increased access points and
- Provide easier and wider access to information resources.

Table 5.25: Impact of IT on Information Services

Rank	Statements	Q. No	Mean	SA	A	U	D	SD
1	Enabled more complex and more specific searches by combination of search terms	Q21.3	4.16	13	40	2	1	-
2	Greatly improved accessibility through increased access points	Q21.6	4.07	12	38	4	2	-
3	Provide easier and wider access to information resources	Q21.4	4.07	12	39	2	3	-
4	Provide rapid access to bibliographic information on-line	Q21.5	4.07	12	37	4	2	-
5	Improved the quality of services	Q21.1	4.05	10	43	-	2	1
6	Enabled multiple users to access simultaneously	Q21.8	4.04	10	40	4	2	-

Rank	Statements	Q. No	Mean	SA	A	U	D	SD
7	Facilitate compilation of bibliographic service on specific topic	Q21.11	3.98	8	41	5	2	-
8	Introduced new range of services not possible before	Q21.2	3.95	10	35	9	2	-
9	Increased users expectations for better services	Q21.13	3.89	7	40	5	4	-
10	Enabled direct access by end-users	Q21.12	3.82	6	36	12	2	-
11	Provide more specialized, need-based and value-added services	Q21.9	3.82	5	39	7	4	-
12	Enabled extended services to remote locations	Q21.7	3.80	10	32	7	7	-
13	Improved users opinion on library services	Q21.15	3.80	5	38	10	3	-
14	Provide more comprehensive retrospective literature at less cost	Q21.10	3.79	4	40	8	4	-
15	Increased users need for staff assistance more frequently	Q21.14	3.43	2	34	6	14	-

SA = Strongly Agree (5); A=Agree (4); U= Undecided (3); D= Disagree (2); SD = Strongly Disagree (1);

Further, the cross tabulation results of chi-square test indicated that

- Staff having master's degree in library science strongly agree with IT enabled more complex and more specific searches by combination of search terms and provide rapid access to bibliographic information online.

- Staff involved in IT implementation strongly agree with provision of rapid access to bibliographic information online and agree with increased users expectations for better services.
- Staff trained in the use of IT agreed with IT enabled extended services to remote locations, direct access by end users and increased users expectations for better services.

5.6 IMPACT OF IT ON LIBRARY STAFF

IT has tremendous impact on various aspects of library staff. Impact can be both positive and negative. Respondents were asked to use a Likert Scale from strongly agree having a data value of 5 to strongly disagree having data value of 1 to respond positively or negatively worded statements. The result of the positively oriented statements is presented in Table 5.26a and negatively oriented statements in Table 5.26b. These findings confirm with Dakshinamurti (1985) and Olrgaard (1989) who stated that effects of technology on library personnel could be both positive and negative.

The highly ranked positive statements are:

- Upgraded my knowledge and skills,
- Made my work more interesting and
- Made it mandatory to learn to use modern technologies.

Further, the cross tabulation results of chi-square test indicated that

- Staff having master's degree in library science agree with IT brought major changes in staff work.
- Staff involved in IT implementation agree with IT reduced staff work load, made their work more interesting, improved their competence and performance, offered new challenges & better opportunities for professional growth and enabled to devote more of their time for user services.
- Staff having master's degree in library science agree with IT became detrimental to creative thinking.

Table 5.26a: Impact of IT on Library Staff (Positive)

Rank	Statements	Q. No	Mean	SA	A	U	D	SD
1	Upgraded my knowledge and skills	Q22.2	4.06	10	48	4	1	-
2	Made my work more interesting	Q22.9	3.92	6	50	1	5	-
3	Made it mandatory to learn to use modern technologies	Q22.1	3.89	6	47	5	4	-
4	Increased my job satisfaction	Q22.19	3.83	5	47	7	3	1
5	Created a better quality of working environment	Q22.12	3.82	5	45	6	5	-
6	Provided more variety in my work	Q22.16	3.79	4	48	5	6	-
7	Added more responsibilities to my job	Q22.8	3.76	4	47	5	7	-
8	Improved my competence and performance	Q22.13	3.76	3	49	4	7	-
9	Offered new challenges and better opportunities for professional growth	Q22.15	3.73	4	45	8	5	1
10	Improved my morale and motivation	Q22.10	3.71	4	43	8	7	-
11	Enabled to devote more of my time for user services	Q22.18	3.68	5	42	7	9	-
12	Brought major changes in my work	Q22.5	3.59	3	42	8	9	1
13	Improved my status	Q22.20	3.56	3	40	11	7	2
14	Forced to employ new staff with IT skills	Q22.3	3.06	5	23	10	19	5
15	Reduced my work load	Q22.6	3.06	1	30	9	18	5

SA = Strongly Agree (5); A=Agree (4); U= Undecided (3); D= Disagree (2); SD = Strongly Disagree (1);

The negative statements identified are: IT became detrimental to creative thinking, de-skilled the job of cataloguers and created health problems etc. From the above results, it can be stated that these problems are not seem to be serious ones, which really hinder the use of IT in CU Libraries.

Table 5.26b: Impact of IT on Library Staff (Negative)

Rank	Statements	Q. No	Mean	SA	A	U	D	SD
1	Became detrimental to creative thinking	Q22.17	3.18	2	30	9	17	3
2	De-skilled the job of cataloguers	Q22.4	2.95	-	25	12	22	3
3	Created health problems (please specify)	Q22.14	2.90	2	19	15	23	3
4	Caused techno-stress (fear of new technology)	Q22.11	2.59	-	18	6	31	6
5	Created fear of loss of job	Q22.7	2.46	1	14	9	28	11

SA = Strongly Agree (5); A=Agree (4); U= Undecided (3); D= Disagree (2); SD = Strongly Disagree (1);

5.6.1. Library Staff comments

Finally library professionals were requested to give their comments on the use of IT in library. The comments are given below.

- all staff members should be given more intensive training and provide an opportunity for hands-on practice and to work in IT based operations.
- Incentives should be given to the staff handling computers, attending training courses and acquiring IT related qualifications.
- The other comments include "IT is essential for libraries, IT provided better opportunities, improved staff skills and image of library".

5.7 IMPACT OF IT ON INFORMATION SERVICES: USERS PERCEPTIONS

UGC has recently given the status of 'University with Potential for Excellence' to the University of Hyderabad (UOH) and provided in the first instance rupees five crores as seed money (UOH, 2001). The UOH library has the distinction of being the first university library in the country to have fully automated all its housekeeping operations. The library started automation activities in 1989. It developed a database for all the book records of 2,35,000 volumes by February 1995 and now has over 2.56 lakhs of volumes including back volumes of periodicals, theses and dissertations. Computers were installed in all the sections of the library. It has replaced its card catalogue with eight Online Public Access Catalogue (OPAC) terminals for users in the library. The library database and seven drive CD Server was hooked on to the campus wide Local Area Network (LAN) to facilitate the network users to search the OPAC and CD-ROM databases from all the Schools / Departments across the campus. The library is using Barcode technology at the circulation desk for issue and return transactions. Recently 16 computers were provided for users to access Internet within the library. It has completed two turnkey projects of computerisation of libraries of Dr.B.R.Ambedker Open University and City Central Library in Hyderabad city. It has initiated the process of becoming a digital library by converting the priority materials into digital media. Users have been using OPAC both within the library as well as through network since 1995 (Rama Reddy, 2001).

The researcher has chosen UOH library as a case and selected a sample of 413 out of 2207 users to make an in-depth study on the impact of IT. Sarojini Naidu School of Performing Arts, Fine Arts and Communication located at Golden Threshold having a total of 150 students and faculty members was excluded from the sample as it was not located in the university campus. Stratified random sampling technique was used to select the sample. Accordingly, the questionnaire was designed and distributed to 413 library users of different categories including faculty members, Ph.D. and M.Phil. scholars and PG students of the UOH during February and May 2000 and received 315 duly filled-in questionnaires with a response rate of 76 percent as presented in Table 5.31. The questionnaire used in the survey divided into two parts. The first part is intended to gather data on users' background and IT facilities accessible to them in the library. The second part is to collect data about the impact of using IT on library, library services and users' satisfaction. Finally, users were requested to state the problems and give their comments relating to the use of IT in their library. The school-wise analysis of respondents is presented in Table 5.27.

Table 5.27: Survey of Library Users

S. No	No of Questionnaires	Schools / No. of Users			
		Social Sciences	Humanities	Sciences	Total
1	Distributed	135	100	178	413
2	Received	116	61	138	315
3	Percentage of response	86	61	78	76

5.7.1. Library Users' Background Information

The characteristics of respondents such as age, designation, residence, frequency of library visits, IT facilities, IT training etc. have been studied and details of data analysis tables are presented below.

5.7.1.1. Gender

Out of 315 respondents, 211 (67%) are male and 100(31.7%) are female.

Table 5.28: Gender – wise Distribution of Respondents

S. No	Gender	No of respondents	Percent	Cumulative Percent
1	Male	211	67.0	67.0
2	Female	100	31.7	98.7
3	Not responded	4	1.3	100
	Total	315	100.0	

5.7.1.2. Age

Of the total 315 respondents, the age of 250 (79.3%) was less than or equal to 30, 23 (7.3%) between 31 and 40, 20 (6.4%) between 41 and 50, 11 (3.5%) are more than 50 years old and 11(3.5%) have not given their age. The average age of respondents was 27.73 years.

Table 5.29: Age of Respondents

S. No	Age range	No of respondents	Percent
1	Less than or equal to 30 years	250	79.3
2	Between 31and 40 years	23	7.3
3	Between 41and 50 years	20	6.4
4	More than 50 years	11	3.5
5	Not responded	11	3.5
	Total	315	100

5.7.1.3. Designation

The designation wise details of the respondents are summarised in Table 5.30. As can be seen from the table that among 315 respondents, 261(82.9%) are students and 54 (17.1%) faculty members (including 17 Lecturers, 23 Readers and 14 Professors). Out of 54 Faculty members, most of them i.e., 51 (94.4%) are Doctorates, 2 (3.7%) have M.Phil. degree and only 1(1.9%) has Masters degree. Among students, 115 (36.5%) are Ph.D. scholars followed by 68 (21.6%). P.G. II year students.

Table 5.30: Designation -wise Distribution of Respondents

S. No	Category	Population	Sample %	Sample	No of Respondents	% of response
1	P.G I yr.	615	10	62	48	77
2	P.G II yr.	478	15	72	68	94
3	M. Phil	187	20	37	30	81
4	Ph.D.	725	25	181	115	64
5	Faculty	202	30	61	54	89
	Total	2,207	100	413	315	76

5.7.1.4 Residential Status

Regarding residential status, out of 315 respondents, a majority of 234 (74.3%) reside in the campus while 67(21.3%) not.

Table 5.31: Respondents' Residential Status

S. No	Campus Residence	No of respondents	%	Cumulative %
1	Yes	234	74.3	74.3
2	No	67	21.3	95.6
3	Not responded	14	4.4	100
	Total	315	100.0	

5.7.1.5. Frequency of Library Visits

When the information about frequency of library visits of respondents is analysed, out of 315 responded, 148 (47%) visit library daily followed by 122 (38.7%) weekly. This clearly indicates the due importance given to the library as well as the interest of users towards studies.

Table 5.32: Frequency of Library Visits by Respondents

S. No	Frequency of Library Visits	No. of respondents	%	Cumulative %
1	Never	1	.3	.3
2	Occasionally	20	6.4	6.7
3	Monthly	7	2.2	8.9
4	Fortnightly	16	5.1	14.0
5	Weekly	122	38.7	52.7
6	Daily	148	47.0	99.7
7	Not responded	1	.3	100
	Total	315	100	

5.7.1.6. Library Use Experience

Users might have been using library for varied periods of duration. The analysis of respondents' library use experience is presented in Table 5.33. Regarding the total length of the library use experience, 233 (74%) respondents have less than or equal to 5 years of experience, 47 (14.8%) between 6-10 years, 17 (5.3%) between 11 –15 years and 9 (2.9%) have more than 20 years of service. The average library use experience of respondents is 4.79 years.

Table 5.33: Library Use Experience of Respondents

S. No.	Library Use Experience	No of respondents	Percentage
1	Less than or equal to 5 years	233	74
2	Between 6 and 10 years	47	14.8
3	Between 11and 15 years	17	5.3
4	Between 16and 20 years	6	2.0
5	More than 20 years	9	2.9
6	Not responded	3	1
	Total	315	100

5.7.1.7. IT Training

The need for orientation/training in use of the new technologies has been emphasized in a number of studies conducted on library users. Respondents were asked to indicate whether they were given any training in the use of IT in their library. Out of 315 respondents, 174 (55.2%) indicated yes and 140 (44.5%) no.

Regarding assessment of quality of training, respondents indicated variations in the quality of training received in their libraries. Out of 174 trained, 4 (2.3%) stated that the training they received was extensive, the largest number of 112 (64.4%) adequate, 18 (10.3%) inadequate and 38 (21.8%) respondents indicated the need for more training. This finding shows that not only more number of users need to be trained but also the mode, module and quality of orientation/

training courses need to be thoroughly revised and improved to suit the different learning styles of users as to make the best use of IT based facilities and services.

Table 5.34: IT Training of Respondents

S.No	IT Training	No. of Respondents	Percent
1	Yes	174	55.2
2	No	140	44.5
3	Not responded	1	0.3
	Total	315	100.0

Table 5.35: Assessment of IT Training by Respondents

S. No	Assessment	No of respondents	Percent
1	Extensive	4	2.3
2	Adequate	112	64.4
3	Inadequate	18	10.3
4	Need more training	38	21.8
5	Not responded	2	1.2
	Total	174	100.0

5.7.1.8. IT Facilities

Most of the departments now have IT facilities. Respondents were asked to indicate the IT facilities accessible to them in their department. The result of the analysis is presented in Table 5.36. According to the Table, 199 (63.2%) respondents indicated having access to the computer in their department, followed by OPAC with 123 (39%) LAN with 72 (22.9%) and Internet with 118 (37.5%). This finding demonstrates that majority of respondents are not having access to OPAC, LAN and Internet in the department. Therefore, there is a need to strengthen IT facilities in the departments in order to provide easy access to IT based information resources and services.

Table 5.36: IT facilities of Respondents

S. No	IT Facilities	Computer		OPAC		LAN		Internet	
		N	%	N	%	N	%	N	%
1	Available	199	63.2	123	39	72	22.9	118	37.5
2	Not available	116	36.8	192	61	243	77.1	197	62.5
	Total	315	100	315	100	315	100	315	100

N=No. of respondents

5.7.2. Impact of IT on Library

In order to assess the impact of using IT on library, respondents were asked to rate the improvement in 15 aspects listed in the questionnaire. The five point scale ranging from '5=Very much improved' to '1=Deteriorated' has been used. Most respondents acknowledged the improvement in all the stated aspects of using IT in their libraries. The average scores on the 15 aspects were high ranging from 3.88 to 3.31. The analysis of responses is summarized in Table 5.37.

Users rated access to collection, status (image/reputation) and efficiency of library as the highly improved aspects of using IT. The other aspects affected by using IT are presented in the decreasing order of their rank in Table 5.43.

Further, the cross tabulation results of chi-square test indicated that

- Male users are in favour of very much improved while female are for much improved with quality of services.
- Users residing in the campus opined that the access to collection is much improved.
- Weekly visitors rated user friendliness as good and daily visitors as poor. Users visiting daily and weekly rated that the services as much improved after using IT.

- Users trained in the use of new technologies in their library rated in favour of very much improved for services, staff competence, staff attitude, user friendliness and user satisfaction.

Table 5.37: Impact of Information Technology on Library

Rank	Statements	Q. No	Mean	SA	A	U	D	SD
1	Information sources/ collection	Q8.1	3.88	69	160	66	18	2
2	Status (image/reputation)	Q8.13	3.84	77	131	88	18	1
3	Efficiency	Q8.14	3.77	58	150	86	17	4
4	User-friendliness	Q8.9	3.75	70	133	77	33	2
5	Aesthetics (pleasant atmosphere/appearance)	Q8.11	3.70	70	125	78	34	6
6	Satisfaction	Q8.12	3.70	59	134	94	25	3
7	Services	Q8.3	3.67	55	130	104	24	2
8	Utilization (Resources/ services usage)	Q8.5	3.65	49	132	114	16	4
9	Collection Arrangement	Q8.2	3.62	47	139	95	31	3
10	Effectiveness (how well library satisfies your demands)	Q8.15	3.59	38	141	111	19	6
11	Physical facilities (Study environment)	Q8.8	3.57	67	104	90	48	6
12	Staff attitude (helpfulness)	Q8.7	3.50	48	129	80	50	8
13	Staff competence (knowledge & expertise)	Q8.6	3.48	36	122	119	34	4
14	Communication (Staff-user interaction)	Q8.10	3.44	52	99	102	60	2
15	Innovation (new ways of service)	Q8.4	3.31	34	89	134	56	2

VI= Very much Improved (5); MI= Much Improved (4); LI= Little Improved (3); NI= Not Improved (2); D=Deteriorated (1);

5.7.3. Impact of IT on Information Services

IT has potential not only to improve the quality of existing services but also to offer wide range of new services. IT enables libraries to provide various benefits in terms of improved services. Therefore, respondents were asked to rate the benefits of using IT in their libraries on a five point scale from strongly agree to strongly disagree. The result of data analysis is presented in Table 5.38. The most recognised benefits of using IT in information services are: enormously saved time and efforts, improved the quality of services and provide more flexible and comprehensive retrieval than manual system.

Table 5.38: Impact of Information Technology on Information Services

Rank	Statements	Q. No	Mean	SA	A	U	D	SD
1	Enormously saved time and efforts	Q9.18	4.15	103	172	26	13	1
2	Improved the quality of services	Q9.2	4.14	88	193	24	10	--
3	Provide more flexible & comprehensive retrieval than manual system	Q9.13	4.14	112	150	38	14	1
4	Found the OPAC (computer catalogue) easy to use	Q9.3	4.13	100	173	29	9	4
5	It is easy and quick to search and find information about collection	Q9.11	4.09	98	172	25	16	4
6	Enabled to borrow, return, renew and reserve documents quickly	Q9.16	3.97	107	137	34	29	8
7	OPAC displays the status of documents instantly	Q9.12	3.94	78	167	48	17	5
8	Created better opportunities	Q9.19	3.90	75	162	54	19	5

	to improve academic pursuits							
9	OPAC has increased the success rate of finding more relevant materials	Q9.10	3.86	67	165	60	19	4
10	Reference / information enquiries answered satisfactorily	Q9.17	3.84	71	162	50	24	8
11	Provided comfortable desk tables and chairs to use OPAC	Q9.4	3.83	74	163	38	29	11
12	Introduced new services	Q9.2	3.81	55	172	64	21	3
13	OPAC provided powerful search facility by combination of terms	Q9.9	3.80	59	170	56	23	7
14	OPAC provided many access points to documents	Q9.8	3.71	46	177	56	26	10
15	Enabled direct access to information	Q9.6	3.61	39	167	60	45	4
16.	Campus network enabled many users to access OPAC simultaneously	Q9.14	3.58	59	130	75	33	17
17	Enabled to publish more publications (articles)	Q9.20	3.37	38	100	128	38	11
18	Campus network enabled easy access to OPAC from remote locations	Q9.14	3.35	51	102	91	46	24
19	There are an adequate number of public access terminals	Q9.5	3.29	26	151	48	69	21
20	IT based services are more complex to use	Q9.7	2.71	24	69	62	112	48

SA = Strongly Agree (5); A=Agree (4); U= Undecided (3); D= Disagree (2); SD = Strongly Disagree (1);

Further, the cross tabulation results of chi-square test indicated that

- Users residing in the campus agreed with IT enormously saved time and effort.
- Daily visiting users strongly agree with the improvement in quality of services and enabling users to borrow, return, renew and reserve documents quickly. Daily visiting users strongly agree, weekly visiting users agree with reference and information enquiries answered satisfactorily and enormously saved time and efforts. Daily and weekly visiting users are towards agreement with the creation of better opportunities to improve academic pursuits.
- Users trained in the use of new technologies strongly agree with improved quality of services, OPAC has increased the success rate of finding more relevant materials, enabled to borrow, return, renew and reserve documents quickly, Reference and information enquiries answered satisfactorily, and enormously saved time and efforts.

5.7.4. Impact of IT on User Satisfaction

Respondents were asked to indicate their satisfaction for the computerised services offered in their library on a five point scale: 1=Not available; 2=Poor; 3=Average; 4=Good; 5=Excellent.

The average scores are ranged from 4.06 to 2.22. The result of data analysis is presented in Table 5.39. The highly rated services are: OPAC (Computer catalogue), Automated lending/circulation and maintaining in-house databases. The other services are listed in the table in the decreasing order of their scores.

Further, the cross tabulation results of chi-square test indicated that

- Faculty members have rated CAS ranging from good to excellent while students rated as average.
- Users trained in the use of new technologies rated good for CDROM database service.

Table 5.39: Impact of Information Technology on User Satisfaction

Rank	Services	Q. No.	Mean	E*	G	A	P	NA
1	OPAC (Computer catalogue)	Q10.1	4.06	95	164	44	5	7
2	Automated lending/ circulation	Q10.2	3.58	62	140	68	9	36
3	Maintaining in-house databases	Q10.3	3.41	37	136	91	22	29
4	Bibliographical service	Q10.8	3.40	53	121	72	36	32
5	Reference Service	Q10.7	3.38	44	121	84	42	24
6	Current Awareness Service (CAS)	Q10.9	3.11	30	108	92	36	49
7	Indexing / Abstracting	Q10.11	2.71	28	85	70	32	100
8	SDI (Personalized Information Service to users)	Q10.10	2.53	24	70	70	37	114
9	Internet Access	Q10.6	2.39	28	58	46	60	123
10	Inter-library loan	Q10.12	2.30	18	38	82	60	117
11	CD-ROM Databases service	Q10.4	2.25	19	50	65	38	143
12	Access to Online External (outside) databases	Q10.5	2.22	21	45	60	45	143

*E= Excellent (5), G= Good (4), A = Average (3), P= Poor (2), NA= Not available (1)

5.7.5. Users' Comments

Finally, users were asked three open-ended questions to indicate their expected IT based new services, the problems they faced and their comments on the use of IT in library.

The new IT based services expected by users include procurement of more CD-ROM databases, improve internet access facility in library, provision of access to external online databases and subscription of electronic journals.

The problems faced by the users in the use of IT include the need for more training in the use of IT based facilities/services including faculty members, increased access to IT based facilities in the departments and OPAC should indicate location of shelf, rack etc.

The general comments of the users in the use of IT in library are given below:

- IT is very useful in libraries as it provides good facilities and saves lot time and efforts.
- Providing access to the resources of other libraries.
- Networking reduced the visits to library.
- Online access to OPAC should be available for all the 24 hours.
- Provision of easy access to OPAC in the departments.
- Staff should have more user-friendly attitude.
- Overall computerized services are good in UOH library.
- IT based services need to be further improved.

5.8 CONCLUSION

The perceptions of staff on the impact of using IT in CU Libraries were studied through distribution of questionnaires to the 100 staff members of eight CU Libraries actively involved in using IT. The rate of response is 64%. The characteristics of the staff are: 73% are male while 27% are female; 50% belongs to 41 to 50 years age group; more than 50% of staff have two masters degrees both in general education as well as in library science; one third of staff are in the UGC cadres of UL, DL and AL while the rest are professional staff. Half of the staff have total experience of more than 20 years. The major findings based on the analysis have been summarised below:

1. There is a significant improvement in the IT skills / knowledge of library staff as the number of library personnel attended training courses, conferences/seminars and presented/ published papers has tremendously increased from 18 (28.2%)

before IT implementation to 61 (95.4%) after IT implementation.

2. More than two-third of the staff members were involved in IT implementation process. All those involved accepted that it helped them to improve their performance in the library. More than half 38 (59.4%) of library staff were provided IT training in their libraries, of which two third felt that training was inadequate and need more training.

3. Regarding IT facilities, almost all staff members reported that they were provided computers while about 50% were provided facilities like printer, LAN and Internet. More than half of the respondents are spending from 26 to 75 percent (two to six hours) of their time working on computer at workplace in libraries. More than three-fourth of library staff is showing enthusiasm towards IT. Most of the respondents have gained IT work experience within the last ten years.

4. Library staff perceive that the highly improved aspects of using IT include efficiency, effectiveness and user satisfaction of the library. The results of Chi-square indicated that the staff involved in IT implementation and attended more training courses have more positive perceptions about the improvement of efficiency, productivity and services of the library.

5. The positive and negative of effects of using IT in library as perceieved by the staff, have been studied. The important positive effects recognized by staff include facilitated networking and resource sharing, eliminated duplication of efforts and improved speed of operations while increased expenditure on systems maintenance, reduced inter-personal communication and increased violation of copyright Act as the major negative effects of using IT in library. The results of chi-square indicated that the staff spending between 50-75% of their time working at computer per day agreed to enormous savings in time and efforts while staff involved in IT implementation agreed to the improved speed of operations. Regarding negative effects, staff trained in the use of IT agreed

to frequent systems breakdown and frequent virus problem.

6. The perception of staff have been studied regarding the benefits of using IT in all house-keeping operations and information services. IT enabled faster pre-order duplicate checking, facilitate easy preparation of purchase orders and enable to keep updated vendor database are rated as the highly acknowledged benefits in computerised acquisition while IT enabled speed and ease in cataloguing, enabled many access points and in-depth subject cataloguing and multiple users to access simultaneously from remote locations and enabled easy checking of previously assigned call numbers, saving time by avoiding frequent consultation of schemes and easy construction of call numbers as the most important benefits of computerised cataloguing and classification respectively.

7. Improved accuracy and control over circulation activities, facilitate easy renewal and reservation of items and sending timely recall notices and reminder letters are the highly recognised benefits in computerised circulation while IT facilitate easy generation of subscription and renewal orders, enabled accurate and up-to-date record of subscriptions and holdings, and faster recording the receipts of journal issues of varied periodicities are the highly acknowledged benefits in automated serials control.

8. The most important benefits in networking and resource sharing as perceived by library staff include IT facilitate better exchange and sharing of resources, enabled easy participation in resource sharing library networks and facilitate the establishment of library networks while facilitate better presentation of proposals and reports, enabled easy monitoring and evaluation of operations and facilitated easy preparation of binding lists as the major benefits in management information.

9. The highly recognised benefits in computerisation of library services include IT enabled more complex and more specific

searches by combination of search terms, greatly improved accessibility through increased access points and provide easier and wider access to information resources. Staff involved in IT implementation strongly agree with provision of rapid access to bibliographic information on line and more specialized, need-based value-added services to users while staff trained agreed to the extended services to remote locations and increased users' expectations for better services as result of using IT in library.

10. The positive and negative effects of using IT on library staff have been studied. The highly ranked positive effects include upgraded knowledge and skills, made work more interesting and made it mandatory to learn to use modern technologies, while IT became detrimental to creative thinking, deskilled the job of cataloguers and created health problems are the major negative effects of using IT on staff. Staff involved in IT implementation accepted that IT has reduced their workload, made their work more interesting, improved their competence and performance, offered new challenges and better opportunities for professional growth and enabled to devote more of their time for user services.

    The perceptions of users on the impact of using IT on library information services has also been studied from user perspective at the UOH library. A sample of 413 users was distributed a questionnaire and received completed responses from 315 users with a response rate of 76%. The characteristics of users reveal that 67% are male and 32% are female; 74% are campus residents while 21% are day scholars. The user community comprises 37% PG students, 46% M.Phil. and Ph.D. scholars and 17% are faculty members.

11. The users reported that they were provided access to Computer (63.2%), OPAC (39%), LAN (23%) and Internet (37.5%) in their departments. This reveals that access to OPAC, LAN and Internet needs to be improved. More than half of the users

(55%) indicated that they had received training in the use of IT in the library. Of these, 67 percent felt that the training is adequate.

12. The users' assessment of the Impact of using IT in library reveals that access to collection, status (image/reputation) and efficiency have been recognised as highly improved aspects of the library.
13. The highly ranked benefits of using IT in library information services are: IT enormously saved time and efforts, improved the quality of services and provide more flexible and comprehensive retrieval than manual system.
14. The highly rated computerized services by the users in UOH Library include OPAC, automated circulation and maintenance of in-house databases.

5.9 REFERENCES

Abifarin, F.P. (1993). Availability and use of information technologies in Nigerian university libraries. *Library Review,* 42(5), 4-14.

Haravu, L. J. (1993). Library automation and networking in India: An overview of recent developments. *Annals of Library Science and Documentation,* 40(1), 32-40.

Jones, D.E. (1989). Library support staff and technology: Perceptions and opinions. *Library Trends,* 37(4), 432-456.

Jones, Dorothy E. (1999). Ten years later: Support staff perceptions and opinions on technology in the workplace. *Library Trends,* 47(4), 711-739.

Kumar, P.S.G. (1987). *Computerisation of Indian libraries.* Delhi: B.R. publishing corporation. 334p.

Lancaster, F. W., & Sandore, B. (1997). *Technology and management in library and information services* .(pp.1). Urbana-champaign: University of Illinois. Graduate School of Library and Information Science.

Rama Reddy, E (2001). University of Hyderabad: University library automation activities (pp.4). (mimeographed)

Shaw, D. (1986). Staff opinions in library automation planning: a case study. *Special libraries,* 77(3), 140-151.

University of Hyderabad (2001). *Prospectus 2001-2002.* Hyderabad: UOH.

6

Strategies For Managing Technological Change in Libraries

6.1 INTRODUCTION

Information Technology (IT) is a driving force for change in libraries. Libraries are experiencing enormous changes due to application of new technologies. The magnitude and speed of technological change in recent years has been phenomenal which may likely to continue at much faster rate in the foreseeable future. The rapid technological change and transformation has tremendous impact on organisation's decision makers, library operations, resources, services, staff and users. A very rapid rate of technological innovations has made it imperative to consider technology as the crucial factor influencing the functioning and management of modern library. Information technology is transforming libraries at a speed unimaginable just a few decades ago. The most pronounced difference between the digital/virtual library of today and the traditional library of yester year is the result of rapid pace of technological change taking place in libraries.

Technological changes have been of such magnitude that it is difficult for individuals and often institutions to follow them. In several technological sectors such as the information sector, more changes have occurred in the last few decades than in the previous few thousand years (Pritchett, 1994).

Information technologies today are characterized by their very dynamic development and increasing complexity. The new technologies allow completely new solutions to old problems, and consequently old services are displaced by new services. In the current turbulent phase of information technological development, this process of displacement of old solutions by new ones is particularly difficult to steer (Hofmann, 1995).

Libraries are undergoing a profound transformation reflecting a sea change in the nature and type of functions and services due to the application of new technologies. According to Cohn et al (1998), the four basic functions of libraries in an electronic age are:

- Providing access to the content of local resources (e.g. books, periodicals, media, electronic resources) that are part of the library's collection.
- Offering gateway access to remote resources (e.g. books, periodicals, media electronic, resources), including the ability to obtain copies in print and electronic formats.
- Facilitating off-site electronic access to local and remote resources from users' homes, offices and schools.
- Providing access to human assistance in locating information.

In conjunction with the rapid pace of technological change, there have been phenomenal rise in users' expectations for higher quality of information products and services. The rapid change in technology coupled with users' higher expectations has forced libraries to shift from the use of traditional methods to the highly powerful new technology. In today's dynamic environment of the rapidly changing nature of technology, strategic planning for managing new technology has become more crucial for harnessing its full potential and benefits. The strategies enable not only in selecting and implementing right technologies but also helps in identifying appropriate automated operations and services that would best meet the users needs and fulfill the mission of the library. Libraries must develop their capabilities and design innovative strategies to keep abreast of technological changes and to harness full potential of new technology. The strategy of libraries to continuously embrace technological change and to manage new technologies has become essential for survival, growth, development and success.

Modern technologies have brought dramatic changes in today's library management and users expectations. Application of IT solutions to library operations and information services is a very complex and challenging process. Libraries are facing variety of issues, problems, threats and challenges in the introduction, use and management of new technologies. Identifying the problems, understanding the issues and formulation of sound strategies are the keys to the successful management of technological change in libraries. Libraries intending to use IT applications should have strategic planning, innovative ideas and intelligent strategies for successful implementation and utilization of modern technologies.

This chapter discusses the rationale for IT applications in libraries, key factors in strategic technology planning and strategies to be adopted for the management of technological changes in libraries.

6.2 RATIONALE FOR INFORMATION TECHNOLOGY APPLICATIONS IN LIBRARIES

Information technology has virtually unlimited potential for variety of applications in libraries. Several people have given varied reasons for IT applications in libraries. The main reasons for IT applications in libraries are to:

- Increase the efficiency of library operations
- Improve the effectiveness of existing services
- Offer a wide range of new services
- Perform tasks which cannot be done by the manual system
- Improve accuracy and control over operations
- Eliminate duplication of efforts
- Enable easy participation in resource sharing library networks
- Enable rapid communication with other libraries
- Generate better management information reports
- Facilitate marketing of information products and services
- Provide gateway access to global digital information resources
- Meet users rising expectations for complex information needs.

In the light of drastically decreasing prices and tremendously increasing capabilities of IT hardware, software and communication equipment, use of new information technologies has become affordable for all types and sizes of libraries. The detailed reasons for IT applications in libraries are given elsewhere at 2.2.

6.3 KEY FACTORS IN STRATEGIC TECHNOLOGY PLANNING

Libraries use IT to increase the efficiency and effectiveness of their operations and services. Information Technology is highly dynamic, fast changing and become obsolete so quickly in such a short span that even before one technology is fully received, understood, implemented and used, an improved version or a new technology is being developed. One cannot service tomorrow's users with yesterday's technology. Constant up-gradations in technology have become essential for survival and success. In fact, keeping up with new technologies is the biggest problem faced by the people around the world. Practically, it is becoming increasingly difficult for the libraries to keep pace with these rapid technological changes especially in developing countries where resources are scarce. Managing new technologies has become an expensive, complex and challenging task requiring the formulation of strategic planning and sound strategies to achieve success.

Strategic planning is a key to the successful management of technological change in libraries. Implementation of IT to library operations is a complex and continuous process. It requires innovative ideas, intelligent planning and huge investment of financial as well as human resources. Libraries intending to use IT have to plan systematically well in advance for successful implementation to derive maximum benefits and to minimise problems. Libraries should develop a sound technology plan to make use of the new technologies in an efficient and cost effective manner.

A number of factors like organizations environment, management support, leadership, financial resources, staff competence, users information needs and expectations need to be studied for designing sound strategies for the management of technological change in libraries.

The following are some of the key factors that should be considered for effective planning and implementation of new information technologies in libraries successfully.

6.3.1. Organisational Environment

The introduction and use of new technologies in libraries will become quite easier and successful only when organisational environment is conducive and supportive. The environment for change is the state of organisation's preparedness for acceptance and introduction of change. An environment that supports technological change in an organization's library would be one in which change is seen as a normal process, and in which the organizations decision makers, library users and library staff are familiar with technological developments and their potential application in the library (Klobas, 1990).

6.3.2. Management Support

Since library is a part of a wider parent organization, librarian alone cannot take decision of IT implementation in library. He has to depend on management for taking such decision. As IT needs heavy investment, the whole-hearted support of management is essential for its successful implementation in library. Top management need to be fully involved right from the beginning of the technology planning process to the decisions concerning IT implementation in library. They should be persuaded, educated and convinced about the potential benefits of IT in various library operations and services to get their support and cooperation. The decision makers in the parent organization need to be made aware of the new developments and opportunities presented by the new technologies, if they are to support the change proposal and implementation process. They should be well informed about the progress of new technological developments through regular management meetings and sending technology update news bulletins periodically.

The responsibility of getting management support however has to be taken by professional librarian who must demonstrate a commitment to modernization including the use of IT for real benefits to the users community. The most effective way of obtaining management support is via user groups (e.g. students, faculty, research scholars, scientists, etc.). Librarians in India need to take a more proactive approach in influencing decisions concerning resource allocation for the modernization of libraries (Haravu, 1995).

6.3.3. Leadership

The success of IT implementation depends to a great extent on the availability of competent leader with in the library. Leader is a driving force for implementation of new technologies in library. Librarian must play the role of a leader who must be committed and shoulder full responsibility from the planning stage to the successful completion of IT implementation process. He has to plan, direct, control and guide the change management process. He must be able to convince decision makers and communicate with all levels of staff members, interact with users and work in a team environment. The leader must forecast the emerging future technologies and strive to implement and promote their effective use in libraries. He should have people skills, communication skills, knowledge of the library's operations and familiarity with various aspects of library technology, financial resources required and human aspects of technological change in libraries. Without librarian's strong commitment, it is difficult to achieve success in introducing, using and maintaining new technologies in libraries. The success of library automation is increasingly dependent on the commitment of a leader in using new technologies.

6.3.4. Financial Resources

Financial resources are one of the most important factors contributing for the successful implementation of new technologies in libraries. IT needs heavy investment for its implementation in the library. Cost involved in acquisition of hardware, software, databases and computerization, networking and their continued maintenance is very large that many organizations are not able to take decisions so easily to invest in IT. Further, it is difficult to anticipate all costs associated with fast changing nature of emerging dynamic technologies. At the time of allocation of funds, library is being given low priority as compared to other departments in most of the organizations. As a result, libraries are not getting adequate resources required for procuring modern information technologies. Due to fast changing technologies, obsolescence in information technology is so high that it is becoming increasingly difficult for libraries to keep pace with these new technologies without adequate resources.

Adequate funds are essential for implementation of new technologies. Funds must be provided annually to install new technology or to maintain existing technology and to update or replace obsolete technology on a regular basis. Financial resources need to be planned carefully taking into account both current and future requirements for managing technological change in libraries. Management must be made aware of the need, usefulness of IT and motivated to allocate more funds for introducing or up gradation of modern technologies in library management.

Today, funds are being provided for modernization and implementation of new technologies in libraries by many external bodies viz. UGC, CSIR, ICAR, ICMR, ICSSR, NISSAT and Department of Science and Technology. These bodies are providing funds for projects related to IT applications in libraries. Librarians must submit well-prepared project proposals clearly indicating the objectives, activities, funds required and time schedules for implementation of new technologies in their libraries.

6.3.5. Staff Competence

One of the most important factors for successful implementation of information technology is the level of competence of the staff (Hofmann, 1995). One of the major problems in effective use of information technology in libraries is the shortage of technically skilled and competent manpower. Without adequate knowledge, staff members working at computers have to spend a lot of time for learning, experimenting and using IT applications in real situations. Staff members feel that these rapidly changing technologies actually interfere with their job. Further, it is found that the staff experience increased techno stress as a result of attending to both routine as well as automation works simultaneously. Working knowledge of IT in library personnel is fundamental for its successful implementation in library. IT has immense potential for handling various library functions. To make full use of this potential in library management, it is essential that the library should have adequate personnel who have thorough knowledge of IT applications in libraries. But in practice, most of the library personnel do not have adequate level of knowledge and competence of IT applications in libraries. Working knowledge can be gained only when one is given an intensive training and gets practical hands on experience in using IT.

IT is one of the most rapidly changing areas in the library environment. Keeping up with changes and trends in library technology involves several tactics. The important include 1) Arrange short term training courses for staff on library automation, databases, LAN, Internet and other timely needed current topics. 2) Arrange staff visit to successfully automated libraries. 3)Attending professional meetings, conferences and seminars. 4) Reading professional literature. 5) Personal contacts with experienced fellow professionals. 6) Brochures of new software packages, products and services. 7) Participation in professional news & discussion groups and 8) Subscribing mailing lists.

6.3.6. Staff Involvement

Staff acceptance is another important factor contributing to the successful use of IT in libraries. No new technologies will be successfully implemented without the acceptance, full support and commitment of all levels of library staff. It is a human tendency to resist change. As some of library staff still lack knowledge of IT, they are not convinced of the use of IT and so not willing to respond positively to the change of new technologies. There is also a psychological fear in the minds of the library staff that the use of IT in libraries may lead to retrenchment/unemployment. It should be made clear to the staff that IT is used to introduce new services and make improvements and not to reduce either the existing library services/ employees. Further they must be convinced that the rapid spread of IT use will lead to a tremendous demand for skilled personnel. Therefore, they must be assured that no one is going to loose his job as a result of the introduction of IT in libraries.

The success of use of IT in library depends on the extent to which supervisory and operational staffs are involved in its planning, design, analysis and implementation. The psychological barriers to change must be cleared in the initial stage involving all the staff in its implementation. Staff involved in IT implementation project need to be trained and must be made aware of the latest developments and be fully involved in the project process and provided guidelines with examples (Msuya, 1990).

Library staff involvement must be multifunctional and multilevel in the technology planning process. Staff involvement in planning process will create interest, improve motivation and ultimately extend full support and cooperation for successful implementation of new technologies. A number of committees and sub committees involving key persons from all levels of library staff are to be constituted in planning, decision-making and implementation of new technologies in libraries. Library staff should be kept informed periodically about the plans, decisions, activities and progress of the IT implementation process in the library.

6.3.7. Staff Training

Most often, emphasis is placed on the hardware and software aspects of the technology without giving due importance to staff training and development that is needed to ensure effective use of potential benefits of technology. Training library personnel and providing facilities for hands on experience in using computers are important aspects to be given serious consideration. Continuous training on emerging technologies is necessary to develop, maintain and improve skills, knowledge and competencies. An intensive need-based practical oriented training should be imparted to library personnel to instill confidence in order to handle and manipulate new technologies. Further, the staff may also be deputed to libraries, which are in advanced state of automation for gaining knowledge and hand-on experience in using IT.

The successful implementation of new technologies can be achieved duly by involving, training and bringing the entire library staff together in a team so that they are motivated to contribute greater levels of performance. Library staff should be provided adequate training to have thorough understanding and knowledge of the IT potentials on library and information products and services. The knowledge, skill and interest in various aspects of IT will need to be constantly upgraded among the library staff. Due to fast changing technological developments, continuous in-service training for working library staff is essential for not only to keep them well informed about the latest developments in their fields but also to learn new skills in the use of modern information technologies.

The introduction of new and advanced technologies into the libraries immediately results in different skill requirements. Once the decision to adopt a new technology has been made, management must anticipate and determine, before implementation, the skills necessary to run the new installations efficiently and effectively. Library staff needs to keep abreast of recent developments in technological innovations through a variety of means such as books and journals, professional meetings, and continuing education programs. They must be sent to automate libraries for personal observation and practical experience in handling different technologies. Management must anticipate the skill requirements of new technologies scheduled for implementation and develop operational plans to match existing staff skills through retraining and relocating measures with minimal disruption to operations and minimal adverse effects on the existing staff.

6.3.8. User Education

The success of IT implementation in libraries depends greatly on the extent of users acceptance and their satisfaction. User is the kingpin of the library. Users should be kept well informed about new technological developments so that they can understand, accept and make more effective use of IT based new services. Informed users can appreciate and may even encourage the library or its parent organisation to adopt new technologies. Active marketing approach is the key for user acceptance. Higher levels of user acceptance and utilization can be achieved by well-designed training programme, effective marketing strategy and improved accessibility to computerized services. These services must be accessible and usable not only in the library buildings but also in academic departments and student hostels/residences round the clock. Effective promotion and marketing campaign strategies need to be planned and adopted so that users are alerted to the new facilities, products and services offered by the new technologies in libraries. Different approaches, modes of teaching skills and time schedules are to be planned for educating different categories of users using manual, lecture and practical demonstration methods. Provide individual instruction and group training programmes in the use of new technologies and electronic reference and information resources.

6.3.9. Communication

Implementation of new technologies in libraries affects different groups of people in various ways. These groups will need to be informed of different aspects of the process and progress of different stages of IT implementation in library. Effective communication at all stages with all the groups viz decision makers, library staff, users and the technology vendors is essential for successful management of technological change in library. There are a variety of communication methods that can be used for different groups for different purposes. They include regular staff meetings, periodical technology update news bulletins and training progarmmes.

6.3.10. Security and Safety

Another important factor that deserves careful attention is the security and safely of data. Fire extinguishers and other safety measures are to be provided. The security problems faced in most of the libraries are theft, physical damage, loss of files etc., Computer viruses are one of the most serious problems affecting the development and use of databases in libraries. The effect of virus ranges from humorous to the catastrophe. Computer users, professionals, organizations and institutions have been seriously affected in terms of losing valuable data and program files by the viruses. As library databases are usually huge and contain valuable data, it is necessary to protect expensive resources and data from mishandling, deletion, unauthorized access and viruses. A well planned security policy and program is essential to protect valuable electronic information resources. Backup facilities for storage and protection of data in the case of corruption of files have to provided on a regular basis. Use of anti-virus programs and passwords are the acceptable means of providing security. The computer room should be secure and accessible only to authorised persons.

6.4 STRATEGIES FOR MANAGING TECHNOLOGICAL CHANGE IN LIBRARIES

Library developments brought by the new information technologies in the past two decades have clearly demonstrated that the application of IT solutions in library is no longer a matter of choice but is a matter of survival in the global digital information era. Successful achievement of library goals and satisfaction of users rising expectations in times of fast-changing technological environment demands the development of sound strategies. The management must formulate innovative and intelligent strategies which will contribute significantly to the successful management of technological change in libraries.

The following are some of the important strategies to be adopted for successful management of technological changes in libraries.

6.4.1. Setting Objectives

For effective implementation of any IT application, the objectives of a new system should be clearly defined. Clearly stated objectives are the keys for successful IT Implementation. The objectives must be revised / redefined and made as user oriented as possible. List the major and specific objectives for different sections of the library that will be accomplished through the use of technology. The objectives should be specific, realistic and easily measurable in quantitative measures. Well-defined objectives will form sound basis for effective strategic planning of financial resources, activities, processes, procedures and services. The objectives can include offering more efficient and effective delivery of current services or to add new services to help carry out the mission of the library.

6.4.2. Assessment of existing system

Introduction of new technologies in libraries is a major complex process, which requires through examination and analysis of various aspects & activities. Before introducing any new technology it is useful to do a formal study to investigate the existing system, find out the limitations, examine various options, assess the potential benefits of new technologies and identify the needed resources for implementation of new technologies. The study collects the basic statistical information about collections, acquisitions circulations, services and users for complete description of the existing system. The assessment of existing system should involve collecting, organizing and analyzing facts about the current system's objectives, functions, processing operations, work flows, size of files, inputs, outputs and resources. It surveys user needs in order to assess their expected services from a new system. User needs assessment can be done either through existing use patterns, interview, observation or surveys. The assessment should be done by a committee consisting of library staff, and computer specialists. Thorough assessment of the existing system will enable us to study and identify the requirements for the development of logical design of the new system.

6.4.3. Identifying Priorities

Based on the information collected in the previous steps, it is necessary to determine which library functions should be automated and in what order of priority. In setting priorities, the factors considered include increased efficiency in manual operations, service improvements, high priority user needs and cost effectiveness.

There are usually three factors that drive automation priorities in the typical library. 1) Manual processes that can be performed more efficiently using technology; 2) Services or service improvements that are a high priority for users 3) New services or service improvements that provide significant benefit in relation to cost. The functions most often automated include development of database, online public access catalogue (OPAC), acquisitions, circulation and serials control (Cohn et al, 1998; 19).

6.4.4. Development of Specifications for the required system

Once the decision has been made regarding what functions are to be automated, the next step is the development of specifications and features required of a system. The detailed system specifications are essential to get the best system suitable for the library. The detailed specifications should outline all of the functional requirements and features required in a system. A committee may be formed to co-ordinate the development of specifications for a required system. Functional subcommittees involving the staff of all user departments may be formed for defining the functional requirements and developing specifications for their respective functions. These specifications will be reviewed and finalised after necessary modifications and revisions. The requirements are to be ranked as mandatory and desirable based on their relative importance. Many problems encountered later can be avoided if the system requirements are clearly identified and specified. The specifications will serve as important guidelines in negotiating with the system supplier as well as a basis for final selection of the software package.

In essence, functional specification defines the capabilities that you want in a system. Specify and prioritize attributes ranging from the required (if it's not there, you won't buy the system) to the desirable (nice to have, but you can live without it). Specifications also cover technical areas such as standards that must be adhered to, system operation, maintenance, and system and data security. Developing clear and accurate specifications that are particular to your library is one of the most important, activity you will engage in as you plan for your automated system. These specifications will carry you through the entire procurement process. The system that most closely matches them will be the most useful and the most responsive to your needs (Cohn et al, 1998; 46).

6.4.5. Evaluation of software options

Having specified the functional requirements of a system, it is necessary to identify suitable hardware and software package. Ideally, software should be selected first which would ultimately decide about the type of hardware required.

Software package is the most crucial for the success of library automation as it has many implications for a library's operations, services, staff and users. The success of library automation depends largely on the selection of right software and its effective implementation. Today, a wide variety of library software packages are available in the market. Selection of an appropriate package suited to a particular library and its intelligent implementation are challenging complex tasks in library automation process. Therefore, libraries should evaluate all the available options carefully in order to select the best possible option that can match both the priority requirements and available financial resources. The various options available for library automation are turnkey systems, stand alone or integrated systems, in-house developed systems and cooperative network systems.

There are two types of library automation software: Stand-alone single function software and integrated library software. Stand-alone software is designed to use for any one of the library functions. In the beginning, most of the libraries have initiated computerisation with a single function. The systems designed for functions such as cataloguing, circulation, acquisition and serials control existed independently from each other and the exchange of data among the systems was not possible. Subsequently, due to limited facilities of stand-alone software and increasing capabilities of hardware, software, and communication technologies, integrated library automation software has emerged. An integrated software is one that computerises multiplicity of library functions using one common database. In this system, all the library functions such as acquisition, cataloguing, circulation and serials control are integrated in such a way that they share common data and files. Integrated library software packages have become increasingly popular as they enabled libraries to computerise many functions and greatly contributed to the success of total library automation mission. These software packages overcome the problems of compatibility, prevents duplication of efforts, improves efficiency in library operations, offers greater scope for staff savings and better provision for comprehensive management information.

A totally integrated system has all principal library functions automated in a network or distributed system. According to Kurtz, the advantages of an integrated system are: 1) all functions are automated at once, and a large amount a manual record-keeping can be eliminated; 2) functions interface with one another; 3) data is not replicated with some integrated systems (data duplication requires a concentrated effort in order to keep records in different files in sync and used more storage than nonduplication); and 4) many access points to data are usually provided.

The evolution of computerised library systems has progressed, since the late 1960s, through the stages of in-house development of software in conjunction with the computing units of the parent institution, the development of centralised automated cataloguing systems in the early 1970s, the commercial availability of turnkey systems for the automation of specific functions in the mid – 1970s, to development of the integrated systems of the 1980s – which added the further advantage of offering software for multiple functions (September, 1990).

There are two methods of acquiring a library software package. Library must either develop software in-house by using local expertise or purchase it form vendors.

As a rule, western libraries have eschewed the option of developing needed software in-house. It has been found that except in rare cases, the cost of the development effort in terms of staff, resources and time required to develop software is higher than acquiring readily available software. In addition to initial development cost, the opportunity cost and the cost of maintaining and updating/ upgrading the software should also be taken into account. The situation in India is no different as the total cost of in house development of software would probably be as high as compared to buying off-the-shelf software (Haravu, 1995).

Rowley (1993:52) stated that in many instances, it is sensible to choose a commercially available package due to the following advantages: (1) They are economical because the investment cost for the initial creation and later maintenance of the package is spread over several users, (2) The package comes as a well-tested set of programs, (3) The software producer is likely to be a specialist in that kind of software, (4) Packages are well documented including detailed system specifications and user manuals, (5) Packages are available readily and can be implemented earlier, and (6) Support and advice services should be available from the package supplier.

Some of the important library software packages used in western countries are BLCMP, BLIS, Bookshelf, DATATREK, DS, DOBIS, DYNIX, GEAC Advance, LIBERTAS, LIBS 100, NOTIS, PALS, REFLION SUPER MAX, Soutron, VRICA and VTLS.

With the great number of potential integrated software packages available on the market today and after considering the advantages and disadvantages of each method, purchasing an integrated software package is far better and more economical than in house development of software by the libraries because of sophisticated functional capabilities.

6.4.6. Requesting proposals

Once the decision to purchase an integrated software is taken, it is necessary to request proposals from prospective vendors whose software's is considered to be potentially useful for the new system. The specifications of the required system form the basis for the formal request for proposal **(RFP)**. The RFP should clearly indicate all the mandatory and desirable functional, technical and performance requirements including the standard format used for submission of proposals. The proposals received in standard form facilitate to compare the functionality, cost, maintenance, support and all other features of software in a systematic and logical manner.

6.4.7. Evaluating proposals for selection of library software

Once the proposals are received, they must systematically be evaluated preferable by a team consisting of library and computer professionals for selecting the best software for the library. The evaluation of proposals can be done based on the standard criteria which include software's functionality, usability, user-friendliness, compliance with specifications, cost, training, documentations, maintenance support, vendor's capacity for software updation/

upgradation and past performance.

The evaluation of proposals for selection of suitable software would be based on three basic criteria, functionality, cost and vendor reputation (September, 1990).

The sources of information for evaluating software include:

- Reading journals and other references works.
- Discussing with other librarians using the same software.
- Personally visit and observe the actual working of software in successfully automated libraries.
- Have informal discussions with potential software suppliers.
- Invite prospective vendors to give demonstration on the software functional capabilities.

Based on the information collected from the responses, demonstrators, current users experiences and other sources, the evaluation team reviews and evaluates all the proposal using standard evaluation criteria and selects the software. Each proposal must be critically evaluated to make sure that all the essential mandatory functional requirements are met by the particular system so selected. After selection, the library needs to negotiate and sign the service contract with the vendor of software selected. Keep good relations with vendors and make maximum use of their full service support. They provide good in house training and help in data entry, migration and conversion.

In today's fast changing dynamic technological environment and ever-rising users expectations, no software package can meet all the current requirements of a given library. Therefore, it is important to select a software package that best suits and meets most of the mandatory functional, technical and performance requirements of a particular library.

6.4.8. Library Automation Software

Today, the phrase library automation can be used for the Library computerization which refers to the use of computers to perform library housekeeping operations and information services. Having learned the advantages of computerization of library operations and services, it is necessary to identify suitable software package for library automation. Library automation software is software designed for automating the housekeeping operations and information services. The success of library automation depends largely on the selection of right software and its effective implementation. Today, apart from a few open source software packages, there are number of commercial software packages available for library automation in the market. These commercial packages are integrated library management software packages which cover all the housekeeping operations such as acquisition, cataloguing, circulation, OPAC, serials control etc. Each package has its own unique features and limitations.

There are two categories of software for Library Automation - commercial software and free open source software.

6.4.9. Commercial Software for Library Automation

Commercial software is software developed and sold for a price by a vendor. There are a number of commercial software packages available for library automation in India. Each package has its own unique features and limitations. Some of the important library automation software packages available in India are presented in Table 6.1

Table 6.1: Important Library Software Packages in India

S.No	Name of Software	Software developer/marketer	Place
1	Alice for Windows	Soft link India	New Delhi
2	Basis Plus/Techlib Plus (Livelink ECM)	National Informatics Center (NIC)	New Delhi
3	CATMAN	INSDOC	New Delhi
4	CDS/ISIS	UNESCO/NISSAT	New Delhi
5	DELPLUS	Developing Library Network (DELNET)	New Delhi
6	Easy Lib	Easy Lib Software Pvt. Ltd	Bangalore

S.No	Name of Software	Software developer/marketer	Place
7	E- Grandhalaya	National Informatics Center (NIC)	New Delhi
8	Granthalaya	INSDOC	New Delhi
9	Libman	Datapro Consultency Service	Pune
10	Librarian	Compusoft Exports Ltd.	Ahmedabad
11	Librarian Suite LIBSUITE ASPT	Soft-Aid Computers	Pune
12	Libris	Frontier Institute of IT	Hyderabad
13	Libsoft	ET & T Corp.,	New Delhi
14	Libsys 7	Libsys Corporation	New Delhi
15	Lims	Data Control Pvt. Ltd.,	Mumbai
16	Maitrayee	Computer Maintenance Corporation	Secunderabad
17	MINISIS	SNDT Women's University Library	Mumbai
18	NexLib - Lib. Auto. Software	Nex_Evolve Logic Solutions Pvt. Ltd	Hyderabad
19	Sanjay	DESIDOC	Delhi
20	SLIM 21	Algorythms	Pune
21	SOUL	INFLIBNET Center	Ahmedabad
22	Troodon	Comtek Services Pvt. Ltd.	New Delhi
23	TULIB	Tata Unisys	Mumbai
24	Virtua I LS	VTLS Software Pvt. Ltd.	New Delhi
25	Wilsys	Wipro India	Bangalore

6.4.10. Open Source Software for Library Automation

Open Source Software is software created by programmers who want to share their source code with anyone who wants to use it. The term open source software refers to software in which the source code is freely available for others to view, amend and adapt. It is maintained by a team of developers cutting across the institutional and national boundaries. To be certified as open source, the license of the program must guarantee the right to read, redistribute, modify and use it freely. Software operated under open source label has to fulfill the criteria such as free circulation, availability of source code and modifications to the source code. Some examples of open source software are – Linux operating system, Mozila web browser, MySQL RDBMS, Apache web server and PERL.

6.4.10.1. Definition of Open Source Software

Generically, *open source* refers to a program in which the source code is available to the general public for use and/or modification from its original design free of charge. Open source code is typically created as a collaborative effort in which programmers improve upon the code and share the changes within the community. Open source sprouted in the technological community as a response to proprietary software owned by corporations. *http://www.webopedia.com/TERM/O/open_source.html*

Open source software is computer software that is distributed along with its source code - the code that is used to create the software - under a special software license. The license allows users to use, change and improve the software's source code, and to redistribute the software either before or after it has been modified. jobsearchtech.about.com/od/techindustrybasics/f / Open_Source_Definition.html

6.4.10.2. Features of Open Source Software

Open source doesn't just mean access to the source code. The distribution terms of open-source software must comply with the following criteria:

- Free redistribution
- Inclusion of source code
- Allowing for modifications and Derived Works
- Integrity of the Author's Source Code
- No Discrimination against Persons or Groups
- No Discrimination against fields of Endeavor
- The license needs to apply to all to whom the program is redistributed.
- License Must Not Be Specific to a Product
- License Must Not Restrict or contaminate Other Software
- License Must Be Technology-Neutral

6.4.10.3. Open Source Software packages

There are many free open source software packages for library automation. Some of the popular **open source software packages** for library automation are briefly discussed below:

i. Avanti Library Systems www.avantilibrarysystems.com/ : Avanti Library Systems grew out of an effort to create a simple flexible open source OPAC for small libraries. The result was MicroLCS, which encapsulates effective simplicity, careful design at all levels and doing one thing really well. Today we are taking some of the ideas and design philosophy developed in the making of MicroLCS and applying them to Nova, a radically different semantic mapping system currently in development that has many potential applications in libraries and other areas.

By focusing on simplicity, basic principles and solid clean design, Avanti Library Systems is dedicated to software tools for the library community that are easy to use, powerful, and that can provide new and effective ways of managing information.

ii. Evergreen http://www.open-ils.org/about.php : The Evergreen is an open source ILS (integrated library system) used by approximately 800 libraries. The Evergreen software is used by libraries to provide their public catalog interface as well as to manage back-of-house operations such as circulation, acquisition of library materials, and sharing resources among groups of libraries. The Evergreen Project was initiated by the Georgia Public Library System in 2006 to serve their need for a scalable catalog shared by approximately 250 public libraries in the state of Georgia. As Evergreen was adopted by a number of library consortia in the US and Canada as well as various individual libraries, it is also adopted by libraries outside of North America. Because of the nature of ILS, Evergreen has an interesting mixture of functionality. For example:

- Evergreen is a metadata search engine
- Evergreen is a transaction processing engine
- Evergreen is just another web application

- Evergreen is based on a robust, scalable, message-passing framework.

iii Koha www.koha.org/ : Koha is an open source integrated library system developed in New Zealand in 2000. Koha is now used by libraries around the world and has been contributed to by over 180 developers. Koha is a 100% web-based system where both the staff and patron functionality is accessible via the browser. It comes complete with modules for circulation, patron management, cataloging, serials, acquisitions, reporting and extensive administrative menu for customizing the system to your library's needs.

LibLime Koha : LibLime Koha is the most advanced open-source Integrated Library System in use today by hundreds of libraries worldwide. LibLime Koha is web based, so there is no software to install on desktop computers, and LibLime hosting services means that no servers are required in the libraries. LibLime's IT experts manage all upgrades, backups and general system maintenance, and the Library's local IT staff can focus on the Library's many other projects.

The development of LibLime Koha is steered by a growing number of libraries throughout the world. These libraries, either on their own, or collaborating in groups, sponsor the development of new features to support their workflows. LibLime Koha's impressive feature set continues to evolve and expand to meet the needs of its sponsoring libraries. Everyone may not use the same features. This freedom to pick and choose from features, through the administration of system preferences, offers librarians the opportunity to tailor their LibLime Koha instance to match their specific workflow needs.

LibLime Koha offers Libraries:

- Easy-to-use circulation policies, strong patron management, intuitive navigation, and extensive permissions for staff accounts.
- Parent-child relationship for patron records, as well as a 'copy' patron feature to quickly add families.

- A Clubs and Services feature that allows libraries to manage reading groups, book clubs, and other other community outreach programs. This feature is easily managed by library staff.
- Extensive support for holds, including an option to 'suspend' and 'reactivate' a hold, an option to place holds from a patron's OPAC account, an option to allow staff to re-organize the holds queue, and an option to place holds at either the title or item level.
- Enhanced matching policy rules for the 001 and 035 tags, allowing libraries to update older records with a newer version.
- Libraries to 'undo' entire import batches from the catalog in a single click, rather than having to delete on a one-by-one basis.
- SIP2 configuration for a wide variety of vendors and their products, including ITG, 3M, EnvisionWare, Talking Tech, Overdrive, TechLogic, and Librarica. LibLime Koha also works with EzProxy as a dual authentication source for remote database access.
- OPAC, staff, administrative features and self-checkout interfaces are all based on standards-compliant World Wide Web technologies—XHTML, CSS and Javascript—making LibLime Koha a completely Web-based solution.

iv. Learning Access ILS http://www.learningaccess.org : The LearningAccess ILS is a Standards-based, Fully integrated, Flexible and Open library automation system, easy to use, yet powerful and completely Web-based for today's demanding information needs. The LearningAccess ILS is uniquely positioned to offer smaller libraries the opportunity to gain access to state-of-the-art library automation, yet at affordable pricing.

The LearningAccess ILS:

- Organizes the library's collections
- Links the collection with enhanced content on the web

- Integrates and controls access to third-party databases and Web-based resources
- Establishes a easy to use library information portal

Main Components : The LearningAccess ILS consists of four modules: the patron or user module (Web OPAC), the cataloging module, the circulation module and the administrative module which are Web based.

Web OPAC : LearningAccess ILS Web OPAC sets a new standard in sophistication and ease of its use. The Web OPAC deploys a revolutionary and unique search system to access local and remote resources.

Powerful searching capabilities : LearningAccess ILS offers three ways to search:

- *EasySearch* gives patrons one space in which to enter search terms and phrases, providing the broadest search results
- *AdvancedSearch* lets patrons search using several terms and using Boolean and proximity operators
- *Zsearch* lets patrons easily search remote libraries, including the Library of Congress

Cataloging: LearningAccess ILS allows quick addition of new material to the database by:

- Copy cataloging using the intuitive build in Zsearch z39.50 copy cataloging tool
- Uploading of book vendor supplied MARC21 bibliographic records
- Original cataloging using one of three MARC21 based cataloging interfaces.

Serials Cataloging: LearningAccess ILS deploys a state-of-the-art and unique serial cataloging interface. This cataloging interface supports the full set of Serial Cataloging requirements. Its unique captions and pattern editor ensure that even the in smallest libraries, managing serials subscriptions becomes easy and fast.

Authority Control: The LearningAccess ILS cataloging system implements full Authority Control at various levels. Authority Control is accomplished through:

- Self learning authority system, using known quality MARC21 bibliographic records already in the system to enforce Authority Control
- Using LCSH, SEARS or other thesauri records imported in MARC21 authority format

Circulation: Circulation has never been easier, using an intuitive Web based interface equally suited for the volunteer as the professional librarian. The circulation system makes it easy to keep track of all types of circulating and non-circulating materials.

v. NewGenLib Library Automation Software 3.0.4 http://www.verussolutions.biz/web/nglAdaptationProgram : NewGenLib is an open source library automation software developed by Kesavan Institute of Information and Knowledge Management (KIIKM) and Verus Solutions Pvt. Ltd., both in Hyderabad, India. NewGenLib is strongly predicated on the use of contemporary and international metadata and interoperability standards. NewGenLib also uses contemporary n-tier based architecture and open source components. These features make the software not only affordable but also scalable and relatively easily maintainable because each of its layers can be sized or upgraded when needed. Unlike other Indian library automation software that have been on the scene for over a decade and a half, NewGenLib is fully based on web technologies in all its versions. Equally importantly, the networking/consortium version of NewGenLib allows cost-effective networking of libraries via the web using a single server and software infrastructure.

NewGenLib has all functional modules of Library management completely implemented. It has the following modules.

- Technical Processing (or cataloging)
- Circulation
- Acquisitions
- Serials Management
- MIS Reports
- Web Online Public Access Catalog
- Administration

A library after implementing can go for full-fledged live implementation. Technologically also NewGenLib uses contemporary technologies compared to other ILS available in the market.

Features

- Functional modules are completely web based. Uses Java Web Start™ Technology
- Compatibility - Complies with international metadata and interoperability standards: MARC-21, MARC-XML, z39.50, SRU/W, OAI-PMH
- Uses chiefly open source components
- Scalable, manageable and efficient
- OS independent - Windows and Linux flavours available
- z39.50 Client for federated searching
- Internationalized application (I18N)
- RFID integration
- Networking – Hierarchical and Distributed networks
- Automated email/instant messaging integrated into different functions of the software
- Form letters are configurable and use XML-based OpenOffice templates

- Extensive use of set up parameters enabling easy configuration of the software to suit specific needs, e.g., in defining patron privileges
- Supports multi-user and multiple security levels
- Allows digital attachments to metadata

vi. OPALS- OPen-source Automated Library System http://www.mediaflex.net/showcase.jsp?record_id=52 : OPALS Open-source Automated Library System is a powerful cooperatively developed, web-based, open source program. This alternative technology provides Internet access to information databases, library collections and digital archives. Many school, college, research, business, religious and library union catalogs use OPALS. There is no need to install software or purchase expensive computer hardware or software licenses to implement this powerful, turnkey Internet accessible system. The "total cost of ownership" of this standards-based, Web-based, feature rich software is demonstrably and undeniably sustainable.

vii. CDS/ISIS database software http://portal.unesco.org/ci/en/ev.php-URL_ID=2071&URL _DO=DO_TOPIC&URL_SECTION=201.html

Micro CDS/ISIS is an advanced non-numerical information storage and retrieval software developed by UNESCO since 1985 to satisfy the need expressed by many institutions, especially in developing countries, to be able to streamline their information processing activities by using modern (and relatively inexpensive) technologies. The software was originally based on the Mainframe version of CDS/ISIS, started in the late '60s, thus taking advantage of several years of experience acquired in database management software development. Several partners contributed to its development through the years.

CDS/ISIS for Windows

The development of the Windows version was the result of

strategic development policy decision aiming at maintaining the leading role CDS/ISIS has played and is still playing on the international scene.

The major features of the CDS/ISIS software are:

- The handling of variable length records, fields and sub fields, thus saving disk space and making it possible to store greater amounts of information;
- The handling of repeatable fields;
- A data base definition component allowing the user to define the data to be processed for a particular application;
- A data entry component for entering and modifying data through user-created data base specific worksheets;
- An information retrieval component using a powerful search language providing for field-level and proximity search operators, in addition to the traditional and/or/not operators, as well as free-text searching;
- A powerful sort and report generation facility allowing the user to easily create any desired printed products, such as catalogues, indexes, directories, etc.;
- A data interchange function based on the ISO 2709 international standard used by leading data base producers;
- An integrated application programming language (CDS/ISIS Pascal and the ISIS_DLL), allowing the user to tailor the software to specific needs;
- Functions allowing the user to build relational data bases, though CDS/ISIS is not based over a relational model;
- Powerful hypertext functions allow to design complex user interfaces.

J-ISIS - Java CDS/ISIS http://kenai.com/projects/j-isis

J-ISIS is a general purpose Open Source database system

entirely written in Java and based on existing and solid FOSS software packages, such as Berkley DB and Lucene, from the Apache Foundation. The project is being supported by the Bibliothèque de l'Ecole du Louvre and INSIA, France.

The *J-ISIS project's* mission and goals are to develop a new multiplatform Free and Open Source Software (FOSS) ISIS suite that would provide the same successful concepts and functionalities as the actual UNESCO ISIS suite while removing the restrictions, being Client/Server, UNICODE, and benefiting of the latest software developments. One of the objectives was also to keep the assets and experience of the users. But the main objective is to develop a long-term solution that would be modular, easy maintainable and extensible.

viii. ABCD Library Automation Software https://sites.google.com/site/abcdlibraryautomationsoftware/home : *ABCD* is an Open Source web-based integrated library management software comprising the main basic library functions developed by BIREME and VLIR (the Flemish Interuniversity Council, Belgium). This kind of library application is a long held aspiration for the ISIS community, since the first MS-DOS version came out more than 20 years ago. Several library automation systems were developed during this period and are still in operation worldwide. The main characteristics of ABCD are the coverage of the main library functions, its web centrality and its development and maintenance under the methodology of Free and Open Source Software.

Main functions:

- Definition of any number of new databases which includes: FDT, PFT, FST, and worksheets directly on the Web,
- Cataloguing of books and serials,
- End-user searching (OPAC),
- Loans circulation,
- Acquisitions,

- Statistics,
- Library services like SDI, barcode printing, quality control, etc.
- Compatible with CDS/ISIS database technology
- Run on both Windows and Linux platforms;
- Use MARC-21, Dublin Core, METS, Z39.50...;

An open source library automation software must be carefully planned and thoroughly researched before implementation in libraries

6.4.11. Open Source Software for Digital Library

Software is crucial for the creation, storage, preservation, retrieval and management of digital information resources in digital libraries. Today, a number of digital library software is available for development of digital library. The initial price, up gradation cost and annual maintenance charges of commercial digital library software is so high that they are beyond the reach of the most of the libraries in India. The best alternative choice available for the libraries is to opt for open source software (OSS). OSS is becoming very popular and widely used in large number of libraries across the globe

OSS is software for which the source code is available to the end-user to modify and use the software according to one's own requirements. The potential users would further improve the software capabilities for their own benefit and also for the benefit of other library community. A brief description of the popular open source software solutions widely used for developing digital libraries is given below.

i. Greenstone Stone Digital Library: [http://www.greenstone.org]: The Greenstone Digital Library software (GSDL) is an important Open source software solution for developing digital libraries promoted by New Zealand Digital Library Project research group headed by Dr. Ian H.Witten at the University of Waikato and is sponsored by the UNESCO. The Software provides a way of building, maintaining and distributing digital library collections. Greenstone builds collections using popular and standard digital formats such as HTML, XML, word, Post script,, PDF, RTF and many other formats which include multimedia. The software is provided with effective full-text searching and meta-data based browsing facilities that are attractive and easy to use. It accommodates different document and metadata types. It incorporates an interface that makes it easy for institutions to create their own library collections. Collections could be built and served locally from the user's own web server or remotely on a shared digital library host. It runs on wide variety of platforms such as windows, Unix/Linux, Apple Mac etc., It has an exhaustive set of well documented and articulated manuals. The main objective of the Greenstone software is to empower users particularly in university libraries and other public service institutions, to build their own digital libraries (Witten, 2003)

ii. Dspace: [http://www.dspace.org] : Dspace is an institutional repository developed jointly by Hewlett Packard (HP) and Massachusetts Institute of Technology (MIT). Dspace software captures, stores, indexes preserves and redistributes the intellectual output of a University's research faculty in digital formats. Dspace accepts all forms of digital materials including text, images, audio and video files. Dspace covers various types of content such as articles, preprints, technical reports, conference papers, books, theses, datasets, audio files, video files, reformatted digital library collections, learning objects and web pages.

iii. Ganesha [http://www.gdl.itb.ac.id] : Ganesha Digital Library is software for managing and distributing digital collection using web technology. The software enables institutions and persons to share their knowledge as well as simultaneously access and utilize knowledge in Indonesian "giant memory" in the form of network of Indonesia DLN digital libraries. It has many useful features and powerful capabilities.

iv. GNUE-Prints Archiving Software: [http://www.eprints.org]: GNU E-prints is open source digital Library software designed primarily to create institutional repositories. It is generic archive software developed by University of Southampton. E

– Prints for research papers but it can be easily used for other content Primary goal is to setup as an open archive such as images, research data, audio archives etc. It works on Linux Operating System and it needs my SQL, Perl modules and Apache Web Server.

v. Fedora [http:/ www.fedora.infol] : Flexible Extensible Digital Object Repository Architecture (FEDORA) is an open source digital object repository management system developed jointly by university of Virginia Library and Cornell University. It is designed to be a foundation on which inter operable web-based digital libraries, institutional repositories and other information management systems can be built. The important features of software include access, control and authentication, XML submission and storage, OAI Metadata harvesting and field specific interface for full text and field specific queries and web services,

vi. ETD-Database [http://scholar.lib.vt.edu/et-dbl] : The ETD database (ETD-DB) was developed jointly by the Digital Library and archives (a division of the University Libraries) of the Graduate School at Virginia Technical University and NDLTAD. It is used for ETD software.submission, archive and search tool. The ETD database is a series of WebPages and perl scripts that interact with a My SQL database. These scripts provide a standard interface for web users, researchers, ETD authors and library staff to enter and manage the files and metada related to electronic theses and dissertations. The ETD-db supports the ETD-MS standard set by NDLTD. ETD-MS is the basic Dublin-case elements with the addition of several elements that further describe parts of the ETD process. This is the only **Metadata standard supported by the**

6.4.12. Implementation of a New System

Implementation of new system involves various activities like site preparation, acquisition of furniture, testing of software, system conversion, data conversion, development of databases, bibliographic standards and digital library.

The activities of system implementation and operation were

identified as: 1) Staffing needs; 2) Space needs; 3) Supply needs; 4) Data Conversion; 5) Database administrator; policy/proceedings; 6) system standards; 7) Procedure development and review; 8) Policy development and renew (Mc Donald, 1984).

System Conversion : Planning for the shift from the existing system to the implementation of new system can take one of following approaches, depending on the size and complexity of the new system (Haravu, 1995).

Phased implementation: In this, the new system is divided into sections. Each section is installed individually and only when it is considered to be operating fully satisfactorily, the next logical section will be installed. This method is suitable in situations where there are a large number of transactions.

Parallel implementation: In this, both the old and new systems are operated in parallel for a specified period of time until of the new system is performing satisfactorily. This method is adopted for complex systems.

Pilot implementation: In this, the system may be installed in a smaller scale, e.g., in a departmental library before it is installed in the main library. This way the problems of the new system can be better understood and tackled without upsetting a major area of operation. This is a useful approach for a multi-site environment.

Complete changeover: In this, the old system is replaced by a new system on a specified day. This is feasible when the new system or application is relatively simple and there is not much preparatory work needed to replace the old system in one operation.

The approach used for change over from existing system to new system depends upon several factors like system potential, type and size of library, financial, human resources available and time limits.

Retrospective conversion : Retrospective conversion (RECON) is a process of converting the library's total collection into computer readable bibliographic database. It is a costly, labour intensive and complex process. The most commonly used data conversion methods include data entry by the existing staff, hiring outside staff on contract basis and importing data from databases. Each of the methods has its own advantages and disadvantages. However, in practice a hybrid approach using combination of all the three methods may be adopted depending upon the situation and the size, nature and type of materials. The library's bibliographic database created through a retrospective conversion need to be effectively maintained subsequently incorporating needed changes like deletion and addition of titles. Since RECON is a large task and existing library staffs are busy with their regular duties, it is better and cheaper to hire temporary staff to enter data into the computer.

Standards : Libraries planning for automation should adhere to standards in the development of databases. Standards for description of bibliographic information in a database are essential for inter changeability and portability of files and to participate in networking for sharing of resources efficiently. Most of the Indian libraries are not being able to follow uniform standard formats while designing and developing in house databases. Each library follows its own formats there by giving a less scope for resource sharing and exchange of information. Communication, exchange of information and resource sharing will not be easily possible without uniform standard entries in a database. Standardization in the data elements, standard procedures of data entry and data storage are essential to ensure compatibility for interconnection, easy transfer of information and sharing of resources. Co-operation in exchange of information and resource sharing is easily possible only when there is uniformity in formats, structures of databases among the participating libraries. Development of uniform technological standards are essential for standardization, networking, communication and sharing resources.

6.4.13. Maintenance of a New System

Maintenance of infrastructure facilities like computers, Printers, UPS, air-conditioning needs to be given due importance while planning for IT implementation. A provision should be made to see that all these machines must be in a working condition at all times. If computers and other equipment have to function properly, they should be protected from environmental hazards, power failure, unauthorized lingering and natural calamities. They cannot give maximum service without favorable environment. They should be kept in a separate room with regular power supply, optimum temperature, humidity and lighting. Places where power cut is more often, use of generators and UPS can help to minimize the effects of the interruptions.

6.4.14. Evaluation of a New System

Having used for considerable period of time after implementation, evaluation needs to be carried out to assess the extent to which new technology meets the goals and objectives set for it. Evaluation process helps to monitor progress toward the specific objectives and make necessary timely revisions responsive to new technological developments, products and opportunities. It is necessary that the library monitors IT activities, evaluates performance and tries to upgrade the existing technology or introduce new technologies. Evaluation has to be done periodically in order to assess the cost effectiveness of new services. The evaluation should include assessment of hardware utilization, staff and users perceptions about new system/services and fulfillment of library's needs and objectives. Regular feedback from users and staff in the form of surveys, interviews and observations will help us to evaluate their satisfaction about new technology based services. Staff and users suggestions will be used as input for future improvements.

6.5 CHANGING ROLE OF LIBRARY PROFESSIONALS IN DIGITAL ENVIRONMENT

In the modern knowledge society, the role of library professionals is adapting to changing technologies, digital information environment and customers expectations. Library professionals are increasingly responsible not only to provide traditional library information services but also to deliver online information services according to the actual user needs. Libraries are functioning under great pressure to become more efficient to deliver more effective services to the users. LIS professionals need to be confident and competent that they can prepare for new challenges, deal with emerging technologies, manage change effectively and claim new professional roles. Well-informed competent and creative Library professionals shall play multiple evolving roles in the 21st century.

Peter Drucker has predicted that the most important profession in the next century will be knowledge workers, and knowledge workers are not the same as computer systems specialists. The most competent ones are likely to be reference librarians using sophisticated hardware and software, tools which the end user does not know how to use.

As the information industry has changed, the expectations of information users have soared and librarians have come to fear for their positions and profession. As we race into the future, librarians should begin to think about the position of the library in the new environment. LIS professionals are functioning under great pressure to keep pace with the constantly changing technological environment. Librarians must serve as technologists with multitasking skills to assist learners in creating individualized information portfolios. Librarians must develop greater technological expertise, advanced research skills and team building competencies to play the new role of library technologist in digital environment.

Libraries must assert their evolving roles in more proactive ways in the context of increasingly competitive markets for information dissemination and retrieval. The library professionals must be multi-skilled Knowledge Navigators constantly interacting with users understanding the diverse needs of different user groups. library professionals have to play multiple evolving and expanding roles to face many new challenges in the dynamic digital environment. A librarian must be a professional expert, techno literate, web usability expert, knowledge manager, navigator, trainer, educator, marketer, service provider and many more.

6.6 COMPETENCIES FOR LIBRARY PROFESSIONALS IN DIGITAL ENVIRONMENT

Today's dynamic digital environment demands new job requirements, new roles, new competencies and skills from LIS professionals in order to utilize innovative technologies and to satisfy changing users expectations and needs.

According to Sarah Houghton, Competencies are the abilities, qualities, strengths, and skills required for the success of the employee and the organization. Competencies are taken to comprise knowledge, skills and attitudes related to effective behaviors and work performance. Knowledge refers to having information about, knowing or understanding something, skill is the ability to apply knowledge effectively, and attitude refers to the individual's mental or emotional approach to something.

In the dynamic digital information environment, the role of Library Professionals has changed from mere custodians of documents to the effective provider of customized, high quality, innovative information products and services using latest technology. Library Professionals have to learn and equip with wide range and variety of skills, knowledge and competencies in order to play multiple future challenging roles responsive to the changing needs of user community. The important competencies required for library professional in digital environment include.

- Experts knowledge of library and information science theory and library profession
- Library & Information Services Skills
- Knowledge about the diverse nature of the library's user community and their needs
- Managerial & Leadership skills
- Information & Communication Technology Skills
- Internet & Web Technology Skills

- Excellent communication Skills
- Teaching and Presentation Skills
- String commitment to excellent customer Service
- Resource generation skills
- Commitment to Life-Long Learning
- Inter personal relations skills
- Marketing and Promotion Skills
- Project Management skills
- Time Management skills
- Copyright, IPR and Cyber laws
- Knowledge Management skills
- Creative and Innovative skills
- Negotiation skills
- Change management skills
- Evaluation and Assessment skills

6.7 IT SKILLS FOR LIBRARY PROFESSIONALS IN DIGITAL ENVIRONMENT

The implementation of new and advanced technologies in the libraries requires competent staff with different IT skills. One of the important factors for successful implementation of IT is the level of competence of the staff. Working knowledge of IT skills for library professionals is fundamental for its successful implementation in library. IT has immense potential for handling various library functions. To make full use of this potential in library management, it is essential that the library should have adequate professionals who have thorough knowledge of IT applications in libraries. But in practice, most of the library professionals do not have adequate level of IT skills in libraries. The knowledge, skill and interest in various aspects of IT will need to be constantly upgraded among the library professionals.

IT has profound impact on the role of Library professionals and offers a numerous opportunities for professional and personal career development. Library Professionals with good IT skills and expertise will have ample opportunities in future and will be crucial to the management of modern libraries in the dynamic digital environment. It has become increasingly important for library professionals to acquire and enhance their IT skills in order to implement new technologies in libraries and to provide new IT based library services to users.

The following are some of the important IT Skills required for the LIS professionals to manage modern libraries in the digital environment:

- Computer hardware basics
- Operating systems (Windows, XP, LINUX etc)
- MS Office (word, Excel and Powerpoint)
- Application software Skills
- Networking (LAN/WAN) skills
- Database development
- Bibliographic Formats (MARC Z39.5, Metadata)
- Internet skills (Email, Discussion groups, Search engines, WWW)
- Web browsers
- Searching strategies
- Library management software
- Open source software
- Electronic databases
- Electronic resources management
- Network consortia access
- Data base management systems (MS Access, MySQL, ORACLE, SQL Server)

- Web designing / Web editors (FrontPage, Dream Weaver, HTML, XML)
- Digital libraries / Institutional repositories
- Digitalization (Scanner, Software and OCR)
- File Formats
- Virtual reference service
- Virtual and E-learning
- Web technologies
- Web based information resources and services
- Digital rights management
- Open access resources
- Barcode and RFID Technology
- Citation Software

Due to fast changing technological developments, continuous in-service training for working library staff is essential for not only to keep them well informed about the latest developments in their fields but also to learn new skills in the use of modern technologies.

6.8 PERSONAL QUALITIES OF A LIBRARIAN

Libraries need to make necessary changes to maintain their continuing relevance in today's digital environment. Libraries must offer user friendly online services like Google and Amazon. Libraries must regularly survey library users to evaluate the utilization of resources and also to find out their changing information seeking behavior/habits. Librarian must possess the following qualities for the successful management of modern libraries in the digital environment.

The Important qualities include:

- Service Aptitude
- Self Confidence
- Flexibility and adaptability

- Create a positive image
- Problem solving attitude – Respond positively to complaints
- Be proactive and positive
- Build good personal relationship with users
- Invite suggestions
- Personal persuasion
- Enjoy your work
- Extend excellent service to users

6.9 SOURCES FOR DEVELOPMENT OF NEW SKILLS

LIS Professionals have a wide range of channels and ways to develop their skills to manage changing technologies effectively. The important methods/ways for improving skills are:

- Acquiring higher qualifications
- Pursuing doctoral research
- Distance and E-learning courses
- Reading professional literature
- Tours and visits to well managed libraries
- Affiliation to professional bodies
- Attending professionals meetings. Conferences & Seminars
- Presenting papers in conferences and seminars
- Writing papers in periodicals and books
- Participation in specialist groups
- Personal interactions with expert fellow professionals
- Attending workplace programs
- Attending Induction Programs

- Attending staff training and development courses
- Undertaking research and development projects.
- Web resources
- Subscribing discussion forums

In an era of ever changing dynamic digital environment, libraries need to reinvent themselves and attempt to equip their staff with multiple new skills required to meet the challenges of new technologies and rising users' expectations.

6.10 CONCLUSION

With the continued trend of emerging high power technologies, it has become increasingly necessary that libraries at all levels need to understand how to plan, evaluate, procure, install and use new technologies successfully. Librarians should take full responsibility and insist on for using IT in their libraries, as it is the most effective tool for managing information. Librarians should make an effort to educate policy makers, administrators and make them to understand the importance of IT and indispensability of information in supporting research, education and in taking appropriate decisions in their day-to-day activities. Appropriate measures involving staff and users should be taken to help understand, accept and adapt to new technologies. Special emphasis should be given to the training of both library staff and users.

Modern technologies would not only make existing library collections available to all as a national resource but would also enable Indian libraries to participate actively in global networks for exchange of information and sharing resources. Implementation of IT to library operations is very complex, stressful and continuous process. It requires an imaginative, intelligent planning and huge investment of financial as well as human resources. Libraries intending to use IT have to plan well in advance for successful implementation and to minimize risks. To survive in the dynamic environment, to meet organizational demands, and users expectations and to keep pace with the unprecedented technological developments, libraries have to accept the change, adapt and manage new emerging technologies successfully.

The use of sophisticated information technology applications will continue to be increasingly a common phenomenon in all types and sizes of libraries in the new millennium. In view of the rapid nature of technological change, libraries must find ways to determine, choose, adopt, and implement appropriate technologies. Librarians must be instrumental in the successful planning, identification, implementation and utilization of emerging new technologies. It is becoming increasingly important for librarians to understand how the technologies work better, what opportunities the technology offers, what new products are emerging and how to effectively utilise them to enhance the capability of delivering high quality of information services to meet the growing expectations of users. In technological dynamic environment, highly trained professionals are needed to evaluate newly emerging technological innovations and will take the lead in stimulating awareness of new technological opportunities and their efficient applications in libraries.

6.11 REFERENCES

ABCD Library Automation Software https://sites.google.com/site/abcdlibraryautomationsoftware/home *(Accessed on 8.8.2012)*

Avanti Library Systems *www.avantilibrarysystems.com/ (Accessed on 8.8.2012)*

CDS/ISIS database software *http://portal.unesco.org/ci/en/ev.php-URL_ID=2071&URL_DO=DO_TOPIC&URL_SECTION=201.html (Accessed on 8.8.2012)*

Cohn, M.John., Kelsey, .Ann L, and Fiels, Keith Michael.(1998). Planning For Library Automation: a Practical Hand Book. London: Library Association Pub, 139p.

Evergreen *http://www.open-ils.org/about.php (Accessed on 8.8.2012)*

Haravu, L.J.(1995). Strategies for the adoption of New Information Technologies in Indian libraries. A paper presented in CALIBER-95: National Convention on Information access through networks held during 10-12, Feb.1995. Hyderabad: HCU.

Hofmann, Ulrich (1995). Developing a strategic planning framework for information technologies for libraries. OCLC systems and services 11(4), 22-32.

J-ISIS - Java CDS/ISIS http://kenai.com/projects/j-isis *(Accessed on 8.8.2012)*

Khalil,Tarek M (2000). Management Technology: The key to competitiveness and wealth creation. Boston:Mc Graw Hill.

Klobas, Jones E (1990). Managing technological change in libraries and information services. The Electronic Library 8(5),344-349.

Koha *www.koha.org/ (Accessed on 8.8.2012)*

Kurz,Sharon. Library Automation (Chap.1). New Mexico: Sandia National Laboratories Albuquerque, 267-296.

Learning Access ILS *http://www.learningaccess.org (Accessed on 8.8.2012)*

Mc Donald,D.R.(1984). Planning the Integrated Library System: A discursion paper for cabinet. University of Michigan Library system office, Ann Arbor.

Msuya, Jangawe. "Planning the automation of libraries in developing countries: A systems analysis approach". Library Review 39(3),29-32.

NewGenLib Library Automation Software *http://www.verussolutions.biz/web/nglAdaptation Program (Accessed on 8.8.2012)*

OPALS- OPen-source Automated Library System *http://www.mediaflex.net/showcase.jsp?record_id=52 (Accessed on 8.8.2012)*

Pritchett, Price (1994). New Habits for a Radically Changing World. Dallas: Pritchett & Associates.

Rowely J.E. (1993). Computers for Libraries.(3rd rev. ed). London Library Association Pub. 311p.

September, Peter E. (1990). Automation and academic library management: A case study. Library Review, 39(3), 6-21.

7

Impact of Using IT in CU Libraries in India

7.1 INTRODUCTION

Information technology has virtually unlimited potential for variety of useful applications in libraries. It has become an integral part of all library information resources, operations and services. Libraries use IT to increase the efficiency, productivity and effectiveness of library operations and services. Because of the numerous advantages of accelerating pace of technological developments, the use of IT applications in libraries has grown tremendously in recent years. Today, the success of library is increasingly dependent upon the effective utilization and management of new technologies in libraries.

The study has been conducted to survey the current state of use of IT in CU Libraries and to assess the perceptions of Library staff and users on the impact of using IT in library operations and information services. The study surveyed 14 CU Libraries, 100 library staff members and 413 library users and received completed responses from 14 (100%) university libraries, 64 (64%) library staff members and 315 (76%) library users respectively. The data has been analysed using both descriptive and inferential statistical techniques including frequencies, percentages, averages, and standard deviation, Chi-Square etc. The analysis of data revealed certain results and trends as presented in the fourth and fifth chapters. This chapter provides a brief summary of findings, conclusions, suggestions, future research areas and future challenges of emerging rapid technological advancements.

7.2 FINDINGS

7.2.1. Central University Libraries

There are 16 Central Universities established in India. Of these, three universities viz. BHU (1916), AMU (1920) and UOD (1922) were established before Independence and 13 after Independence. The first university established after Independence was VB in 1951 and the recent one was MANUU in 1998. Regarding the growth trend of universities, there were seven universities in six decades from 1916 to 1975 at the rate of about one university per decade, which has increased significantly by three in 1980s and by six in 1990s.

Out of 16 CU Libraries, 14 were surveyed on the use of IT and received duly filled-in questionnaires from all the 14 (100%) libraries. The remaining two CU Libraries viz. MGAHV and MANUU were not included in the survey as they were established recently in 1997 and 1998 respectively.

Of the 12 responded, eight central universities started their libraries within the same year, two within one year and the remaining two within two years of their establishment. Out of 16 universities, 14 have separate buildings exclusively for library and five universities have even separate names for their libraries. These factors demonstrate a good sign of giving due recognition to libraries in central universities in India.

All the 14 CU Libraries have a huge collection of about

46,48,431 books, 4,63,176 back volumes of periodicals, 40,636 theses, 11,046 audio-visual materials and 34,402 others. In electronic form, six libraries reported having 205 CD-ROM databases. The size of collection of CU Libraries vary widely from 1000 (in BBAU) to 14 lakhs (in DULS).

CU Libraries subscribe to 10,169 periodicals. Only four CU Libraries viz. AMU, BHU, UOD and JNU subscribe to more than 1000 periodicals while five subscribe more than 500 and the remaining libraries subscribe less than 500 periodicals.

The user community of CU Libraries comprises 42.6% P.G. Students, 14.8% Faculty, 13.1% Research scholars, 15.5% Administrative staff and 14% others including students of under graduate and distance learners.

CU Libraries have a total of 1,214 staff members comprising 11.2% supervisory cadres, 54.6% middle level professionals and 34.2% other staff including semi-professional and supporting staff.

The annual books budget of CU Libraries is ranging from seven lakhs to 60 lakhs. DULS consisting 30 libraries has spent about 4 crore rupees for both books and periodicals during the year 1997-98. IGNOU has spent 60 lakh rupees while NU, UOH, VB and AU have spent more than 20 lakhs for books during the year 1997-98. The highest amount of budget spent for periodicals was Rs. 1.2 crores by JNU, followed by BHU with Rs.1.04 crores and UOH with Rs.0.93 crores. The other CU Libraries are spending in the range of five to Rs.77 lakhs each for periodical subscriptions. Nine CU Libraries reported IT budget figures, have spent Rs.677.87 lakhs for IT only during three years from 1995-96, 1996-97 and 1997-98.

7.2.2. Use of IT in CU Libraries in India

With regard to infrastructural facilities used in CU Libraries, telephone, fax, internet, email, xerox, TV and multimedia are the common facilities used. Two CU Libraries viz., UOH and PU have websites, homepages and V-SAT.

Regarding the objectives of library automation the top goals of CU Libraries are to improve access to their collection, improve the quality of existing services and reduce routine and time consuming clerical operations.

Library Automation planning is done by both library professionals and computer personnel. However UL, DL and AL are rated as the key persons involved in planning library automation in CU Libraries.

To cope up with the implementation of technological changes, the important steps recognized by CU Libraries include sending staff for training courses, visits to automated libraries and consultations with the other librarians.

CU Libraries have considered the user-friendliness as the most important factor in selecting the software for library automation followed by supporting the cataloguing format and successful use in other libraries.

The three most important constraints faced in IT implementation in CU Libraries include inadequate financial resources, lack of standard and well accepted software package and lack of IT trained personnel.

Most of the CU Libraries are using personal computers for their library automation while only UOH library has minicomputer and none had mainframe computer. UOD, UOH, JNU and PU are using large number of computers ranging from 18 to 53.

Regarding software usage in CU Libraries, MS-DOS, Windows and UNIX are the most common operating systems while Wordstar, Word processing and MS-word are the widely used word processors. dBase III+ / IV is used by five libraries. The programming languages viz. Basic, Pascal and C are also used by very few libraries. The major library application software used in CU Libraries include CDS/ISIS, LIBSYS, BASIS/TECHLIBplus, ILMS/SOUL etc., CDS/ISIS promoted by NISSAT is used by almost all CU Libraries. LIBSYS is used in eight libraries, followed by ILMS/SOUL in five libraries and BASIS/

TECHLIBplus and Troodon in one library.

More than half of CU Libraries reported database creation, acquisition, cataloguing, OPAC, retrospective conversion etc. are computerized operations. Word processing is used for office automation by most of the libraries while budgeting and management information are the other areas reported by some CU Libraries. Regarding method of implementation, more than half of CU Libraries adopt computerisation in phases in an integrated way. Some libraries are maintaining cataloguing, circulation and serial control operations parallally both in manual as well as in computerised system.

About half of CU Libraries have created databases for books, back volumes of periodicals, theses etc. altogether ranging from 10,000 to 2.5 lakh records while others are in the process of development. One university library viz. UOH has completed the creation of database for the total collection of more than 2.5 lakh volumes. CU Libraries are using mainly CCF format. More than one third of CU Libraries have made some progress in retrospective conversion of their catalogue into electronic form mostly through manual data entry by staff rather than using CD-ROM databases and networks.

Nearly half of CU Libraries have been offering computerised information services such as accession list, CD-ROM and internet search service while, reference service, CAS, SDI and Indexing service are offered by a few libraries. Nearly half of CU Libraries use CD-ROM databases and internal databases for information retrieval services while a few use INFLIBNET databases and Online databases including DELNET.

Nearly half of CU Libraries provide access to computers ranging from two to eight to the end-users. These computers are used for searching OPAC, Online, and CDROM databases, Email and Internet services.

Regarding accessability to various networks, five CU Libraries have accessibility to INFLIBNET followed by four libraries ERNET, three libraries NICNET, DELNET each and two INET. Nearly half of CU Libraries participate in LAN while five participate in MAN.

7.2.3. Impact of IT on CU Libraries in India

The perceptions of staff on the impact of using IT in CU Libraries were studied through distribution of questionnaires to the 100 staff members of eight CU Libraries actively involved in using IT. The rate of response is 64%. The major findings based on the analysis have been summarised below:

The characterstics of the staff are: 73% are male while 27% are female; 50% belongs to 41 to 50 years age group; more than 50% of staff have two masters degrees both in general education as well as in library science; one third of staff are in the UGC cadres of UL, DL and AL while the rest are professional staff. Half of the staff have total experience of more than 20 years.

There is a significant improvement in the IT skills / knowledge of library staff as the number of library personnel attended training courses, conferences/seminars and presented/published papers has tremendously increased from 18 (28.2%) before IT implementation to 61 (95.4%) after IT implementation.

More than two-third of the staff members were involved in IT implementation process. All those involved accepted that it helped them to improve their performance in the library. More than half 38 (59.4%) of library staff were provided IT training in their libraries, of which two third felt that training was inadequate and need more training.

Regarding IT facilities, almost all staff members reported that they were provided computers while about 50% were provided facilities like printer, LAN and Internet. More than half of the respondents are spending from 26 to 75 percent (two to six hours) of their time working on computer at workplace in libraries. More than three-fourth of library staff is showing enthusiasm towards IT. Most of the respondents have gained IT work experience within the last ten years.

Library staff perceives that the highly improved aspects of using IT include efficiency, effectiveness and user satisfaction of the library. The results of Chi-square indicated that the staff involved in IT implementation and attended more training courses have more positive perceptions about the improvement of efficiency, productivity and services of the library.

The positive and negative of effects of using IT in library as perceived by the staff, have been studied. The important positive effects recognized by staff include facilitated networking and resource sharing, eliminated duplication of efforts and improved speed of operations while increased expenditure on systems maintenance, reduced inter-personal communication and increased violation of copyright Act as the major negative effects of using IT in library.

The results of chi-square indicated that the staff spending between 50-75% of their time working at computer per day agreed to enormous savings in time and efforts while staff involved in IT implementation agreed to the improved speed of operations. Regarding negative effects, staff trained in the use of IT agreed to frequent systems breakdown and frequent virus problem.

7.2.4. Impact of IT on Library Operations

The perceptions of staff have been studied regarding the benefits of using IT in all house-keeping operations and information services. IT enabled faster pre-order duplicate checking, facilitate easy preparation of purchase orders and enable to keep updated vendor database are rated as the highly acknowledged benefits in computerised acquisition while IT enabled speed and ease in cataloguing, enabled many access points and in-depth subject cataloguing and multiple users to access simultaneously from remote locations and enabled easy checking of previously assigned call numbers, saving time by avoiding frequent consultation of schemes and easy construction of call numbers as the most important benefits of computerised cataloguing and classification respectively.

Improved accuracy and control over circulation activities,

facilitate easy renewal and reservation of items and sending timely recall notices and reminder letters are the highly recognised benefits in computerised circulation while IT facilitate easy generation of subscription and renewal orders, enabled accurate and up-to-date record of subscriptions and holdings, and faster recording the receipts of journal issues of varied periodicities are the highly acknowledged benefits in automated serials control.

The most important benefits in networking and resource sharing as perceieved by library staff include IT facilitate better exchange and sharing of resources, enabled easy participation in resource sharing library networks and facilitate the establishment of library networks while facilitate better presentation of proposals and reports, enabled easy monitoring and evaluation of operations and facilitated easy preparation of binding lists as the major benefits in management information.

7.2.5. Impact of IT on Information Services

The highly recognised benefits in computerisation of library services include IT enabled more complex and more specific searches by combination of search terms, greatly improved accessibility through increased access points and provide easier and wider access to information resources. Staff involved in IT implementation strongly agree with provision of rapid access to bibliographic information on line and more specialized, need-based value-added services to users while staff trained agreed to the extended services to remote locations and increased users' expectations for better services as result of using IT in library.

7.2.6. Impact of IT in Library Professionals

The positive and negative effects of using IT on library staff have been studied. The highly ranked positive effects include upgraded knowledge and skills, made work more interesting and made it mandatory to learn to use modern technologies, while IT became detrimental to creative thinking, deskilled the job of cataloguers and created health problems are the major negative effects of using IT on staff. Staff involved in IT implementation accepted that IT has reduced their workload, made their work more interesting, improved their competence and performance, offered new challenges and better opportunities for professional growth and enabled to devote more of their time for user services.

7.2.7. Impact of IT on Library Users

The impact of using IT on library and information services has also been studied from the users, perspective at the UOH library. A sample of 413 users was taken and distributed questionnaire. Responses were received from 315 users with a response rate of 76%.

The characteristics of users reveal that 67% are male and 32% are female; 74% are campus residents while 21% are day scholars. The user community comprises 37% PG students, 46% M..Phil. and Ph.D. scholars and 17% are faculty members.

The users reported that they were provided access to Computer (63.2%), OPAC (39%), LAN (23%) and Internet (37.5%) in their departments. This reveals that access to OPAC, LAN and Internet needs to be improved. More than half of the users (55%) indicated that they had received training in the use of IT in the library. Of these, 67 percent felt that the training is adequate.

The users' assessment of the Impact of using IT in library reveals that access to collection, status (image/reputation) and efficiency have been recognised as highly improved aspects of the library.

The highly ranked benefits of using IT in library information services are: IT enormously saved time and efforts, improved the quality of services and provides more flexible and comprehensive retrieval than manual system.

The highly rated computerized services by the users in UOH Library include OPAC, automated circulation and maintenance of in-house databases.

7.3 CONCLUSIONS

Central universities have given due recognition and importance to their libraries as reflected in establishment and construction of separate buildings for libraries.

CU Libraries, in general, are better placed in terms of resources viz. collection, staff, budgets, users and infrastructural facilities.

The major reasons for using IT are to improve access to the collection, to improve quality of existing services and to reduce routine and time consuming clerical operations.

In adequate funds and lack of IT trained personnel are the major problems faced by CU Libraries.

Most of the CU Libraries use computers and the rest are also in the procurement process.

Most of the CU Libraries are using integrated library automation software packages, which include LIBSYS, ILMS/SOUL, BASIS/TECHLIB Plus etc. CU Libraries using commercial software are more actively involved in computerisation of more number of operations than others.

The computerized library operations in CU Libraries include database creation, acquisition, cataloguing, OPAC, retrospective conversion etc.

Some libraries developed databases for significant size of their collection while others need to make serious efforts to develop databases. CU Libraries, because of huge volume of collection and transactions, are partially computerised and taking longer time for its completion.

Most of CU Libraries are doing retrospective conversion of their catalogues into electronic form manually rather than using CD-ROM and network databases.

Some CU Libraries are offering computerised information services and providing computers to users within the library.

Few CU Libraries have campus-wide LAN as well as access to INFLIBNET databases.

CU Libraries have technology but are not able to utilize them to the desired extent due to lack of properly skilled and competent personnel.

IT has started to make an impact on the computerization of CU Libraries in India. Most of the CU Libraries surveyed have one computer-based application or more. But on the whole, they need to be more active in computerisaton of other library operations and services.

Library staff in general have inadequate knowledge about the potential of IT and its application in library operations and information services. However, IT has brought about significant improvement of IT knowledge skills in library personnel.

Staff with more training programmes, grater working experience on computers and involvement in IT implementation would be in a better position and more positive than others to assess the impact of new technologies on library operations and services.

Library personnel realised that IT has a great potential and offers various benefits in library operations and information services, if utilized effectively in libraries.

The highly acknowledged benefits by users are that IT has improved the access to collection, the quality of services, and enormously saved time and efforts.

Users of UOH have rated high for computerized services of OPAC and automated circulation.

In most of the CU Libraries, the fruits of computerisation are yet to reach adequately to the user community.

Overall, library staff and users have more positive perceptions about IT applications, potentials and benefits of using technology in CU Libraries in India.

7.4 SUGGESTIONS

Based on the above findings, the following suggestions are offered.

7.4.1. Libraries

In view of shrinking library budgets, rapidly increasing capabilities and dramatically decreasing cost of IT and explosive growth of electronic information sources, it has become not only essential but also more useful, economical and effective for CU Libraries to make best use of IT in house-keeping operations and information services to users.

The newly emerging technology will eventually have an impact on every aspect of library and therefore libraries should create appropriate environment as well as prepare staff for this change. CU Libraries need to have a long term planning and well defined strategy for IT implementation in order to reap maximum benefits and to minimise the problems of using IT.

IT applications for total library computerisation requires heavy investment at the initial stage. Therefore, adequate funds in the form of special grants should be made available for university libraries to modernize their operations and services. Further, CU Libraries need to restructure their budget policies by allocating a part of their annual budget for IT related purposes including acquisition/upgradaion of hardware and software as well as maintenance and training of staff and users.

As large number of information sources are now available in electronic form, CU Libraries need to adopt a hybrid collection development policy in order to build resources with appropriate combination of both print and electronic media.

Majority of CU Libraries have good infrastructural facilities for IT while a few of them need to develop multimedia, internet, and other facilities. Only two CU Libraries viz., UOH and PU reported to have their websites/home pages and VSAT. Therefore, the other libraries need to design their websites and install VSATs to facilitate easy communication and access to library resources and services.

Planning for library automation is done mostly by top level library professionals. The library professionals of all levels need to be involved to improve their morale and motivation for successful implementation of IT.

CU Libraries should prefer to purchase integrated library software package, which has already been in use successfully in other university libraries in the country. As integrated library softwares are now available, it is suggested that CU Libraries can opt for simultaneous implementation of total library automation rather than in phases.

Majority of CU Libraries are using IT mainly to house-keeping operations which need to extend and concentrate more on need-based value added user services.

It was observed that the database development activity in some libraries seems to be very slow. Therefore, CU libraries need to make rigorous efforts using INFLIBNET databases for retrospective conversion of their catalogues rather than duplicating the efforts through manual data entry in each individual library. Development of databases including retrospective conversion of catalogues should be done on contract basis to enable libraries to render computerized services with in the stipulated right time.

CU Libraries should follow established standards for compatibility, exchange and sharing of resources as well as economy in costs and efforts.

Campus-wide LAN is suggested in all CU Libraries to link various departments in the campus with the library in order to facilitate easy access to library OPAC and to gain maximum benefits from computerised services.

CU Libraries may plan their separate network called CU Libraries Network (CULIBNET).

CU Libraries should subscribe to important national, regional and international library networks in order to provide access to a wide range of information sources and services to users.

Fully automated CU Libraries should offer consultancy and advisory services by way of sharing their IT expertise and experiences to other university libraries.

As CU Libraries contain rare and valuable documents as well as rich research these and dissertations, digitization of these documents may be taken up in a phased manner for preservation and for future use.

CU Libraries should priorities and implement new technologies into the areas where their contribution is significant as well as cost and performance effectiveness has already been well established.

CU Libraries operating under shrinking budgets, increasing costs and greater user demands need to make more serious efforts in using new technologies to enable them not only to continue to provide existing service but also make possible a greater range of innovative services.

7.4.2. Library Staff

Effective utilization of new technologies in libraries is possible only with the skilled and competent personnel. It has become essential for library to have staff with IT skills. The persons with IT expertise and a vision for new and innovative services using new technologies would be able to bring significant improvement in IT implementation in libraries.

University Librarians should constantly keep in touch with new and emerging technologies, their applications and utility, so that they can convince the policy decision makers about the benefits of using latest technology and plan for their successful implementation.

Staff involvement is regarded as crucial to the final success of IT implementation. Therefore, all levels of staff should invariably be involved in planning, decision making, installation and implementation of the project in order to achieve higher levels of acceptance as well as to improve their morale, motivation, efficiency and enthusiasm.

IT implementation is one of the most rapidly changing areas in the library environment. Some CU libraries do not seem to fully utilize technologies that are available due to inadequate IT training for staff. Intensive training, retraining and sensitizing the staff need to be largely increased and more funds and staff time are to be allocated in order to exploit the full potential of IT applications for the development of innovative services.

The staff of CU Libraries may form online Newsgroup / Listserv to have regular interaction with fellow professionals in order to share ideas, experiences, innovations and to keep abreast of new developments.

Staff should be encouraged by liberally deputing them to attend training programmes, conferences and by providing incentives in the form of reimbursement of course fee as well as additional increments on completion of courses / acquisition of additional qualifications related to IT.

As the staff and users of CU Libraries appreciate the technological facilities available to them, more advanced technological equipment, devices, and products should be added to offer improved user services.

Comfortable ergonomic design of IT workstations, extensive efforts in job design and organizational development should be made to improve working conditions and job satisfaction among library staff.

7.4.3. Library Users

CU Libraries should provide more number of computers exclusively for users to access OPAC, CDROM databases and Internet facilities not only within in the library but also in the departments as well as in students hostels.

A well-designed marketing strategy is a backbone for higher levels of user acceptance and utilization. Therefore, CU Libraries should organize intensive user education programs for optimum utilization of IT based facilities and services.

CU Libraries should develop current awareness program in the form of lectures, demonstrations, bulletins etc. for user community to make them aware of the importance and utility of computerised services.

CU Libraries should make periodic studies to evaluate IT based services in order to measure user satisfaction for further modifications and improvement.

7.4.4. UGC INFLIBNET

INFLIBNET should suggest UGC to issue policy guidelines for university libraries to allocate a part of their annual budgets for IT implementation on regular basis.

INFLIBNET in collaboration with IT professional bodies should provide support co-ordinate and promote the use of IT by devising well-designed strategies, developing appropriate standards and offering expert consultancy services to assist university libraries to adopt IT successfully.

INFLIBNET should prepare a clear and comprehensive documentation and manual of guidelines, procedures and standards to provide direction and guidance in all aspects of IT implementation in university libraries.

INFLIBNET should provide SOUL software freely or at conscessional rate to all university libraries in order to promote their computerisation.

INFLIBNET should make the existing union databases easily accessible on wider scale at the earliest by all university libraries for retrospective conversion of catalogues and promote the development of local databases. It should also develop optical disks for union databases and distribute to universities for retrospective conversion of their catalogues at their local sites.

INFLIBNET should setup training centers in different regions to conduct more intensive need-based training courses, workshops, seminars and user meets on IT applications for library professionals in order to become more proficient in the use of modern technology.

INFLIBNET should encourage the development of campus-wide Local Area Networks (LANs) in universities.

University libraries in India have rich resources of Ph.D. theses and Dissertations. INFLIBNET should initiate digitization of this research output of the country that can be shared and put to optimum use for the benefit of academic and research community.

Incentives should be given to the university libraries which have fully automated / achieved significant progress in IT implementation.

7.4.5. Government

Government should evolve a national policy on IT use in university libraries and should allocate more funds and provide more incentives for IT implementation in university libraries.

Government should provide more funds to UGC for speedy completion of INFLIBNET Project and for effective sharing and utilization of library resources.

Government should strengthen and develop national information infrastructure and enhance national capacity for information handling and services.

Government should support and encourage IT firms to develop indigenous user-friendly library automation software packages suitable to the needs of university libraries.

Government should nominate library professionals in the IT task force in order to represent the problems of libraries as well as offer suggestions / advices for the promotion of IT use in libraries.

7.5 FUTURE RESEARCH AREAS

Information Technology has become an integral part of all

library operations and services. IT has huge potential for variety of applications in libraries. It has profound implications in library management, information resources, operation future functions, services staff and users.

There is a greater need to initiate, support and encourage research and development efforts directed towards applications of new technologies and their effective management in libraries in order to find out more effective IT based solutions and provide more innovative and intelligent need based library and information services to the users. IT offers numerous opportunities and challenges in a wide range of areas for further research and investigation to discover new processes, methods, products and better solutions. The present study covered central university libraries in India. Based on the results of this study, the following areas are suggested for future research.

- Use and impact of IT on state universities' libraries in India.
- Use and Impact of IT on libraries of the Institutes of National importance viz. Indian Institutes of Management, Indian Institutes of Technology, CSIR, ICAR, ICMR, DRDO research organizations etc.
- A study of staff attitude towards IT implementation in different types of Library and Information Centers (LICs) in India.
- A study on user attitude towards IT based information services in different computerised Library and Information Centers (LICs) in India.
- Impact of Internet on information access to users in LICs in India
- A study on the use of electronic resources in libraries in India.
- Use of library application software packages in India: An evaluative study.
- A study on the use of OPAC in Library and Information Centers in India.
- Impact of Networks on resource sharing among LICs in India.

- A study of users attitude towards accessing web based information resources and services.

7.6 FUTURE CHALLENGES

Today, libraries are functioning in a highly dynamic and frequently turbulent technological environment. The rate of technological change in libraries is increasing exponentially with the high rate of change in technology. The complexity of emerging technologies will continue to increase at much faster pace in future. They will have greater impact on all aspects of libraries. Libraries should have a vision to embrace change and must always be on the look out for implementation of emerging technological innovations that can offer new opportunities to provide better quality solutions and user services. This will require a higher level of technologically competent and skilled staff to deal with complex technology. In a dynamic environment of fast-paced technological change, library manager's role expands beyond the traditional role of managing the optimum use of available resources to a new role of managing technological change in libraries successfully.

A wealth of information resources is available on the Internet. Accessing right information on the Internet is becoming very difficult for end-users due to lack of systematic structured organization of information and also paucity of adequate effective search engines. The need for experts in identifying and evaluating potential web resources, designing interfaces and finding relevant information on the web has tremendously increased. Librarians being the intermediaries between the information resources and users have to act as technological gatekeepers to develop catalogue of websites, resources and design interfaces that provide direct access to information to the users at their desktop. Library professionals will need to keep abreast of the new technological developments and act as an information consultants advising end-users on the best use of access tools, search engines, techniques, methods and ways to deliver high quality of information services.

The accelerating pace of new technological developments, emergence of virtual libraries, distributed electronic information resources and development of digital reference services demand different types of managerial, professional, technological, presentation and communication skills for library professionals. Technology is changing so rapidly that what you know today will be outdated tomorrow. The explosive growth and wide usage of web resources has made it imperative for the library staff to equip new skills in the use of latest techniques, tools and strategies needed for the development of a virtual library. Each library must serve as intelligent and innovative gateway to access the global network of information resources and services. As technology continues to advance at phenomenal speed, one needs to keep up-to-date and learn new set of skills to keep pace with and ahead of the technological developments. An utmost attention needs to be given to upgrade staff skills in improving their ability to identify, access and use electronic information resources from the web. They should have good knowledge of the latest trends in emerging technologies, and be aware of innovative ideas and intelligent strategies for effective exploitation of the full potential of future technologies in libraries. Otherwise, there will be no good prospects for librarians in the emerging digital/virtual libraries of the future. Librarians must take the role of technological gatekeepers, navigators', intermediaries and trainers actively involved in helping the users in accessing and making the best use of the web resources. The library profession must attract, retain and retrain the individuals who can master the increasingly complex information technology skills and manage the modern libraries in a challenging and ever changing dynamic technological environment.

If libraries are to be successful in future, they have to be more proactive to the technological change, manage the complex challenges and exploit the opportunities offered by the new technologies in order to meet the rising expectations of their user community.

Select Bibliography

Adams, Roy J. (1986). *Information technology & libraries: A future for academic libraries.* London: Croom Helin. 177p.

Agha, S.J. (1986). Library automation in Nigeria: Achievements and constraints on progress. *Program,* 20(4), 409-414.

Alabi, G.A. (1986). Library automation in Nigerian universities. *Information Development,* 2(3), 163-164.

Alemna, A. A. (1993). CD-ROMs in Ghanaian libraries:A survey. *International Forum for Information and Documentation,* 18(2), 26-8.

Alemna, A. A. (1999). Library evaluation: Some options for academic libraries. *Aslib Proceedings,* 51(7), 243.

Ali, S. N. & Young, H. C. (1992). Information access through CD-ROM and its impact upon faculty research output: A case of a university in third world countries. *Microcomputers for Information Management* 9(3), 177-89.

Andre, Pamela Q.J. (1989). Optical disc applications in libraries. *Library Trends,* 37(3), 326-342.

Anjana Chattopadhyay. (1998). University libraries. In P.B. Mangla, D.R. Kalia and Neela Jagannathan (Ed). *50 years of library and information services in India.* Delhi: Shipra Pub.

Awogbami, Popoola A.(1995). Staff openion on library automation planning in Nigerian university libraries. *Library Herald*, 33(1-2), 34-37.

Bajaj, Rajinder Prashad., & Lal, Bhooshan. (1986). Computerised circulation control: an I.I.T. Delhi experiment. *Library Science with a Slant to Documentation*, 23(3), 152-161.

Barrentine, James., & Kontoff, Trudy.(1990). Library automation software. *Library Technology Reports*, 26(4), 475-483.

Bednar, Marie. (1988). Automation of cataloging: Effects on use of staff, efficiency and service to patrons. *The Journal of Academic Librarianship*, 14(3), 145-49

Blagden, J & Harrington, J. (1990). *How good is your library:A review of approaches to the evaluation of library and information services*. London: Aslib.

Blank, Karen L. (1984). Library automation in Australia. *Library Hi Tech* 2(3), 47-54.

Blunden-Ellis, J.A. & Graham, M.E. (1994). A UK market survey of library automation system vendors (1992-1993). *Program*, 28(2), 109-124.

Bobp, M. E., Richey, D., & Kratzert, M. (1993). The emergence of systemwide electronic access to information sources: Experience of two California state university libraries. *Reference Librarian*, (39), 111-30.

Boss, R.W. (1984) *The library manager's guide to automation* (2nd ed.) White Plains, NY: Knowledge Industry Publications.

Bossers, Anton., Muyen, Martin Van., & Muyen, M. Van.(1984). Library automation in the Netherlands and Pica. *Electronic Library*, 2(2), 87-99.

Branin, J. et al. (1997). The evaluation of the IIC Project. *Journal of the American Society for Information Science*, 48(5), 472-3.

Braude, R. M. (1993). Impact of information technology on the role of health sciences librarians. *Bulletin of the Medical Library Association*, 81(4), 408-13.

Breeding, M. (1996). Library technology: highlights from the National online meeting & IOLS '96. *Computers in Libraries*, 16(7), 8-20.

Brightman, Richard .W. & Dimsdale, Jeffery M. (1991). *Using microcomputers (pp.*14). New Delhi; Galgotia Publication (p) ltd.

Brown, D. (1995). New technologies in music libraries: Their impact on support staff. *Library Mosaics*, 6(3), 13-14.

Buckland, M. (1992). *Redesigning library services: A manifesto.* Chicago: American Library Association.

Burke, J. (1986). Automation planning and implementation: Library and vendor responsibilities'. In *Human aspects of library automation: Helping staff and patrons cope* (pp. 46-58). Urbana, IL: Graduate School of Library and Information Science, University of Illinois.

Craghill, D., & Wilson, T.D., & Neal, C. (1989). *The impact of IT on staff deployment in UK public libraries.* Boston Spa: British Library.

Chopra, Hans Raj. (1980). Automation of university libraries in India. *International Library Movement*, 2(3&4), 62-67.

Chowdhary, G.G & Chowdhary, Sudalta. (1994). Text retrieval and library management software in India. *NISSAT Newsketter*, July-September, (3), 13-18.

Chou, Nancy Ou-lan. (1991). Library automation in the Republic of China. The development of a National Bibliographic Network. *Journal of Library and Information Science* (USA/Taiwan*)*, 17(2), 24-35.

Cibbarelli, P. (1996). Library automation alternatives in 1996 and user satisfaction ratings of library users by operating system.

Computers in Libraries, 16(2), 26-35.

Clear, Fiona. (1986). Library automation at UMIST, using ADLIB. *Program,*20(3),264-74.

Clyde, Laurel A., & Middleton, Michael. (1990). Library automation in Western Australia. *LASIE* 21(1), 5-15.

Collier, Mel W. (1988). Library automation today. *International Forum on Information and Documentation,* 13(3), 14-20.

Corbin, John. (1985). *Managing the library automation project.* Phoenix (USA): Oryx.

Cowan, B *et al.* (1992). Training and the impact of information technology on work groups in public libraries in Canada and England. *Journal of librarianship and information science* 24(3), 139-148.

Crawshaw, Tom. (1991). Library automation at the Universty of Oxford. *Program* 25(4), 291-301.

Davies, E. J. (1992). *Data protection and LIS management in academic libraries (pp.* 121-151). Adershot; Ashgate Publishing.

DESIDOC Bulletin of Information Technology. (1996). 16(2&3). (Special issue on Library Networks in India).

DESIDOC Bulletin of Information Technology. (1997). 17(6). (Special issue on Digital Libraries).

DESIDOC Bulletin of Information Technology. (2000). 20(1&2). (Special issue on Information Technology).

Dillion, A., & Morris,M.G. (1996). User acceptance of information technology: Theories and models. In M.E. Williams(Ed.). *Annual Rreview of Information Science and Technology* (pp. 3-32). Medford, NJ: Information Today, Inc.

Doty, P., & Bishop, A,E. (1994). The national information infrastructure and electronic publishing: A reflective essay. *Journal of the American Society for Information Science,* 45, 785-799.

Dyer, Hilary & Morris, Anne. (1990). *Human aspects of library automation.* Aldershot: Gower.

Edwards, C., Walton, G. & Day, J. M. (1995). The IMPEL Project at the University of Northumbria at Newcastle: background, methodology and progress. *Library and Information Research News,* 19(62), 5-10.

Evald, Pierre. (1996). Information technology in Danish public libraries. *Program,* 30(2), 121-131.

Fisher, T. (1995). Impact of computer technology on library expansions. *Library Administration and Management,* 9(1), 31-6.

Gore, A. (1995). Infrastructure for Global Village. *Scientific American* (Spl issue), 156-9.

Government of India, National Task Force on Information Technology & Software Development (1998). *Information Technology action plan.* New Delhi: PMO. (http://www.nic.in).

Grosch, Audrey N. (1976). Library automation. In M.E. Williams (Ed.). *Annual review of information science and technology,* volume 11 (pp. 225-266). Washington (DC): American Society for Information Science.

Grosch, Audrey N. (1995). *Library information technology and networks* (384p). New York: Marcel Dekker Inc.

Gupta, O.P. (1992). *University libraries in India after Independence* (pp. 24-26). New Delhi: Concept.

Hanson, Heidi., & Pronevitz, Gregory. (1989). Planning for retrospective conversion: A simulation of the OCLC TAPECON service. *Information Technology and Libraries,* 8(3), 284-294.

Heaton, S., & Brown, J. M. (1995). Staff perceptions of incentives and hurdles to the use of technology. *Computers in Libraries,* 15(2), 28-31.

Heseltine, R. G. (1991). Library automation in the 1990s: the open systems future. In I. C.McIlwaine (Ed.). Standards for the international exchange of bibliographic information (pp. 162-8). London: Library Association Publishing.

Inamdar, N.B. & Ramaiah, L.S. (Eds). (1984). *National policy for university libraries in India.* Delhi: Concept.

Jones, S., & Wallace, D. (1993). The role of a bibliographic utility in resource sharing; an ISM Library Information Services perspective. Dalhousie University. *Occasional Papers* (54), 16-22.

Kamath, V. A. (1990). Computer application in library and information services: A brief survey of the world and Indian Scenario. In H-A-Khan and S.R.Ijari (Eds.).

Current problems and trends in Library and Information Services. Varanasi: Indian Bibliographic Centre.

Kanamugire, A. B. (1994). Developing a CD-ROM service in Saudi Arabia: Some lessons for developing countries. *Journal of Information Science,*20(2), 99-107.

Kaul, H.K. (1992). *Library networks: An indian experience.* New Delhi: Virgo.

Keeka, P. M. (1981). *Computer applications in indian libraries: A survey.* M.Lib.Sc Dissertation. SNDT Women's University, Bombay.

Kumar, P.S.G and Vashishth, C.P. (Eds.). (1999). *CALIBER-1999: Academic Libraries in Internet era.* (Papers presented at the Sixth National Convention for the automation of libraries in education and research, Nagpur, 18-20 February 1999) (524p). Ahmedabad: INFLIBNET Centre.

Kumar, R.P. (1993). Application of modern technologies in health science libraries in India: a survey. *ASLIB proceedings,* 45(3), 63-67.

Kurtz, Sharon. *Library Automation: Sandia laboratories Albuquerque.* New Mexico, 268.

Lancaster, F. W. (1977). *Measurement and evaluation of library services.* Virginia: Information Resources press.

Lancaster, F. W. (1978). *Towards paperless information system.* New York: Academic Press.

Lancaster, F. W., & Sandore, B. (1997). *Technology and management in library and information services.* Urbana-Champaign: University of Illinois. Graduate school of Library and Information Science. 1.

Leggate, p. & Dyer, H. (1986). The microcomputer in the library: VI Implementation and future development. *Electronic Library,* 4(6), 332-343.

Library Association (1983). *The impact of new technology on libraries and information centers.* (Library Association Pamphlet: 38). London: Library Association.

Library Trends. (1989). 37(3), 265-384 (special issue on Contemporary Technology in Libraries).

Library Trends. (1999). 47(4), 605-827 (Special issue on Human response to Library Technology).

Lim, H.T. (1985). New technology and the university library in a developing country: the Malayasian experience. *Journal of Library and Information Science (India),* 10(2), 122-137.

Loarer, Pierre Le., & Loarer, P. Le. (1987). Library automation in France. In Verina Horsnell & Jacqueline Cooper (Eds.). *European Conference on Library Automation* (pp. 20-32). London: Library Association Publishing Ltd.

Lynch, Mary Dykstra. (1997). Information highway. *World Information Report* (1997-98) (pp. 296). Paris: UNESCO.

MacDougall, Susan. (1992). Networkshop '91, and the impact of AARNet on academic libraries. *Australian Academic and Research Libraries,* 23(1), 35-39.

Maier, John H. (1986). Library automation in the People's Republic of China. *Information Technology and Libraries,* 5(2), 106-111.

Malwad, N.M. (1995). Selection criteria for library automation software. *DESIDOC Bulletin of Information Technology,* 15(2), 17-26.

Manish, Bhatia (comp). (2000). *Directory of libraries in Delhi.* New Delhi: Reliance Pub. House. 462p.

Matthews, J. (1980). *Choosing an automated library system: A planning guide.* Chicago: American Library Association.

McCarthy, Cavan. & McCarthy, C. M. (1983). Library automation in Brazil: the state of the art. *Program,* 17(4), 233-240.

Mittal, R. L. (1983). *Library Administration: Theory and practice* (5th ed.). New Delhi: Metropolitan.

Modernisation of libraries. (1988). Papers of 33rd All India Library Conference, Tiruchirapalli.

Morita, Ichiko T. (1988). The impact of OCLC on a large research library. *International Symposium on New Techniques and Applications in Libraries,* Xian, Chinese People's Republic, 8-11 Sept 88, 152-162.

Msuya, Jangame. (1990). Planning the automation of libraries in developing countries; A systems analysis approach. *Library Review 39(3), 29.*

Moorthy, A.L & Mangla, P.B (Eds). (1997). *CALIBER-1997: Information Technology Applications in Academic Libraries.* (Papers presented at the Fourth National Convention for the automation of libraries in education and research, Patiala, , 6-8 March 1997), Ahmedabad: INFLIBNET Centre. 214p.

Moorthy, A.L & Murthy, S.S. (1998). Information technology and Indian libraries. In M.K.Jain (Ed.). *Library and information services in India* (pp. 249-260). Delhi: Shipra Publications.

Munasinghe, Mohan. (1995). Policy and infrastructure for information technology. *UNCTAD's Advanced Technology Assessment system,* issue 10, 476.

Murthy, S.S. (1999). Role of libraries in the new millennium of information technology, *DESIDOC Bulletin of Information Technology,* 19 (4-5), 3-10.

Neela Jagannathan (1995). *Role of UGC in academic libraries, university college and other institutions in Academic library system.* New Delhi: IGNOU. (Block 2, Unit 3, 5-20).

Nixon, Paul E. (1990). A university library's OPAC on CD-ROM: Various views on the technology. *Inspel* 24(3), 120-127.

Oh, D., & Woods, G. (1994). The future of Australian academic libraries. *Australian Academic and Research Libraries* 25(3), 149-58.

Patterson, P.J. (1995). Information technology and development in Jamaica. *UNCTAD's Advanced Technology Assessment System,* Issue 10, 9.

Peake, Dorothy G. (1981). Library automation in Australia: The state of the art. *Program,* 15(1), 11-23.

Powell, Ronald R. (1991). *Basic Research methods for librarians.* Norwood, NJ: Ablex.

Pradeep, C ; Ganesan & Rama Reddy, E (1999). In CALIBER-99: Academic Libraries in Internet era. *In CALIBER-1999: Academic Libraries in Internet era.* (Papers presented at the Sixth National Convention for the automation of libraries in education and research, Nagpur, 18-20 February 1999) *(pp. 26-36).* Ahmedabad: INFLIBNET Centre.

Prince, B. & Burton, P.F. (1988). Changing dimensions in academic library structures: the impact of information technology. *British Journal of Academic Librarianship,* 3(2), 67-81.

Raizada, A. S. & Satyanarayana, R. (1980). *Report of the Survey on Computerised Selective Dissemination of Information Service.*

New Delhi: INSDOC. (Mimeographed).

Raju, A. A. N.; Laxman Rao, N & Sudharshan Rao (Eds.). (1997). *Information Technology and its impact on LIS education and Library Management.* Delhi: Delta Publishing House, 211p.

Rama Reddy, E & Pradeep C (1997). Document image processing and management system: Experience at Indira Gandhi Memorial Library. *In CALIBER-1997: Information Technology Applications in Academic Libraries.* (Papers presented at the Fourth National Convention for the automation of libraries in education and research, Patiala, , 6-8 March 1997) *(pp. 63-67).* Ahmedabad: INFLIBNET Centre.

Rama Reddy, E & Varada Rajan,N (1997). Internet Facilities and connections: Experience of IGM Library. *In CALIBER-1997: Information Technology Applications in Academic Libraries.* (Papers presented at the Fourth National Convention for the automation of libraries in education and research, Patiala, 6-8 March 1997). Ahmedabad: INFLIBNET Centre.

Ramsden, Hilary. (1988). Library automation and software. *Aslib Information,* 16(7-8), 177.

Ravichandra Rao, I. K. (1990). *Library automation.* New Delhi: Wiley-Eastern.

Rehman, S. (1992). Library automation in Pakistan: myths and realities. *Pakistan Library Bulletin,* 13(4), 10-17.

Reid-Smith, E. R. *Information technology in Australian libraries: A state-of-the-art report on their application and impact.* Charles Sturt University, School of Information Studies, New South Wales. AUSTRALIA

Reynolds, D. (1985). *Library automation: issues and applications.* New York: Bowker.

Richmond, Phyllis A. (1981). Library automation in the United States of America. *Program,* 15(1), 24-37.

Rowley, Jennifer E. (1988). *The Basics of information technology.* London: Cline Bingley.

Saffady, William. (1989). Library automation: an overview. *Library Trends,* 37(3),269-81.

Satalkar, Vasudha., & Kunte, Pravia. (1988). Micro-based relational database for a special library. *Electronic Library,* 6(1), 18-22.

Schraml, M.L. (1981). The psychological impact of automation on library and office workers. *Special Libraries,* 72(2), 149-156.

Seshagiri, N. (1984). *Modernization of library services and informatics for the Seventh Five Year Plan 1985-90.* Report submitted to the Government of India by the working group of the Planning Commission.

Sethi, A.R. (1982). Jawaharlal Nehru University Library: a decade of development. *Delhi Alis Bulletin,* 6(12), 33-37.

Sewa singh. (1992). Information technology and academic libraries in India. *Journal of Information Science,* 3(1), 11-24.

Sharma. C.K. (1977). *University library: Its management and organisation.* Delhi: Metropolitan Book Co.

Siddiqui, M. A. (1995). A study of the effect on online searching of CD index in a science and engineering library. *Library Review,* 44(7), 45-54.

Siddiqui, M. A., & Mirza, M. I. (1994). Impact of CD-ROM searching on reference and information services in a university library. *Program,* 28(4), 405-13.

Simkins, M.A. (1983). The impact of new technology on the information profession. *Aslib Proceedings,* 35(2), 92-98.

Singh, A. (1993). Declining finances and collection development in university libraries: challenges and strategies. A study based on university libraries of Madhya Pradesh. *Proceedings of the 19th All India Conference of IASLIC,* Calcutta, India, 26-29 December 1993. Indian Association of Special Libraries and

Information Centres (IASLIC), 53-62.

Soerensen, Boerge. (1983). Library automation-its impact on library services, working conditions and employment. *Scandinavian Public Library Quarterly* 16(1), 8-13.

Storey, C. (1995). The impact of information technology on management and organization: the case of Hong Kong Polytechnic University Library. *Library Management,* 16(2), 22-33.

Sturges, R. P. (1991). *Impact of information technology in advanced developing countries: case study of the State of Kuwait.* Loughborough, Loughborough

University of Technology, DLIS, Leicestershire December 1986 - December 1991.

Subba Rao, S. (1996). CD-ROM technology: World scenario and indian experience. *Information Today and Tomorrow,* 15 (2), 3-16.

Suryanarayana, N., & Hugar, N. C. (1988). Planning an automated circulation system for an academic library. *Lucknow Librarian,* 20(2), 72-80.

Tedd, L. A. (1977). *Introduction to computer-based library systems.* London: Heydon.

Tedd, L. A. (1993). *An introduction to computer-based library systems* (3rd ed.). Chichester: John Wiley & Sons.

Tedd, Lucy. (1997). Computer Developments. *World information report 1997/98.* Paris: UNESCO, 193-205.

United Kingdom, University Grants Commission. (1921). *Report of the Committee on libraries.* London: HMSO.

Valauskas, Edward J. (1987). Library automation with workstations: Using Apple Macintoshes in a special library. *Information Technology and Libraries,* 7(1), 73-78.

Varalakshmi, K.S.R. (1992). Emerging trends in information

technology and its impact on library environment. *INCAE,* 11(2), 232-243.

Veaner, A. (1991). *Automation and oganizational change in libraries.* Boston: G.K.Hall.

Vengan, R., Mohan, H.R. & Raghavan, K.S. (Eds.). (2000). CALIBER-2000: *Information Services in a Networked environment in India.* (Papers presented in the Seventh National Convention for the automation of libraries in education and research, Chennai, 16-18 February 2000). Ahmedabad: INFLIBNET Centre.

Venkataramana, P. (1997). *Use of information technology in indian libraries: Problems and prospects.* In L.S.Ramaiah *et al* (Eds), Information and society (pp 298-308), New Delhi: Ess Ess Publication.

Venkataramana, P. (1999). Role of digital libraries in the electronic information era. In J.L.Sardana (Ed.), *Libraries and information servicesin the electronic information era* (pp 189-195) (Seminar papers of forty fourth All India Library Conference, Hyderabad. 25-28 February, 1999). Delhi: ILA.

Venkataramana, P (2000). Impact of internet on library and information services in T. Ashok babu et al (Eds). *Vision of future library and information systems* (pp.109-117). New Delhi; Viva books pvt.ltd.

Venkataramana, P. & Chandrasekhar Rao, V. (1998). Multimedia technology and its impact on education. In B.Satyanarayana et.al (Eds.) *Multimedia: Its applications in library and information science* (pp. 243-250). Chennai: T.R.Publications Pvt. Ltd.

Venkataramana, P. & Ramesh, L.S.R.C.V. (1998). Role of multimedia applications in libraries. In M.Sankara Reddy (Ed.) *Library and information science:Some perspectives* (pp. 243-250). Hyderabad: Vaibhav Agencies.

Viswanathan, T. (1995). Overview of communication technology. In *application of information technology,* Block1, Unit 2, (pp. 31-55). New Delhi: IGNOU.

Vyasamoorthy, P. (1995). Database industry in India: A current scenario. *DESIDOC Bulletin of Information Technology,* 15(4), 11-22.

Walker, James Thomas. (1985). *Using statistics for psychological research: An introduction.* New York: Holt, Rinehart & Winston.

Weber, David C. (1988). University libraries and campus information technology organisations: Who is incharge here ?. *Journal of Library Administration Series,* 9(4), 5-19.

White, Carl M. (1965). *Survey of University of Delhi Library.* Delhi: University of Delhi.

Wilson, J. (1995). Enter the cyberpunk librarian: future directions in cyberspace. *Library Review,* 44(8), 63-72.

Wilson, Wayne. (1983). Computer-assisted instruction in an academic library. *Information Technology and Libraries,* 2(4), 389-393.

Woods, R.G. (1982). *Library automation.* London: British Library, Research and Development Department, 32p.

Wright, Stephen. (1991). Library automation in Papua New Guinea. *Libri,* 41(1), 37-50.

Yeates, R. (1996). Library automation: the way forward. *Program,* 30(3), 239-53.

Zorkoczy, Peter. (1989). *Information technology: An introduction.* 2nd ed. New Delhi: Affiliated East-West.

List of Library & Information Science Technology Journals

1 Advances in Internet of Things
2 African Journal of Library, Archives and Information Science
3 American Libraries
4 Annals of Library and Information Studies
5 Asian Libraries
6 Aslib Proceedings
7 Australasian Public Libraries and Information Services
8 Australian Academic & Research Libraries
9 Australian Library Journal
10 Campus Technology
11 Campus Wide Information Systems
12 Code4Lib Journal
13 Collaborative Librarianship
14 Collection Management
15 College & Undergraduate Libraries
16 College and Research Libraries
17 Community & Junior College Libraries
18 Computers in Libraries
19 DESIDOC Journal of Library and Information Technology
20 D-Lib Magazine
21 Econtent
22 Electronic British Library Journal
23 Electronic Journal of Academic and Special Librarianship
24 Electronic Library
25 Evidence Based Library and Information Practice
26 Gyankosh- The Journal of Library and Information Management
27 IFLA Journal
28 Information Development

29 Information Management & Computer Security
30 Information Resources Management Journal
31 Information Retrieval
32 Information Services and Use
33 Information Systems Frontiers
34 Information Technology
35 Information Technology & People
36 Information Technology and Libraries
37 Information World
38 Informing Science
39 Infoscience
40 International Information and Library Review
41 International Journal of Digital Curation
42 International Journal of Digital Library Systems
43 International Journal of Library and Inf. Science
44 International Journal of Library Science
45 International Journal of Special Libraries
46 International Journal on Digital Libraries
47 International Journal on E-Learning
48 International Research: Jl. of Library & Inf. Science
49 Internet Reference Services Quarterly
50 Internet Research
51 Italian Journal of Library and Information Science
52 Journal of Academic Librarianship
53 Journal of Access Services
54 Journal of Digital Contents
55 Journal of Documentation
56 Journal of Electronic Resources Librarianship
57 Journal of Information and Organizational Sciences

58 Journal of Knowledge Management Practice

59 Journal of Librarianship and Information Science

60 Journal of Library & Information Services in Distance Learning

61 Journal of Library & Information Studies

62 Journal of Library and Information Science

63 Journal of Library Innovation

64 Journal of Library Metadata

65 Journal of Web Librarianship

66 Lib. & Inf. Research : Research into Practice for Inf. & Lib. Services

67 LIBER Quarterly

68 Librarian Career Development

69 Library

70 Library & Information History

71 Library & Information Science Research

72 Library Collections, Acquisitions, and Technical Services

73 Library Consortium Management

74 Library Herald

75 Library Hi Tech

76 Library Hi Tech News

77 Library Journal

78 Library Leadership & Management

79 Library Management

80 Library of Congress Information Bulletin

81 Library Philosophy and Practice

82 Library Review

83 Library Review

84 Library Student Journal

85 Library Technology Reports

86 Library Trends

87 Libres
88 Libri: International Jl of Libraries and Information Services
89 Multimedia Information and Technology
90 National Library of Australia Gateways
91 New Library World
92 New Review of Academic Librarianship
93 New Review of Information and Library Research
94 New Review of Libraries and Lifelong Learning
95 NewBreed Librarian
96 OCLC Systems & Services
97 Online Information Review
98 Open and Libraries Class Journal
99 Open Information Science Journal
100 Partnership: Canadian Jl of Lib. and Inf. Practice and Research
101 PEARL - A Journal of Library and Information Science
102 Performance Measurements and Metrics
103 Perspectives in International Librarianship
104 Portal: Libraries and the Academy
105 Practical Academic Librarianship: The Intl Jl of the SLA Acad. Division
106 Program: Electronic Library And Information Systems
107 Public Services Quarterly
108 Reference Librarian
109 Reference Reviews
110 Reference Services Review
111 Research Strategies
112 Resource Sharing & Information Networks
113 Russian Digital Libraries Journal
114 Singapore Journal of Library & Information Management
115 Slavic & East European Information Resources

116 South African Journal of Libraries and Information Science
117 SRELS Journal of Information Management
118 Sri Lankan Journal of Librarianship and Information Management
119 Web Semantics
120 World Libraries

Index

D

O

P

R

S

T